The
Soldiers
Fell Like
Autumn
Leaves

ALSO BY RICK M. SCHOENFIELD

The McGraw-Hill 36-Hour Negotiating Course
Legal Negotiations: Getting Maximum Results

The Soldiers Fell Like Autumn Leaves

The Battle *of the* Wabash, The United States' Greatest Defeat *in the* Wars against Indigenous Peoples

RICK M. SCHOENFIELD

WESTHOLME
Yardley

Westholme Publishing, LLC
904 Edgewood Road
Yardley, Pennsylvania 19067
Visit our Web site at www.westholmepublishing.com

ISBN: 978–1–59416–423–1

Printed in the United States of America.

*To my brother Mark, for the fun and the guidance,
for as long as I can remember.*

"We see your intentions, you are drawing so close to us that we can almost hear the sound of your axes felling our trees & settling our country. According to the lines settled by our forefathers, the Ohio is the boundary, but you are encroaching on the grounds given to us by the Great Spirit. . . . It is clear to us that your design is to take our country from us."

—Kekewepelethy (Captain Johnny), response to American treaty commissioners, 1785

"When our ancestors arrived, they found the trees of the forest the great obstacle to their settlement, and cultivation. The great effort was of course to destroy the trees. It would seem that they contracted and transmitted an antipathy to them; for the trees were not even spared around the dwellings. . . . In fact, such has been the inconsiderate and indiscriminate use of the axe, that this country is beginning to feel the calamity as much as some of the old countries of Europe; and it will soon be forced to understand the difficulty of curing it. . . . It is high time for many farmers, even in this quarter, and still more so in the country below us, to take this subject into serious consideration. Prudence will no longer delay to economize what remains of wood land."

—President James Madison, address to the Agricultural Society of Albemarle, May 12, 1818

CONTENTS

Illustrations

INTRODUCTION

The largely forgotten Battle of the Wabash was the greatest Native American triumph and the US military's greatest disaster in more than a century of Indian wars. It was fought in November 1791, close to the Ohio-Indiana border at what is now Fort Recovery, Ohio. This was part of the vast expanse of the Old Northwest Territory. The frontier, and hence the line of conflict in the ongoing struggle between expanding American settlements and Native Americans, had been pushed into Ohio from western Pennsylvania, western Virginia, and Kentucky. At stake were ways of life, economies, and the environment itself.

Having been personally selected by President George Washington, General Arthur St. Clair led an American army to attack Indian towns in and around what is now Fort Wayne, Indiana. It is where the St. Marys and St. Joseph Rivers meet to form the Maumee.[1] The army numbered more than 2,100 on October 4, 1791, when it embarked on its mission. It was supplemented by more than four hundred militia. With artillery and wagons, it moved slowly. Well aware that they were coming, a confederation of Shawnee, Miami (Myaamiaki), Delaware, Wyandot, Seneca-Cayuga (then known as Mingo), Ottawa, Ojibwe (also known as Ojibwa and Chippewa), Potawatomi, and Cherokee met and decided on their strategy.[2] Rather than waiting, a little over one thousand warriors moved to intercept St. Clair's force.

When the army camped on the night of November 3, although reduced by deployments, desertions, discharges, and a few casualties, it still numbered approximately 1,800 officers and men, including militia. In the early hours of November 4, in a crescent shaped, "half-moon" attack formation, the confederation warriors moved into position to assault St. Clair's camp. Despite being outnumbered, they killed over six hundred troops and inflicted over nine hundred casualties before those still able to do so escaped and fled. The battle is sometimes simply called St. Clair's Defeat, a name unlike any other in American military history. Here it is referred to by another of its names, the Battle of the Wabash, because battles are usually named for where they were fought, and because St. Clair's Defeat implicitly absolves everyone else of fault while failing to credit the victorious Native Americans.

The story of the battle is one of dysfunctional, flawed military and civilian leadership, in contrast to a high degree of cooperation, coordination, and efficiency by the war chiefs of the Maumee Confederation. As at the Battle of the Little Big Horn eighty-five years later, no one Indian leader was in overall command. But at the forefront of leadership were Blue Jacket (Waweyapiersenwa or Weyapiersenwa) of the Shawnee, and Little Turtle (Mihsihkinaahkwa) of the Miami.[3] Beyond the top leadership, the actions of individual soldiers and Indian warriors, a few of them adopted whites, account for what happened.

Despite the condemnation leveled at St. Clair, as well as other key Americans involved in organizing, supplying, and leading the campaign, both contemporary criticisms and critiques written over the years have failed to focus on the critical planning errors that ultimately doomed the American army. Examining both the American and the Native American planning brings into focus a deeper, more meaningful analysis of the judgments, beliefs, and assumptions that resulted in the bloody devastation along the Wabash that November morning. Beyond the intrinsic historical interest, though weapons and battlegrounds have changed, lessons can be drawn both from the sound decision making and from the dismal failures and omissions. Through a deeper analysis of why decisions were made and why oversights occurred, the campaign and the life-and-death fight at the Wabash provide timeless lessons in leadership and analytical thinking.

Compared to the far better known Battle of the Little Big Horn (Greasy Grass to the Lakota), St. Clair's dead numbered more than twice as many as were killed with Lieutenant Colonel George Armstrong Custer, while St. Clair's total casualties were approximately three times those of Custer.[4] No other purely Native American victory inflicted such high casualties on opposing troops. Unlike the Battle of the Wabash, where St. Clair's troops outnumbered the Indian confederation almost two to one, Custer's Seventh Cavalry was substantially outnumbered. In both engagements, Indian casualties were probably in the dozens, not the hundreds.

Numbers aside, wiping out Custer on June 25, 1876, only gained the Lakota (popularly known as the Sioux) and the Cheyenne a respite for the rest of the summer.[5] By September, the army's renewed offensive resulted in the Battle of Slim Buttes, known to the Lakota as "The Fight Where We Lost The Black Hills."[6] By January, Lakota leaders Sitting Bull and Gall had retreated to Canada with their followers. By May, the most renowned Lakota war leader, Crazy Horse, and his followers surrendered and came to the reservation. Just four months later, Crazy Horse was killed.

In contrast, the Wabash battle stymied American expansion into Ohio and the rest of the Old Northwest for almost four years before the United States obtained the treaty concessions it demanded. Routing St. Clair preserved much of Ohio and Indiana for its Native American inhabitants during those years. By extension, it did the same for the rest of the Northwest Territory and the timeline of Indian life across the northern plains. Thus, it affected the lives of tens of thousands, both white and Native American.

Yet the Battle of the Little Big Horn is far better known than the Battle of the Wabash and is the subject of far more history books—not to mention the numerous depictions, albeit inaccurate, of Custer's defeat in popular media.

St. Clair's defeat was fought in the new republic's first war. Only a year after the Constitution was ratified, George Washington's decision to go to war set the precedent for a president taking sustained, large-scale military action without a formal declaration of war by Congress. That precedent remains relevant and controversial to this day. The scope of the rout launched the first congressional investigation, as well as the first claim of executive privilege. It also triggered early examples of American history being distorted to meet what self-interest needed and the public preferred.

Policy and psychological issues that set the stage for St. Clair's campaign and for the subsequent congressional investigation also echo in present-day issues. Are decisions made based on true knowledge, after considering their potential consequences, or are they based on beliefs, wishful thinking, unconscious assumptions, and biases, as if those reflected actual facts? Are plans made that account for uncertainties, or are they made with fallacious certitude? In evaluating leadership, how should courage, audacity, or brash confidence compare to the process and quality of decision making?

Americans' vision of settling the Old Northwest imagined substantial deforestation. There was conflict over the existence of the dominant forest landscape. There was no equivalent issue in the Great Sioux War. One can still walk the grassy prairie where the Lakota and Cheyenne overwhelmed Custer and the Seventh Cavalry. Fundamentally, the Great Plains remains the Great Plains. In contrast, millions of acres of Ohio forest are gone. The site of the Wabash battle is now the town of Fort Recovery. Even the river itself, an integral feature of the battlefield, has been rerouted three times, though parts of the original channel can still be seen.

Conflicting cultural, philosophical, religious, and economic views, then, as now, created a struggle over the fate of the environment. To what extent should nature be valued and preserved? Are forests primarily sources of timber and obstacles to be cleared, or are they essential for maintaining the balance of nature and human well-being? Which people would live on, control, and profit from the land of the Old Northwest would determine the fate of the forest, its wildlife, its biodiversity, and the environment for generations to come. Even in the 1970s, the noted anthropologist and ethnobotanist Wade Davis "was raised to believe that the rain forests existed to be cut," and that was taught as the foundation of "scientific forestry." That, in contrast to indigenous peoples' "deep attachment to the land . . . [and their] profound sense of belonging and connection."[7]

Not until after the turn of the eighteenth century did Alexander von Humboldt sound the first alarm in the white world regarding environmental destruction. Humboldt was a leading scientist and author whose many accomplishments spanned what are now classified as multiple disciplines, including physical geography, ecology, and oceanography. Locating the magnetic equator was among his discoveries. As part of the science we now call climatology, he recognized that deforestation affects local climate and charted how air and water flows create diverse climate bands at different latitudes and altitudes. His "revolutionary theory" of "the 'unity of nature'" conceptualized the inseparable links between all aspects of the earth, from the outer atmosphere to the ocean floors.[8]

Not until 1818, ten years after meeting Humboldt and a year after his presidency, did one of America's founders join in sounding his alarm. In a speech given to the Agricultural Society of Albemarle and widely published in newspapers, James Madison voiced a prescient warning against deforestation and soil erosion. His thesis was that there is a balance to nature, a balance that maintains plants, animals, and ultimately humans, and that the unlimited, short-sighted exploitation of soil and timber collapses that balance.[9] Madison warned that it was critical to alter the widespread attitude that the forest was a "great obstacle to . . . settlement" that should largely be destroyed.[10] He emphasized the need to preserve what was left and to replant much of what was gone.

Though our twenty-first century context is quite different than that of the late eighteenth century, the mental lens through which we view forests was, and is, of critical importance. Then, it was an inextricable part of the conflict over tens of thousands of square miles, over who would live there, and how they would live. Now, the fate of forests is an essential element of whether climate change and the loss of biodiversity will continue to worsen or be brought under control. Madison's sagacious counsel remains highly relevant.[11]

As much as possible, I have tried to describe the perspectives of post-Revolutionary War Americans and Native Americans. Whenever possible, I have relied on original sources. In doing so, I have been cognizant that at times, misperception or self-interest affected their accuracy. Also problematic, descriptions in some sources are inaccurate or incomplete. Examples of the former are claims that Little Turtle, the Miami war chief, was in overall command and that Indian "sharpshooters" led by William Wells, an adopted white, were a key factor in the battle. When critically examined, some supposedly first-hand accounts appear to be fictitious or highly exaggerated.[12]

To give voice to those who went through the lethal turmoil of the campaign, I have quoted extensively from journals, official correspondence, and the accounts that are reliable, or at least reflect honest memories. In the interest of authenticity, when quoting eighteenth-century documents, I have generally maintained the original spelling, punctuation, and capitalization, though often quite different from our modern practices. Indeed, they can best be described as flexible.

I have had the advantage of new information. In recent years, researchers at Ball State University in Indiana have completed and published an archaeological study of the battle site.

After examining the context of the conflict, detailing the setting and drama of the battle, and exploring its aftermath, I end with a brief analysis of the planning and decision making that resulted in the course of events at the Wabash. Human nature being what it is, the lessons of that analysis are readily applicable to our twenty-first-century events.

A final introductory note: when the army camped by the river where it would be attacked the next morning, St. Clair and his officers believed they were at the St. Marys, about fifteen miles from their objective at the Maumee. It was a mistake worthy of an antiwar satire by Paddy Chayefsky or Joseph Heller.[13] The army was camped along the Wabash. Due north, the St. Marys was some twenty-five miles of wilderness away; to the northwest, the Maumee more than fifty. Hence, the fight has also been called The Battle with No Name.[14] Surprisingly, the omission that caused this mistake has largely been ignored in histories of the campaign: St. Clair's expedition lacked a guide capable of recognizing where they were.

Chapter One

The Fate of the Forest

PICTURE IN YOUR MIND'S EYE A DENSE, old-growth forest stretching as far as you can see, broken here and there only by a river, small streams, and perhaps a meadow, a prairie, a bog, or a well-established narrow Indian trail. Being only twelve to eighteen inches wide, such trails had no effect on the trees or the forest canopy. There are centuries-old trees. There are tree trunks three or four or even six or seven feet in diameter, sometimes towering seventy feet before limbs have sprouted. Visualize a leaf-filled canopy a hundred feet up, with some trees rising to a hundred and fifty feet. Prominent within this virgin, predominantly deciduous forest might be oak, maple, basswood, hickory, elm, ash, and beech.[1] Buckeye (now Ohio's state tree), cedar, walnut, sweetgum, aspen, cherry, hemlock, pine, chestnut, cottonwood, willow, tulip, and poplar are some of the other species that might be seen. Ground vegetation is limited to mosses that thrive in the shade. Some pioneers said they walked for days under the thick forest canopy without seeing the sky.[2] Fauna along the water include river otters, beavers, minks, and muskrats. Among the trees, or in a meadow, there are whitetail deer, badgers, porcupine, elk, and perhaps woodland bison. Natural predators like black bears, bobcats, cougars, lynx, foxes, and wolves still thrive. Of course, there are countless birds.

In the midst of the vast forest, outside of scattered Native American villages and a handful of trading posts and forts, few, or more likely, no people are to be seen. There is "a continuity of woods without end."[3]

Before American settlement, this was nearly all of what became Ohio and Indiana, as well as much of Michigan, Wisconsin, and the land along the rivers of Illinois.[4] Farther north in Michigan, Wisconsin, and northeastern Minnesota, the trees were coniferous, or a mix of coniferous and deciduous, with spruce, fir, and pine. There, moose, badgers, and wolverines flourished. In Illinois and part of southern Wisconsin, grasslands with forest predominated. This was the Old Northwest Territory, the frontier stretching north from the Ohio River to Canada, and west from Pennsylvania to the Mississippi. In 1783, the Treaty of Paris recognized American independence with a border that placed the Old Northwest forest within the new American republic.

It is estimated that when the first settlers came to Ohio, as much as 95 percent of Ohio's 44,825 square miles was forested.[5] That is more than 28 million acres. Approximately ninety percent of Indiana's 36,418 square miles was wooded.[6] Together, the forest covered more than 48 million acres. Estimating conservatively, it likely contained between 2.4 billion and 2.9 billion trees.[7]

For the tribes, the natural landscape, its flora, and fauna, supported their traditional way of life. With indigenous understanding born of generations, the observation of animal behavior warned of an oncoming hard winter, or of a more immediate, oncoming storm. Observing the moss, the lean of treetops, and the pattern of branch growth distinguished north from south. Native knowledge encompassed which plants could be used to make dyes, and which bark, berries, and roots provided medicinal benefits.[8]

Woodland Indians "learned ecological principles and relationships directly from nature." With hunting and fishing essential, the necessity of having enough game and fish for the next generation was evident. "Whites who observed Indians in early times rarely reported any instances of wasteful hunting. . . . Pregnant animals were spared, as were all females during the breeding season. . . . Predators were hunted . . . but never persecuted with the idea of destroying them all." In a given year, many tribes utilized only part of their hunting grounds, allowing the animal population in other sections to recover.[9]

Corn and other crops were grown around the villages and were a staple of the food supply. Around Kekionga and Miamitown, the Miami villages where the confluence of the St. Marys and the St. Joseph form the Maumee, the corn fields were "vast . . . in almost every direction."[10] In addition to corn, pumpkins, squash, melons, beans, and tobacco were commonly grown around Native American villages. This was the domain of the women. The land selected was the easiest to cultivate, typically along river bottoms and terraces.[11] "Forest clearings were used for many years, because Indians knew several ways of preserving the fertility of the soil." For example, maize and beans were planted together. The cornstalks provided climbing poles for the beans, and the roots of the beans contained bacteria with soil-enriching nitrogen for the corn.[12]

While the First Peoples used and cleared some trees, they did so only on a limited basis. They viewed the forest as the foundation of their environment, never as an obstacle to eliminate. Tree bark was utilized to make wigwams, canoes, toboggans, and containers. But when bark was gathered, it was only stripped from one side, so as not to kill the tree. Unless there were none to be found, dead trees were used for firewood. Controlled fires were sometimes used to clear fields for planting, to drive game to hunters, or "to clear undergrowth and encourage food plants for deer and game birds. Indian forest fires were calculated in season, weather, and location to burn over the surface of the ground, not to spread into the forest canopy in destructive crown fires."[13] Of course, campfires were carefully put out.

Thus, early whites felt they had entered an unspoiled wilderness because Native Americans were "effective stewards of the earth," maintaining a natural balance without depleting nature's bounty. "The Indians' way was to move carefully through the natural environment, merging themselves into the landscape, leaving as little trace of themselves as possible. . . . Feeling themselves to be part of the organic cycles, they cooperated with nature and refrained from drastically altering the environment."[14] The forest literally stood as a testament to this.

Through the fur trade, manufactured goods had become a part of Native American life. The fur trade had grown through the eighteenth century. In an early manifestation of a global economy, European demand made the fur trade economically important on an international scale. As the ones who provided the fur, the First Peoples hunted not just for food and for the skins and furs they used but also for the business of trade. The manufactured goods they received had long since become a part of their life. Trade goods included guns, powder, and lead for war and hunting; knives, axes, and flints; cloth, beads, and silver ornaments; kettles and pots; rum and more. While some of those goods were also provided as gifts from governments seeking to secure tribal goodwill, much was received in trade for fur. Just as the forest fauna had long been essential to the Woodland Indians for food and for protection from the cold, fur-bearing animals were the essential component of the long-established trade and the material benefits it brought.

Had Native Americans maintained control of the ecosystem, perhaps they would have limited the fur trade to a sustainable level. Perhaps short-term profits would not have blinded them to long-term environmental and economic destruction. Beyond their traditional understanding of the need to conserve animal populations for future generations, there is reason to think they would have limited the fur trade. In late 1805, Lalawethika (later Tenskwatawa), a hitherto inconsequential thirty-one-year-old Shawnee, had a dream. In his dream, Waashaa Monetoo, the Great Spirit, warned that the First Peoples must return to traditional ways and values. Lalawethika woke up a changed man and began to preach the message that had come to him. His teachings broadly addressed how Native American society should live. Some were environmental. By now, the wildlife was noticeably diminished. Lalawethika taught that traditional values included not killing animals just to acquire fur for trade.[15] Another environmental teaching was to preserve maple trees by not overharvesting their syrup just to sell it to whites. Lalawethika rapidly gained followers and became known as the Prophet. His older brother and the chief of his band was Tecumseh. They voiced these environmental warnings at about the same time Humboldt was starting to publicize his broader environmental concerns. Already a noted war leader, in the coming years, Tecumseh would create the broadest of all Native American confederations.

Britain was another player in this drama. Despite ceding the Northwest Territory to the United States to establish peace in 1783, the British continued to maintain Fort Lernoult at Detroit and Fort Mackinac at the straits between Lake Superior and Lake Huron. These forts provided close, direct contact with tribes, including the Potawatomi, Wyandot, and Ottawa around Detroit and the Ottawa and Chippewa around Mackinac. By 1790, Shawnee and Delaware opposing American expansion also lived in Maumee towns. The forts maintained the vital fur trade between Canada and the tribes, both those in the Old Northwest and those even farther west.

Britain's defeat of France in the Seven Years' War, known as the French and Indian War in North America, resulted in its acquisition of Canada and complete control of the fur trade. Consequently, all of the fur trade became licensed by the British Crown and was routed through London to British merchants. They reaped the profits of sales in England and the rest of Europe. Prior to the Revolution, some fur traders were Americans, often frontier Pennsylvanians, and furs might be routed through Montreal or New York. After the Revolution, nearly all of the lucrative fur trade was a British enterprise that excluded Americans. It operated through Canada, to the benefit of Montreal merchants.[16] Not surprisingly, the magnitude of profit increased as furs moved from the forest, through Detroit or Mackinac, to Montreal, and then to London. Further increasing the economic importance of the trade, the manufactured goods that went to the Indians were all British made.

The essential groundwork was in the hands of the traders who received the furs and, in return, distributed the trade goods. As trade goods became an integral part of everyday Indian life, the identity and loyalty of the traders acquired critical economic and political significance. In the Old Northwest, these men lived in, or within easy reach of, Indian villages, maintaining the vital connection between the First Peoples and the white world. Through loyalty or necessity, they continued to work with the Indians and the British, be they of English, Scotch, Irish, French-Canadian, or biracial heritage. Britain's continued control of its forts in the Old Northwest and its ties with the most influential traders allowed it to encourage the tribes to resist giving up their lands. More important than encouragement, the British, often through the traders, supplied tribes with the means to resist American demands for land with guns, gun powder, and ammunition. Maintaining most of the Old Northwest as Indian country secured two significant benefits for Britain. One was economic: the flow of fur trade profits continued to run through London. The other was military and political: the forest and its indigenous inhabitants provided a strategic, de facto buffer zone between Britain's Canadian colony and its former American colonies. The British had not forgotten the invasions of Canada, their own from the colonies during the French and Indian War and the Americans' during the Revolution.

In contrast to the indigenous relationship with the forest, settlers did not view the woods as home. Rather they were an impediment where danger might lurk. The consequence of that perspective is well described by the US

Department of Agriculture's Forest Service. "As settlers acquired land, one of their first concerns was to clear the land of trees. The forest was an obstacle to be conquered." Trees were cleared to make room for buildings, crops, and pasture, and to provide building material and fuel. Trees were also cleared to provide a feeling of increased security from the possibility of Indians or wild animals approaching unseen.[17] Ohio tribes like the Wyandot, Delaware, Seneca-Cayuga, and Shawnee had seen this pattern on a large scale in Pennsylvania and Kentucky where much of the forest was replaced by farms and settlements, and the First Peoples had been forced out. The same pattern of land clearance was evident in Ohio since the first settlers crossed the Ohio River. Indeed, when Captain Johnny (Kekewepelethy, also Great Hawk or Tame Hawk), a Shawnee chief, complained of ongoing settlement efforts in 1785, his description was one of clearance and deforestation. "We see your intentions, you are drawing so close to us that we can almost hear the sound of your axes felling our trees & settling our country."[18]

Thus, when the subject was Indian land, it was understood that Indian land was the natural woodland ecosystem. There was no need to describe it as wooded or as forest. Conversely, when the subject was land where there were, or would be, settlers, it was understood that settled land had been, or would be, largely cleared of trees. There was no need to describe its deforestation.

The drive to clear forests and to hunt most wildlife to extinction, or near extinction, was perhaps ingrained from centuries of English culture. By the time of the Norman invasion in 1066, more than 80 percent of England was already deforested.

We sometimes describe the deep political divisions that exist today as tribalism. It is not pejorative to recognize the settlers' drive to acquire land as a tribal migration under the veneer of civilization. With relatively few exceptions, the former colonists and new Americans lacked respect for the indigenous race, religion, and culture, for the wildlife, and for the forest. From George Washington and national leadership to land speculators and settlers, of course they felt justified. Justified in seeking land and better economic circumstances, whether they were poor, wealthy, or in between. Justified by convenient feelings of racial and cultural superiority. Justified that settlement with its concomitant displacement of the tribes meant progress and national growth.

A century and a half later, in 1937, no less a titan of the twentieth century than Winston Churchill, expressed his belief in their justification: "I do not admit ... that a great wrong has been done to the Red Indians of America. ... I do not think the Red Indians had any right to say, 'The American Continent belongs to us and we are not going to have any of these European settlers coming in here.' They had not the right, nor had they the power."[19]

Ironically, had Churchill been born a "Red Indian," it is unimaginable that he would not have aggressively led the fight to protect his tribe's way of life from European and American settlement.

Conflict between the Indian population north and west of a vague, disputed line of separation and the whites to the south and the east hung over the land like an ominous specter. Conflict over who would control and inhabit the land intertwined with conflict over the very existence of the massive, ancient forest itself and of the animals within it. As the eighteenth century entered its last decade, the conflict was focused in Ohio, eastern Indiana, and northern Kentucky.

Congruent with his lifelong appetite for land acquisition, George Washington understood that the desire for land fueled expansion. In a 1771 letter, he rhetorically asked, "What Inducements have Men to explore uninhabited Wilds but the prospect of getting good Lands?"[20] For Washington, good lands meant lands that would generate profits—profits from fields of crops, pasture for cattle, cutting trees to sell timber, or from reselling the land itself.

The Indians grew crops for food, not profit. Bark was used to construct wigwams, and some now lived in wood cabins, but the forest was not timber to be sold for profit. Nor was the land itself a commodity to be sold for profit. Such concepts were alien to the First Peoples—as alien as it would have been for Washington to know to the core of his being that the forest was home and that its animals and plants supported life.

Thomas Jefferson, Washington's secretary of state from March 1790 to the end of 1793, had promoted the benefits of an agrarian republic since at least the early 1780s. And an agrarian republic meant western expansion and displacing the tribes. Though Jefferson acknowledged that Native Americans were not racially inferior, he viewed them as so culturally inferior as to not be worthy of maintaining their way of life in the forest ecosystem.

A Library of Congress exhibition describes Jefferson's impact on indigenous peoples. "In seeking to establish, what he called 'an empire for liberty,' Jefferson influenced the country's policies toward Native Americans and the extension of slavery into the West. Despite a life-long interest in Native Americans culture, President Jefferson advocated policies that would dislocate Native Americans and their way of life."[21]

In a written address issued in 1788, Arthur St. Clair, governor of the Northwest Territory, focused on "subduing a new country" and "reducing a new country from a state of nature to a state of civilization." Virtually rhapsodizing on the "very sensible pleasures" of doing so, he wrote that "the gradual progress of improvement fills the mind with delectable ideas; vast forests converted into arable fields and cities rising in places which were lately the habitations of wild beasts, give a pleasure something like that attendant on creation." The text of St. Clair's address then shifted to the dangerous obstacle in the way of altering the land and its inhabitants. "But you have upon your frontiers numbers of savages, and too often, hostile nations." He counseled the whites of Ohio, as good Christians, to treat the Indians with justice and kindness. With surprising naivety for a man of his experience, St. Clair suggested this would lead the Indians to "soon become sensible of the superior advantages of a state of civilization . . . and a way be opened for introducing amongst them the gospel of peace."[22]

The Washingtonian-Jeffersonian ideal of farms and plantations carried over to envisioning that Indians who accepted peace, and the limited land that would remain for them, would convert to being primarily farmers. This would mean altering gender roles, with men joining or replacing women who had been responsible for planting and harvesting their crops. From our twenty-first century view, this was cultural imperialism. But a balanced perspective should also consider that Washington, Jefferson, and others who agreed with them probably imagined that "civilizing" the Indians was in the Indians' best interests. Of course, more importantly, they believed it was in the best interests of white Americans. For the times, this was a relatively moderate view, certainly compared to those who wanted all Indians dead or at least banished from sight. The former was the view of many of the time, especially Kentuckians.[23]

For the tribes of the Old Northwest, the tidal wave of settlement that flowed west from the Alleghenies toward the Mississippi was an invasion akin to a plague, imposing a choice to fight or move out of its path.

Under the circumstances that existed, it is not surprising that the worst human instincts of greed and aggression fueled what was to come—indeed, what had already been happening for over a century, as evidenced by the lack of Native Americans east of the Appalachians, where once tribes had thrived. The Woodland Indians of the Old Northwest knew how some of them had been pushed out of western Pennsylvania and out of western Virginia (now West Virginia), and how the hunting grounds of Kentucky had been lost. During colonial times, no tribe claimed Kentucky as its home. Instead, it was a hunting ground for many tribes. Decades later, they still spoke of how once it was only "possessed by the wild animals of the forest . . . in great abundance," including buffalo.[24]

This is not to say that the First Peoples were not the aggressors—both economic and cultural—when it served their purposes. Certainly, they were. Tribes warred with each other long before Europeans came and long before they were enlisted as allies by the French and British in their North American conflicts. In the hunting grounds of Kentucky, parties from hostile tribes "often met or overtook each other, and many a rencounter sprinkled the ground with their blood."[25] Even when there was a defensive goal to stop colonial or American incursions, simultaneously there might be aggressive motives to attack for glory, for captives, and for plunder.

Too often, revenge motivated murderous attacks, by Indians and by whites. Too often, innocents paid the price as revenge was taken not on those who had done the prior killing but on any member of the tribe, or sometimes any Indian, for white revenge, and on any white, for Indian revenge. Also, too often, an act of revenge triggered a cycle of reprisals by both aggrieved peoples.

After the Revolutionary War, from a micro perspective, Indian war parties might have those same reasons to seek targets to kill or capture. However, by then, the tribes of the Old Northwest had decades of experience resisting first colonial, then American expansion. Those bitter experiences had proven the enormity of the challenge they faced. From a macro perspective, tribal leadership would have opted for peace and trade, not war and raids, if peace had meant keeping the land in which they lived and hunted. But the fundamental American choice was always for more land, for more farms, and for more towns. That was also a choice for less and less of the Old Northwest forest, for hunting most of the wildlife to near or actual extinction, and for the indigenous tribes to move out of the settlers' way, voluntarily or by force.

Chapter Two

Quagmires of Hate,
Oases of Humanity

IN 1763, AFTER THE FRENCH AND INDIAN WAR, Britain's King George III issued a royal proclamation that forbade settlement, and forbade governors from issuing land grants, west of the Alleghenies unless the Crown properly purchased the land from the Indians.[1] It was an effort by Britain to secure peace with Native American tribes and maintain the valuable fur trade.[2] Many colonists were outraged. Some were noncompliant, and the proclamation was not enough to stop them from pushing across the mountains into lands inhabited by the Indians. The proclamation remained a point of contention in the years that led to the Revolution. Adding to colonial discord, in 1774, Parliament passed the Quebec Act, which placed the Old Northwest under the governance of Quebec.

Though already part of Virginia's landed gentry and a member of the colony's legislature, George Washington had an abiding interest in acquiring large swaths of land west of the Alleghenies, which the royal proclamation did nothing to abate. Washington viewed the proclamation as a transient nuisance. The lieutenant governor of Virginia had promised land to Washington, as well as to those who served under him in the Virginia militia, for their military service during the French and Indian War. Four years after the proclamation, Washington wrote: "I can never look upon the Proclamation in any other light . . . than as temporary expedient to quiet the minds of the Indians. It must fall, of course, in a few years, especially when those Indians consent to our occupying those lands. . . . [M]y plan is to secure a good deal of land." It seems Washington assumed the Indians would cooperate and agree to part with their land because he wanted to believe it. Washington did succeed in acquiring more than 40,000 acres west of the Alleghenies: 3,051 in Ohio, 5,000 across the Ohio River in Kentucky, and 33,085 near the Ohio and the Great Kanawha Rivers in West Virginia.[3]

William Johnson came to the colonies in his early twenties. Rising on merit, in part because of the deep bond he developed with the Mohawk people, he became wealthy and powerful as Sir William Johnson, the northern superintendent of Indian affairs for the Crown. Extraordinarily, Johnson was equally at home living with the Mohawk and living in the white world as one of the king's highest officials in the American colonies. His relationship with the Mohawk was mutually beneficial. As the Mohawk were part of the Iroquois confederation, this also gave Johnson ties to the Iroquois.

In the 1768 Treaty of Fort Stanwix, influenced by their close relationship with Johnson, the Iroquois agreed to sell a vast amount of land, including Kentucky, most of present day West Virginia, and southwestern Pennsylvania.[4] This despite the Iroquois not actually owning those lands and Kentucky being an extremely important hunting ground for other tribes, including the Shawnee and the Cherokee. They and others refused to accept the legitimacy of the Iroquois' sale. Nevertheless, this transaction provided a legal veneer for expanding colonial settlement.

Thus, the frontier moved west of the Alleghenies, to western Pennsylvania and the western portion of the Virginia colony. In the latter 1770s and early 1780s, the Revolution came, and the frontier continued to shift west, farther into Kentucky, to Tennessee, and into Ohio. By 1790, the bloody conflict over land west of the Alleghenies—first with colonists, then with newly independent Americans, and the Native Americans who opposed them—was more than two decades old. Muskets and tomahawks, rifles and knives, had left thousands dead.

Hundreds of Indian raids and ambushes over those years left the bodies of men, women, and children to be found, usually scalped. Stories of torture were sometimes true, sometimes exaggerated. Property was plundered or destroyed, horses were taken, and cattle were stolen or killed. Those raids also took captives that numbered in the thousands.[5]

The Declaration of Independence is appropriately known for stating, "We hold these truths to be self-evident, that all men are created equal, that they are endowed by their Creator with certain unalienable Rights, that among these are Life, Liberty and the pursuit of Happiness." The Declaration goes on to list the colonies' grievances against the king. The last listed grievance proclaims, "He has excited domestic insurrections amongst us, and has endeavoured to bring on the inhabitants of our frontiers, the merciless Indian Savages, whose known rule of warfare, is an undistinguished destruction of all ages, sexes and conditions."[6] Most Americans of the time, including government and military leaders, referred to "Indians" and "savages" as if they were synonymous. Certainly, much of Indian warfare was savage. For most whites, already starting with racial and cultural biases, the bodies and destruction left in the wake of that warfare created a visceral reaction that blocked any capacity for objectivity.

What of the frontiersmen's mode of warfare as they pushed toward, and into, the Old Northwest? Contrary to what is popularly remembered now, scalping was commonly practiced not only by Indians but also by whites. Scalping was actively encouraged by "civilized" governments as early as the 1600s. The Dutch, the French, the British, and colonies such as Massachusetts, Connecticut, New Hampshire, and Pennsylvania all paid scalp bounties. During the French and Indian War, the famed Rogers' Rangers, including their commander, engaged in scalping.[7] Many Virginians and Kentuckians routinely scalped the Indians they killed.[8] That Kentuckians returned from a raid into Ohio with six scalps was reported as a detail, not worthy of comment, by Governor St. Clair to the secretary of war.[9] In 1792, after repulsing an attack on an isolated blockhouse along the Great Miami River in Ohio, the lieutenant in command wrote to General Josiah Harmar, enclosing two Indian scalps and expressing the hope that he would soon have more to send.[10]

While Indians "massacred" settlers, whites also "massacred" Indians. Though less frequent, the latter occurrences were usually on a larger scale.

One of the most horrific happened late in the Revolutionary War. An Indian village was taken and its inhabitants captured. Ninety-six men, women, and children were killed, their heads smashed with mallets, tomahawked, and scalped. All of the horses were taken. The village was looted and burned. Two children survived, despite being scalped. This was the Moravian or Gnadenhutten Massacre of Delaware Indians by Pennsylvania militia. These Delaware were known to be peaceful, Christian converts. Pennsylvania took no action against any of its militia.

Several months later, Pennsylvania militia launched another, larger raid, targeting Indian villages. This time the targets were in hostile territory, and the militia were met by a combined force of Delaware, Wyandot, Shawnee, and British. In a series of fights, the militia suffered serious losses. Most were able to retreat and return home, but a number were captured, including their commander, Colonel William Crawford. The prisoners were taken to various villages. With the massacre of the Moravian Delaware a fresh, raw wound, they were marked for death. Crawford was famously tortured and burned at the stake.

As terrible as the slow deaths of Crawford and others were, and with the bodies of women and children often found after Indian raids, Americans of the late eighteenth century were not inclined to dispassionately consider whether this justified labeling Indians as "savages." If they had, they would have had to consider that England did not abolish burning at the stake until 1790. That in New York, convictions for an alleged slave/Catholic uprising resulted in thirteen blacks being burned at the stake in 1742. And that in earlier centuries, in England and elsewhere in Europe, those deemed or suspected of being traitors were frequently tortured, and those declared to be heretics were often tortured and burned at the stake.

While settlers were the usual Indian target, frequently any Indian served as the target to quench a thirst for revenge or to satiate murderous racism. In 1786, an army officer, William North, observed, "The people under [George Rogers] Clark are back woodsmen, as much savages as those they fight against. An immortal hatred subsists in the heart of the one against the other, and whenever a Virginian back woods man meets an Indian he will kill or be killed."[11] Virginia and Kentucky militias were known to the Indians as Big Knives.[12]

Governor St. Clair wrote to President Washington of Kentuckians' "habit of retaliation, perhaps, without attending precisely to the nations from which the injuries are received."[13] To express it more bluntly, killing any Indian would do. Major John Hamtramck shared that opinion of Kentuckians and noted that they could do so without fear of punishment. At the end of 1790, Hamtramck wrote that if a treaty could be made in the spring, "the people of our frontier will certainly be the first to break it. The people of Kentucky will carry on private expeditions against the Indians and kill them whenever they meet them, and I do not believe that there is a jury in all of Kentucky who would punish a man for it."[14]

Secretary of War Henry Knox agreed that anti-Indian passions on the frontier were so strong that even if a white was brought to trial, there was no chance of conviction or punishment for killing Indians. Knox believed that this lack of justice worsened the cycle of revenge killing. He concluded that a "principal cause" of this cycle of murderous attacks, often on the innocent, began with "too many frontier white people" seizing Indian lands "by force or fraud." Although white violence against Indians was not reported or talked about, St. Clair found "much reason to believe that at least equal if not greater Injuries are done to the Indians by the frontier whites."[15]

These opinions came from observation, not from sympathy for the Indians. Writing about what would be needed to subdue the Indians, Hamtramck opined "the thirst of war is the dearest inheritance an Indian receives from his parents," while St. Clair wrote that Indian "depredations on the Ohio River . . . gratify . . . their passions of avarice and revenge, and their desire for spiritous liquors . . . every boat carrying . . . that commodity."[16]

Of course, not every frontiersman was willing to shoot any Indian, hostile or not. Nor was every Native American inclined to kill or torture every prisoner. The latter included the two most renowned Shawnee leaders, Tecumseh and Blue Jacket.

An inspiring leader politically and militarily, Tecumseh created a renewed Indian alliance in the early 1800s and led its warriors in the War of 1812. Tecumseh was a young warrior when he first spoke out against burning prisoners. Stephen Ruddell, an adopted white and a close friend from the time they were twelve, told the story: When they were fifteen, or possibly twenty, Tecumseh distinguished himself in an attack on a boat traveling the Ohio River, the Great Sepe, "river," to the Shawnee.[17] A prisoner was taken and burned alive. Disgusted, Tecumseh spoke against it. It was agreed that no more prisoners would be burned. After that, Ruddell maintained, if Tecumseh was present, prisoners were never burned or tortured.

There are multiple accounts from whites and blacks of how well they were treated by Blue Jacket when they were captured or held captive in his village. Under his protection, they might work in conditions as good as or better than before they were captured. Jacob Hubbs, a white man, worked as a clerk for Blue Jacket's trading business. A black man whose name is unknown worked as a steward or manager for Blue Jacket's trading business. A Mrs. Honn lived with his family, taking care of the cows and making butter.[18]

Blue Jacket, however, did not have unilateral authority to spare prisoners, unless he personally had a clear claim to the captive. Nevertheless, he could use his influence and powers of persuasion. For instance, in 1786, Jerry Hays was captured at Drinnon's Lick, Kentucky, by a raiding party led by Blue Jacket. No one warrior captured Hays, so no one had the sole right to decide what to do with him. Despite others wanting to kill Hays, Blue Jacket refused, explaining that Hays was needed to carry their swag back home. Once they returned, Blue Jacket's wife, presumably with his approval, bought Hays from the raiding party with gallons of rum, thereby saving his life.[19]

Certainly, the fate of those who were captured by the Indians was precarious. Some were quickly killed for convenience, or because pursuit was imminent, or for immediate revenge. Others, particularly smaller children or the wounded, might be killed on the trail when they proved to be a hindrance. If they were brought back to their captors' village, death, sometimes by torture, remained a threat for adults, more so for men. Torture and death were most often used to slake a desire to avenge slain relatives. Children who reached their captors' village were normally spared and usually adopted. Most women and some men were also spared. For them, adoption was possible, though much less common. Adoptions might be motivated by taking a liking to a captive or to replace a family member who had died. Even if not adopted, some captives found a place in village life. Many were held to be ransomed, frequently through the British. Occasionally, a prisoner might be released to the British at their request.

The fate of some captives was not decided until they were brought back to a village. One such case occurred in February 1790, when a young man named McMullen was captured by Shawnee while hunting near the Ohio River. The Shawnee were out to avenge an attack on a hunting party the prior spring in which men, women, and children were killed. McMullen's face was painted black, an ominous sign that he might be burned at the stake. There was also the possibility of his being given to a family for adoption, probably to replace a relative who had died. The villagers, men and women, gathered in council. As Henry Hay, a visiting trader described, McMullen's captor gave "a very minute Report of all what passed—which they are obliged to do."[20] The war party had not lost anyone and had gained a number of horses. With a consensus reached that McMullen should be adopted, his face was washed clean of the black paint. As part of the adoption ceremony, his body was washed, and he was given clean clothes and a wampum belt.

For some, the decision might not be made until after they were forced to run a gauntlet, which meant running through two lines of villagers, men, women, and children, who might strike with clubs, sticks, or switches. It was a test of the captive's bravery and pain tolerance. After the gauntlet, captives might be allowed to live, or they might be killed, perhaps slowly.

Oliver Spencer, captured as a boy by Shawnee, told of a gauntlet run by William Moore. It happened at Blue Jacket's town. Men, women, and children, not only from Blue Jacket's village but also from neighboring villages, came for the show. Moore was about six feet, two inches tall, quick, and strong. Spencer knew him to be "fearless and lawless . . . naturally good-humored and obliging, but when roused a perfect savage." More than two hundred men, women, and children "armed with clubs, switches and other instruments of punishment . . . arranged themselves facing each other in two rows, about seven feet apart . . . each distant about four or five feet from each other." Chiefs and principal warriors were at the head of the lines near the cabin that Moore ultimately had to reach. Moore was stripped to the waist, with his wrists tied together, though his left wrist was wounded when he was captured. He was to run the course, then turn and run back through it again to the cabin. "Starting a short distance from the head of the lines, he soon bounded through them; and breathing for a few moments, returning with the same speed had reached the middle of his course, when the Indians, fearing that from his fleetness he would run through with little injury, (as most of their blows, instead of falling on his back, fell clattering on each other's sticks,) half closing their ranks attempted to obstruct his progress." Kicking, punching, and headbutting, Moore broke through the attempted blockade and completed his run. "[H]e was congratulated as a brave man."[21] Moore's performance won his life and acceptance in the village. Other than being longer than average, this gauntlet was typical. Moore's degree of success in getting through it was not typical.

Being an expert in the woods was no guarantee against capture. Simon Kenton, a contemporary and peer of frontiersman Daniel Boone, Boone himself, and even Blue Jacket, experienced capture. Each of their experiences was unique.

Kenton fared the worst. He was captured while trying to steal horses from a party of Shawnee. Treated harshly, he was forced to run multiple gauntlets. Several times, Kenton's face was painted black, a sign that he was condemned to die by being burned at the stake. He survived through the intercession of Simon Girty, a British Indian agent. Years before, Kenton and Girty had become close friends on the Virginia frontier. Now it was 1778. The Revolutionary War raged in Kentucky, and Kenton and Girty were on opposite sides. Fortunately for Kenton, Girty happened to come to the village where Kenton was being held. Girty's friendship remained undiminished. Girty was well known to the Shawnee. First through persuasion and later through British influence, he succeeded in having Kenton spared and turned over to the British.[22] Months later, having healed from his ordeals, Kenton escaped from Detroit and made his way back to Kentucky.

In winter 1778, Boone was surprised by Shawnee while he was hunting. With immediate death the only other option, Boone surrendered. He had led men from Boonesborough to gather salt from a salt lick. With a much larger party of Shawnee ready to surprise and overwhelm them, Boone agreed to have his men surrender in return for a promise they would be spared. More than two dozen were taken prisoner. Impressed with Boone and with nothing personal against him, a Shawnee chief adopted him after Boone successfully ran a gauntlet. Adopting a grown man into the tribe was far less common than adopting a child or a woman. Surprisingly, most of his men were also adopted. Four months later, Boone escaped and made his way back from Ohio to warn that the Shawnee were planning to attack Boonesborough.

Ten years later, Blue Jacket was captured while leading a horse-stealing raid in Kentucky. Surprised and pursued by a larger group of Kentuckians, he found himself alone and cut off from escape. Like Boone, seeing no alternative other than being shot, he surrendered. Struck in the head and threatened with death, Blue Jacket protested that he was only taking horses, not killing anyone, and spoke of his good relationship with Boone. This convinced his captors to take him to Limestone. A night of drinking by captors and captive followed. The next morning, some of the hungover Kentuckians discharged gunpowder from their muskets at Blue Jacket. It is likely that Blue Jacket gave them little reaction to enjoy. After another night, Blue Jacket managed to undo his restraints and escape into the woods, leaving no trail for the Kentuckians to follow.[23]

Despite the enmity between them, the Shawnee and Kentuckians were twice led by self-interest to negotiate prisoner exchanges. The first occurred the year before Blue Jacket's capture. Negotiations stretched for months until there was an agreement to meet just south of the Ohio, at Limestone, in August 1787. Captain Johnny led the Shawnee delegation, which included Blue Jacket and other chiefs. Negotiating for Kentucky were Benjamin Logan, who had taken Shawnee captives during a devastating raid ten months earlier, Daniel Boone, John Crow, and Isaac Ruddell.

Ruddell, his family, and more than one hundred others had surrendered to a large force of British and Indians at Ruddell Station in 1780. Most, including Ruddell and his wife, were released by the British in 1782. But two of their sons, Stephen and Abraham, were adopted and remained with the Shawnee. Twelve and six when they were taken, neither they nor the Shawnee considered them prisoners to be exchanged. The Ruddell brothers lived as Shawnees for fifteen years.

During the talks, Blue Jacket took one of Boone's sons hunting. The meeting was successful in that some white captives and most of Logan's Shawnee captives were released. Blue Jacket expressed his appreciation to the people of Limestone and to Boone. He tangibly showed his appreciation when he returned home by arranging for the release of another white captive who was from Limestone.[24]

Notwithstanding ongoing conflict and the inability to hold a peace council, the following year, Kentuckians and Shawnee negotiated another prisoner exchange. To initiate negotiations, Isaac Freeman was sent to the Maumee towns. There, Freeman met with Blue Jacket and stayed in his home. Freeman observed gunpowder and lead arriving by packhorse from Detroit, as well as British flags flying over some homes. He also learned that other Maumee villages were receiving gunpowder and lead from Detroit. With a shared desire to exchange prisoners, an agreement was reached. Six whites were returned to Freeman. Two, however, did not want to return and fled before Freeman could start back. Once the other four were safely in Kentucky, ten of fifteen Shawnee prisoners were freed.[25]

That two of the whites released to Freeman would not leave the Shawnee was not an isolated phenomenon. Among our largely forgotten history is that it was not unusual for eighteenth-century whites who had been captured, then adopted, to want to remain with their Indian lives and families. Once adopted, their former state of captivity was extinguished and of no import. When treaties were made that required the return of all captives, including those who had been adopted, many did not wish to return. That adoptees who had been captured in raids could come to feel that way must have triggered bewilderment, disgust, and disbelief among many who thought of Indians as "savages."

As eminent an observer as Benjamin Franklin noted this phenomenon in 1753. Contrasting Indian children who were brought up by colonists "and habituated to our Customs," choosing to return to their tribe if ever given the opportunity to do so, Franklin observed:

"[T]hat when white persons of either sex have been taken prisoners young by the Indians, and lived a while among them, tho' ransomed by their Friends, and treated with all imaginable tenderness to prevail with them to stay among the English, yet in a Short time they become disgusted with our manner of life, and the care and pains that are necessary to support it, and take the first good Opportunity of escaping again into the Woods, from whence there is no reclaiming them."[26]

In 1764, when Pontiac's War ended, the English compelled the defeated tribes to return more than two hundred whites who had been captured and adopted. The commanding officer, Colonel Henry Bouquet, documented that many did not want to return, some of them so much so that they were forcibly restrained. Thus, whites captured by Indians became prisoners to compel their return. Bouquet also documented that some, who were clever enough to protest less, escaped back to their Indian lives.[27]

Lieutenant Ebenezer Denny observed the Shawnee return a number of whites they had captured in prior years. Denny described the reaction of one of the boys. "[W]hen he found there was no way of escaping [back to the Shawnee] he cried, and appeared to leave the Indians with more regret than he could have done if they had been bearing him away a prisoner from his mother." A few weeks later, several of the boys and a young woman "made their escape and returned to the Indians."[28]

Why did some whites who had been taken captive, usually in violent, bloody circumstances, want to stay with their adopted families and live as Indians? Franklin's answer was that "human Nature" naturally gravitated to the Indians' "life of ease, of freedom from care and labour" where "almost all their Wants are supplied by spontaneous Productions of Nature, with the addition of very little labour, if hunting and fishing may indeed be called labour when Game is so plenty."[29] Franklin's answer greatly exaggerated the ease of Indian life, omitting the rigors of being a warrior and ignoring the work of women, including raising crops. But there was truth in the idea that Indian life could be more attractive than the often rigid, ordered lifestyles of many colonists and early Americans. The most noted and successful Indian fighter of the French and Indian War, Robert Rogers, described these aspects of typical Indian life:

[W]hen sick, the woods and the lakes furnish them with all the drugs they make use of; in the application of which some indeed are allowed to excel in skill, but ask no fee or reward for their trouble. And altho' there is such a thing as private property among them, which they transfer to one another, by way of bargain and exchange, and if taken out of the compass of fair dealing, the aggressor is stigmatised, and punished with distain: yet no individual or family is allowed to suffer by poverty, sickness, or any misfortunes, while their neighbors can supply their wants; and all of this from the simple natural consideration.[30]

In today's terms, each village provided a social safety net. In contrast, in America, as in England, debtors' prisons were common.

Honesty, cooperation, and personal choice were prized. While these were also valued in white society, it is fair to say that personal choice was more restricted and less prioritized. For the most part, Indian life was substantially one of individual choices. Chiefs, especially war chiefs, were followed by choice, not by law. Decisions were accepted based on agreement, consensus, and the influence a chief had earned. Rising to leadership was largely based on merit. Thus, tribes generally enjoyed the benefits of pure democracy, while also being disadvantaged by its attendant structural weaknesses.

Also intrinsic to most Eastern Woodland Native American cultures were, to use modern terms, social mobility and social equality. America's work toward making these principles norms had begun as colonies and continued at a faster pace after the Revolution. The lives of men like Benjamin Franklin and Alexander Hamilton are notable examples of social mobility. However, though valued, these principles were not as fundamental, nor as widespread, in the early United States as they were among the Eastern Woodland tribes. This was true even for white society, racial inequality and prejudice obviously being pervasive. That states restricted the vote to white men with property is a prime example of social inequality and a concept alien to Native Americans.

Stockholm syndrome is the phenomenon of captives developing positive feelings toward, and identification with, their captors, while simultaneously developing negative feelings toward those trying to find and rescue them. It is not a mental health diagnosis but is considered a survival or coping mechanism. However, the overwhelming majority of captives do not develop the syndrome.[31] That significantly contrasts with the substantial number of Eastern Woodland Indian adoptees, albeit still a minority, who wanted to remain with their adoptive tribe.

Another factor to consider, though not specifically mentioned in primary sources, is that some Eastern Woodland tribes viewed premarital sex as natural and not improper.[32] That might well have been a factor for some adoptees.

While some who were captured as young men wanted to stay with their adopted families, most males who wanted to stay had been taken as children. The younger they were taken, the more likely they did not want to leave the life they knew. Women who consented to marry and had children, whether taken as children or as young women, also more often resisted returning to white society. They knew that unlike Indian society, their children would not be fully accepted in white society. Of course, if forced to leave their children behind, the motive not to return was even stronger. It was contemporaneously observed that the marriages of these women were the product of consent, not compulsion, and certainly not of rape.[33]

A French-American, John Hector St. John de Crevecouer, wrote of the Indians' "social bond [being] something singularly captivating." Whatever the reasons, the strength of the social bonds felt by many white adoptees is evidenced by "the large number of English colonists who became, contrary to the civilized assumptions of their countrymen, white Indians."[34]

Chapter Three ●

The Drive for Land,
the Descent into War

I N THE 1780S, THE UNITED STATES ACHIEVED independence and transitioned from the Articles of Confederation to the Constitution. In 1789, the Constitution took effect, Washington was inaugurated as the first president, the Bill of Rights was submitted to the states for ratification, and the Federal Judiciary Act created the Supreme Court as well as the lower federal courts. In the course of the decade, the frontier moved west from Pennsylvania into Ohio, and settlement multiplied exponentially to engulf Kentucky. The white population of Kentucky mushroomed from three hundred in 1775 to seventy-three thousand in 1790.[1]

Native American confederations, such as the Iroquois (originally five nations and later six) and the Huron, predated European arrival. They understood the value of tribes uniting, both to secure peace among their members and to strengthen the confederated tribes against others.

To promote unity and alliances, intertribal councils could be called. Calumets—long-stemmed tobacco pipes—could be sent to signal that a peaceful meeting was desired. Beaded belts of wampum, with lengths measured in feet or even yards, could be sent to signal the purpose of the meeting. Purple meant an agenda to discuss alliance or confederation. Red traditionally meant war was to be proposed. A red hatchet was a clear signal war would be proposed.

Since England's defeat of France, astute tribal leaders had seen the necessity for alliances to gain the strength needed to resist first colonial and then American expansion. Whether a tribal confederation could be formed, and if so, among which tribes, were political questions. The answers would determine the power of the tribes' diplomatic and military capabilities. Pontiac formed the first such confederation in 1763. After initial military success through a series of coordinated attacks, he was defeated by the British. In Dunmore's War, in 1774, the Shawnee had allies, but lacked the support of a true confederation. Dunmore's War was a conflict between the colony of Virginia and the Shawnee, who were joined by the Seneca-Cayuga (Mingo) and small groups of Delaware, Miami, Ottawa, Wyandot, and others. It was named after Lord Dunmore, the governor of Virginia. The conflict culminated in a bloody day-long battle at Point Pleasant, at the juncture of the Ohio and Kanawha Rivers.

During the American Revolution, discussions of forming a confederation abated, as the issue became whether to be neutral, ally with England, or ally with the revolutionary colonists. Initially, some tribes sought to remain neutral. As the war continued, most tribes of the frontier and of the Old Northwest became active British allies. The fundamental reason for doing so was simple: the British promised to limit settlement and preserve Indian homes and hunting grounds. Then the fighting ended, followed by the formal recognition of American independence in the Treaty of Paris. The tribes had not lost their part of the war, but England surrendered its claim to the land where they lived and hunted.

With England's defeat, the political question of tribal confederation arose again, more important than ever. Subsumed within that question was the issue of tribal unity. Which, if any, tribes could truly unify to fight? Which would agree on a diplomatic policy? To what extent would tribes splinter?

The earliest American settlers entered Ohio even before the United States achieved independence. They notched trees at each corner of the land they claimed and began to clear trees and build. After independence, the numbers increased. These early settlers were designated by the government as squatters because they were occupying land without having acquired any legal title. They were subject to eviction by the army, and those efforts began as early as 1779. They were also subject to attack for being on Indian land. The squatters were numerous enough to be a concern for both the new American nation and the Native American nations. In 1787, Secretary of War Knox considered the "extremely imminent" threat of large numbers of squatters usurping the government's authority over the land to be the greatest threat to the plans for the Northwest Territory.[2]

When Captain Johnny complained about settlers in 1785, the first legal settlement was still three years in the future. Legal, organized settlements began in 1788, as first Marietta and then Losantiville were established. The latter was renamed Cincinnati in 1790. Marietta was built on the east bank of the Muskingum River and the north bank of the Ohio. It was established across the Muskingum from Fort Harmar, which had been constructed three years earlier. The following year, Fort Washington was established at Losantiville.

Like Marietta and Cincinnati, the legal settlements tended to be along, or close to, the Ohio River. Squatters tended to venture farther from the Ohio and are known to have been in what are now Columbiana County, Jefferson County, and Belmont County on the eastern edge of Ohio, as well as more numerously along rivers in southern Ohio, including the Muskingum, the Hockhocking (now simply the Hocking), the Scioto, and the Great Miami. While the number of squatter families over time numbered more than a thousand, not all were successful in establishing permanent farms.[3]

Understanding that the new nation of former colonists would continue to clear more forest and settle more land, a large intertribal council was held in late summer 1783, along the lower Sandusky River. The Wyandot hosted participants who included Iroquois, Shawnee, Delaware, Ottawa, Ojibwe, and Potawatomi. Some interested Cherokee and Creek also came. At the forefront was the widely respected Mohawk leader Joseph Brant (Thayendanegea). The Mohawks were one of the Six Nations of the Iroquois. Concurrently, across the Atlantic, American and British negotiators were moving toward concluding the Treaty of Paris.

Joseph Brant had familial ties to Sir William Johnson. Those ties came through Joseph's older sister, Molly Brant (Degonwadonti, or Several Against One). Molly Brant and William Johnson enjoyed a twenty-one-year relationship, beginning when he was thirty-eight and she was seventeen, until his death in 1774. Over those years, they had eight children. Living together, Molly Brant presided over their homes, and her "status as Johnson's partner [was recognized] in both white and Indian societies."[4] As a result of their relationship, Joseph Brant grew up educated as a Mohawk warrior with a deep understanding of English ways. Allied with the British, as the Mohawk war chief, Brant was the scourge of upper New York during the Revolution.

The Iroquois, who had once dominated militarily and politically far beyond their homes in upper New York, were drastically weakened in the Revolutionary War. The diminished power of the Iroquois and of the English led many Indian leaders to consider a fundamental shift in their thinking. They began to envision a broader perspective than that of their own tribe's interests—a perspective that gave weight, even priority, to the cooperative interests of as broad a confederation as could be formed, because that was ultimately in their long-term tribal interest.

At the intertribal council of 1783, Brant and others promoted three intertwined propositions. First, that the tribes should act together in a confederation—something that had never been proposed on such a grand scale. Second, that only the new confederation, not any one tribe or combination of tribes, should enter into treaties with the United State. That concept was strengthened by the third proposition: that all tribes had rights in all of the different tribal lands. This was a radical change in thinking in response to the new reality they faced. Many tribal leaders saw, or began to consider, the wisdom of and necessity for this fundamental change.

From 1783 through the decade and into the 1790s, a confederation was formed among many tribes, albeit not always unified tribes, for diplomatic purposes. Their principal position was that land could not be sold without the consent of all. From the beginning, this new confederation involved the Wyandot, Iroquois, Shawnee, Delaware, Ottawa, Ojibwe, and Potawatomi. Nevertheless, though tribes might agree in principle, the coming years would see the United States obtain new treaties conceding land, purportedly from some of the individual tribes, despite the confederation's tenets. But through pressure and coercion, these concessions came from chiefs who were not empowered to speak for their entire tribe, an inconvenient political fact disregarded by the government and its negotiators.

Winning independence left economic and political pressures on the new American republic. Revenue was needed to pay off a war debt approaching $40 million. Veterans of the Continental army had been promised land. These burdens fueled the drive for more land, as the Northwest Territory presented opportunities for the federal government to lessen its debt and fulfill its promises. As the territory was under federal control, land could be sold to nonveteran settlers and to land speculators, while other parcels could be given to veterans.

In 1783, the United States operated under the Articles of Confederation and the first presidential election was five years in the future. Like the new tribal confederation, George Washington was also looking ahead to the future of "the Western Country." His immediate focus was on the land from where the Great Miami River empties into the Ohio, north to the confluence of the Mad River with the Great Miami, northwest to the Miami villages on the Maumee, northeast on a line that included Detroit (still held by the British) to Lake Erie, east to Pennsylvania and back south to the Ohio.[5] Washington saw the need for government control across these lands, in part, "to receive . . . a large population of Emigrants," to create future new States, and to avoid emigrants roaming "at least 500,000 Square Miles contributing nothing to the support, but much perhaps to the Embarrassment of the Federal Government." Washington concluded that

the Settlemt of the Western Country and making a Peace with the Indians are so analogous that there can be no definition of the one without involving considerations of the other. . . . [P]olicy and economy point very strongly to the expediency of being upon good terms with the Indians, and the propriety of purchasing their Lands in preference to attempting to drive them by force of arms out of their Country; which as we have already experienced is like driving the Wild Beasts of the Forest which will return [to] us soon as the pursuit is at an end and fall perhaps on those that are left there; when the gradual extension of our Settlements will as certainly cause the Savage as the Wolf to retire; both being beasts of prey tho' they differ in shape. In a word there is nothing to be obtained by an Indian War but the Soil they live on and this can be had by purchase at less expence, and without that bloodshed, and those distresses which helpless Women and Children are made partakers of in all kinds of disputes with them.[6]

Thus, for Washington, large-scale emigration by white settlers into the Indian land of the Old Northwest was a given. This necessarily meant that acquiring millions of acres of Indian land was a given, preferably by purchase, possibly by war.

Implicit in Washington's view was that the Indians should agree to sell when the government offered to purchase their land. While thinking that war would be neither wise nor just without seeking to buy the land, Washington ultimately felt that the Indian nations had no right to say no and refuse to move aside. He expressed this to Thomas Jefferson, opining that if the land "is thinly occupied by another nation . . . a principle of the law of nations . . . there are but two means of acquiring the native title. 1. War; *for even war may sometimes give a just title.* 2. Contract, or treaty."[7] (Emphasis added.)

To understand the mindset of most Americans of the time, Washington's likening the Indians to "the Wild Beasts of the Forest" and referring to them as "beasts of prey" should not be overlooked. When Others are viewed as evil, or savage, or lesser, human nature instinctively finds it easier to justify war. Killing or driving the Others away becomes more palatable, especially if the land they inhabit is desirable.

Today, at least our theoretical sense of conflict of interest is more acute than it was in the late eighteenth century. Acquiring Ohio land was further driven by land speculators' avarice and the financial interests of influential, powerful investors. Among them were Arthur St. Clair, Winthrop Sargent, and William Duer. All were involved with companies speculating in millions of acres of Ohio land, and the future of their investments depended on an absence of Indians.

St. Clair invested in the Ohio Company when he was president of Congress, before the Constitution was ratified, while the government operated under the Articles of Confederation. He continued to be invested after he was appointed governor of the Northwest Territory. Sargent was the secretary of the Ohio Company when it was formed in 1786. A year later, he was appointed secretary of the Northwest Territory. Duer invested while he was secretary of the Confederation Treasury Board. He became an assistant to Secretary of the Treasury Hamilton and a business associate of Secretary of War Knox's. Duer also became the War Department's general contractor, a position jointly overseen by the War and Treasury Departments.

Burdened with debt and with barely any army, the federal government had good reason to seek Indian land without the expense and difficulty of war. Congress found little money to spend on maintaining a standing army. By mid-1784, the army had shrunk to three officers and seventy-five enlisted men, split between Fort Pitt and West Point. The following year, without a meaningful standing army, Congress obtained eight militia companies from Connecticut, New Jersey, New York, and Pennsylvania for service on the frontier.

In 1785, the government began its efforts to acquire Indian land in the Northwest Territory. The Confederation Congress sent commissioners, including George Rogers Clark and Richard Butler, to obtain the desired land.

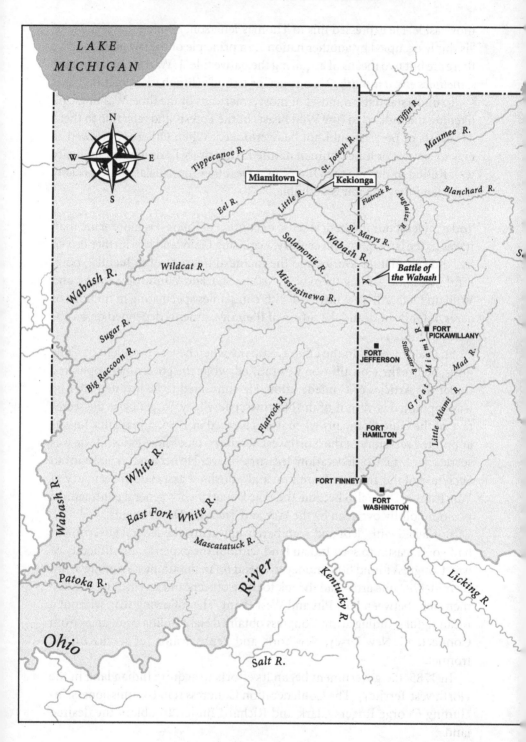

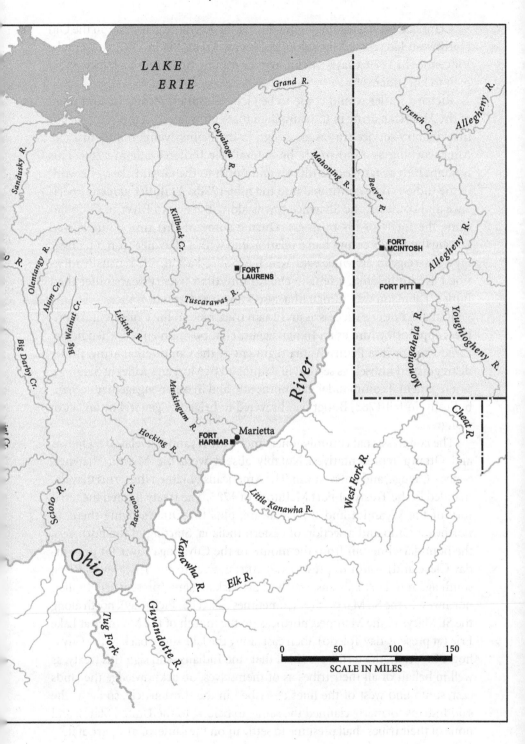

LAKE
ERIE

Grand R.

French Cr.

Allegheny R.

Cuyahoga R.

Mahoning R.

Beaver R.

Sandusky R.

FORT
MCINTOSH

Killbuck Cr.

FORT
LAURENS

Allegheny R.

o R.

Olentangy R.

FORT PITT

Alum Cr.

Tuscarawas R.

Youghiogheny R.

Big Walnut Cr.

Licking R.

Monongahela R.

Big Darby Cr.

Muskingum R.

River

Cheat R.

Hocking R.

FORT
HARMAR

Marietta

West Fork R.

Scioto R.

Raccoon Cr.

Little Kanawha R.

Ohio

Kanawha R.

Elk R.

Tug Fork

Guyandotte R.

0   50   100   150

SCALE IN MILES

Clark had been a leading figure during the Revolutionary War in the Old Northwest. He crossed the Ohio to capture Kaskaskia in 1778 and to take Vincennes in 1779. Clark was known for leading his Virginian backwoodsmen to kill Indians.[8]

Richard Butler would come to be General Butler, second in command of the American army in the campaign that culminated on the Wabash. His first military service was as an ensign in the Pennsylvania militia in 1764. After working as a gunsmith, he entered the Indian trade in 1766. This brought him as far west as Illinois and north to the Great Lakes. His work in the Indian trade continued into the mid-1770s. As Butler gained experience and contacts, the Shawnee towns along the Scioto River in Ohio became the focus of his business. During some of this time, Butler lived among the Shawnee and had a relationship with a Shawnee woman, possibly a marriage in Shawnee eyes, which produced a son. She is usually identified as Nonhelema, a female chief, more than twenty years older than Butler. Their son was Tamanatha, also known as Captain Butler.[9]

Richard Butler's success as an Indian trader led to the Continental Congress appointing him as an Indian agent. That position ended when he became a major in a Pennsylvania regiment of the Continental army. Butler distinguished himself as second in command of Morgan's Rifles at Saratoga, as a regimental commander at Monmouth, and in other engagements. Symbolically, in fall 1783, Butler was breveted to brigadier general by an act of Congress.[10]

The congressional commissioners met with Wyandot, Delaware, Ojibwe, and Ottawa representatives. Notably absent were the Miami, Shawnee, Seneca-Cayuga, and Potawatomi. The Americans obtained the terms they demanded in the Treaty of Fort McIntosh of 1785. The treaty limited the territory of the Wyandot and the Delaware, plus the Ottawa living there, to northwest Ohio and a section of eastern Indiana. Starting in the northeast, the boundary line ran from the mouth of the Cuyahoga River (at present-day Cleveland) south to present-day Akron, west to the Tuscarawas River, south again to Fort Laurens, west to Fort Pickawillany (present-day Piqua), northwest to the St. Marys River (sometimes called the Pickaway), north along the St. Marys to the Maumee, northeast to the mouth of the Maumee at Lake Erie (at present-day Toledo), then east along the lake shore back to the Cuyahoga. Critically, the terms provided that "the Indians who sign this treaty, as well in behalf of all their tribes as of themselves, do acknowledge the lands east, south and west of the lines described in the third article, so far as the said Indians formerly claimed the same, to belong to the United States; and none of their tribes shall presume to settle upon the same, or any part of it."[11]

These were the terms the United States wanted from all the tribes. This would make most of Ohio and Indiana white territory, available for settlement. It would separate the Miami, Shawnee, Delaware, Wyandot, and Seneca-Cayuga from the Potawatomi, Ojibwe, and most of the Ottawa. It placed some important Miami villages outside the boundary line because they were on the west bank of the Maumee, rather than on the east bank.

A year later, Clark and Butler, with Commissioner Samuel Holden Parsons, continued their efforts. This time they focused on the Shawnee, who had once extended their hospitality to Butler in his years as a trader. Reluctantly, some Shawnees came to meet with Clark, Butler, and Parsons at Fort Finney. Moluntha was the hereditary, principal civil chief of the tribe, by virtue of his being chief of the Mekoche, one of five Shawnee clans. Moluntha headed the Shawnee delegation. He was elderly, probably in his nineties. Most of the Shawnee who came to the fort were members of his clan. They did so despite a consensus among the tribes that only the Confederation should negotiate with the United States, not individual tribes. Nevertheless, believing that war was unwinnable, Moluntha was at Fort Finney.

At the conference, the Shawnee initially refused to surrender any land. The commissioners responded with an overt threat of war. Richard Butler displayed no good will toward the Shawnee. For Moluntha, the choice was between the lesser of two evils. With sadness and resentment, he and his followers acceded to the American demands. The paramount provision limited where the Shawnee (spelled Shawanoe in the treaty) could live or hunt to an area immediately south of the Wyandot/Delaware reservation, with the southwest corner at the confluence of the de Panse and Wabash Rivers. (The de Panse is now called Wildcat Creek and runs from near Kokomo to Lafayette, Indiana.) Most Shawnee, other than the Mekoches, never accepted the treaty's terms, and Moluntha had neither the authority nor the power to make them do so. A biographer concluded: "It was evident that Richard Butler had discarded his empathy for the plight of the Indians. In his early years he had gone out of his way to help Native Americans. Now he uncompromisingly dispensed the harsh policy of conquerors."[12]

The Fort McIntosh and Fort Finney treaties were worse than worthless in achieving the goal of agreeing on boundaries that both the United States and the indigenous tribes would accept.

Months later, in October, Moluntha and the Mekoche were peacefully in their village. Moluntha displayed the American flag when they were attacked by Kentucky militia led by Colonel Benjamin Logan in what is known as Logan's Raid. Most of the warriors were away for the fall hunt. Without them, there was little resistance to the Kentuckians.

After surrendering, the old chief was asked by militia Colonel Hugh Mc-Gary if he had been at Blue Licks, where 170 Kentuckians had walked into an ambush in 1782. Waiting for them, positioned across the trail at the summit of a ridge and on both flanks, were hundreds of Indians and fifty British rangers led by Captain William Caldwell, Alexander McKee, and Simon Girty. More than half of the Kentuckians were quickly killed or captured. The survivors retreated.

Moluntha's response was short. He may have said Blue Licks, either as an affirmation, or as a question. Whatever Moluntha said or meant, McGary struck him twice in the head with a hatchet, killing him. Then McGary scalped the old chief.

Logan had ordered that prisoners were not to be harmed, but he took no action against McGary. Article 3 of the Fort Finney treaty provided that a Shawnee who murdered, robbed, or injured an American citizen, and any American citizen who injured a Shawnee, would "be punished according to the laws of the United States." After Logan's Raid, McGary was court-martialed. His punishment was a year's suspension from the militia. This example of the laws of the United States further hardened Indian hostility.

Logan's Raid was not limited to Moluntha's village. The Kentuckians went on to sack at least four, and possibly six, more Shawnee villages around the headwaters of the Great Miami and its confluence with the Mad River. These included Blue Jacket's Town. Most of the warriors from these villages were also away hunting. Homes were looted and burned. Thousands of bushels of corn were burned. As many as thirty women and children were taken prisoner.[13]

The goal was to make the Shawnee suffer and force them farther west. In that, the Kentuckians succeeded. Logan's Raid demonstrated the vulnerability of the villages along the Great Miami and its tributaries. With the consent of the Miami, most Shawnee relocated their villages near Kekionga and the other Maumee towns. Blue Jacket was among those who led their followers west to the Maumee. Many Delaware and Seneca-Cayuga did the same.

Other Shawnee and Delaware gave up and chose to migrate across the Mississippi to Missouri, which was still part of Spain's colonies. A small Shawnee band decided they could best resist the Americans by joining the Chickamauga Cherokee's fight in Tennessee. The Chickamauga were based around Lookout Mountain, near present-day Chattanooga. The Shawnee who joined them were led by Cheeseekau (Chiksika), a war chief of the Kispoko clan. With him was his younger brother, Tecumseh. Both of those moves depleted the warriors available to fight for the Wabash country, the

Maumee, and Ohio. In summer 1791, Tecumseh returned north. The next year, Cheeseekau was killed leading an attack. It was said that he predicted his death.[14]

Less than a month after Logan's Raid, Blue Jacket and the Shawnee began to strike back, launching limited raids into Kentucky. According to Shawnee history, that summer, angry warriors "killed many and took many scalps."[15]

There was an eerie coincidence to the revenge killing and scalping of Moluntha in Logan's Raid. Until April 1774, a Seneca-Cayuga (Mingo) leader, Talgayeeta, was well known for being hospitable to whites and an advocate for peace. That changed when his family, including the women and children, were among the victims of a killing raid by whites. Their deaths triggered a series of revenge raids by a disconsolate Talgayeeta, which left numerous white men, women, and children dead. Talgayeeta was known to whites as Logan.

In late November and December 1786, another large, intertribal conference was held by the incipient Indian Confederation. Originally intended to be held among the Shawnee villages, in the aftermath of Logan's Raid it convened instead at Brownstown, a Wyandot village at the mouth of the Detroit River. The Wyandot hosted Iroquois, Shawnee, Miami, Delaware, Seneca-Cayuga, Potawatomi, Ottawa, Ojibwe, and others. Again, Joseph Brant was at the forefront. Urging everyone to learn from the past, he forcefully advocated for unanimity in policy. "If we make a war with any nation, let it result from the great council fire. If we make peace, let it also proceed from our unanimous councils.... The welfare of the one should be the welfare of all the others."[16] Sagacious words, but left unanswered was how to achieve unanimity.

Addressing Congress as our "Brethren" and as "Brothers," the council said it desired and hoped for peace, based on the 1768 Fort Stanwix treaty that the Iroquois, through Sir William Johnson, had made with the British. While that treaty ceded immense areas to settlement, significantly it set the Ohio River as a boundary line, maintaining the land north and west of the Ohio for Native American tribes.

The name Ohio comes from the Iroquois and translates to Beautiful River. The nearly nine hundred mile long Ohio begins in far western Pennsylvania at the confluence of the Allegheny and Monongahela Rivers. It soon turns south-southwest, and from that point on it becomes first the eastern and then the southern border of Ohio as it flows to the Mississippi.

The council's position on subsequent treaties and on any new treaties, unless they were made with the Confederation, was clear:

"[A]ll treaties carried on with the United States, on our parts, should be with the general voice of the whole confederacy. . . . And especially as landed matters are often the subject of our councils with you . . . we hold it indispensably necessary that any cession of our lands should be made in the most public manner, and by the united voice of the confederacy; holding all partial treaties as void and of no effect."[17]

There was a request: "We beg that you will prevent your surveyors and other people from coming upon our side of the Ohio River." There was also a warning: If a grand council was not held, and if the surveyors and others kept coming across the Ohio River, the Confederation would defend the "rights and privileges which have been transmitted to us by our ancestors; and if we should thereby be reduced to misfortunes, the world will pity us when they think of the amiable proposals we now make to prevent the unnecessary effusion of blood."[18]

To establish a governing system for the territory, the Northwest Ordinance was enacted in 1787. Pursuant to the ordinance, Arthur St. Clair was appointed the territorial governor. St. Clair was born in Scotland, though his name indicates an English heritage. More than thirty years earlier, he had bought a commission as a lieutenant in the British army. Posted to America during the French and Indian War, he served proudly under Generals James Wolfe, Robert Moncton, and James Murray. St. Clair was with Wolfe when Quebec fell to the British. Leaving the army in 1762, he moved to the Pennsylvania frontier. There he became wealthy and politically prominent. As such, St. Clair led an effort to avert Dunmore's War between Virginia and the Shawnee, and to maintain Pennsylvania's neutrality.[19]

In January 1776, St. Clair joined the Continental army as a colonel in command of a Pennsylvania regiment. He was promoted to brigadier general and served under Washington, most notably in the Delaware crossing to attack Trenton and Princeton, critical victories for the Continental army. Promoted to major general, St. Clair was sent to take command of Fort Ticonderoga, strategically located on Lake Champlain along the New York-Vermont border. In the face of a major British offensive, St. Clair decided the fort could not be successfully defended. Accordingly, he ordered an evacuation and retreat. Surviving the ensuing criticism, St. Clair maintained his rank and continued to serve through the remainder of the war.

Returning to Pennsylvania business and politics, he was elected as a delegate to the thirteen states' Confederation Congress. In early 1787, Congress elected him its president, which gave him the responsibility for moderating congressional discussions. St. Clair still held that position when he was named governor of the Northwest Territory. Fifty years old, with money and political prominence, St. Clair had begun to indulge his taste in food and to lead a more sedentary life.

Before considering the provisions relating to Native Americans, the Northwest Ordinance's provision on slavery is worth noting:

There shall be neither slavery nor involuntary servitude in the said territory, otherwise than in the punishment of crimes, whereof the party shall have been duly convicted: provided always, that any person escaping into the same, from whom labor or service is lawfully claimed in any one of the original states, such fugitive may be lawfully reclaimed and conveyed to the person claiming his or her labor or service as aforesaid.[20]

Thus, the Northwest Territory was to be free of slavery, but it would not be a safe haven for escaped slaves. The ordinance's key provision on Indian rights stated:

The utmost good faith shall always be observed toward the Indians; their lands and property shall never be taken from them without their consent; and in their property, rights, and liberty they never shall be invaded or disturbed unless in just and lawful wars authorized by Congress; but laws founded in justice and humanity shall, from time to time, be made for preventing wrongs being done to them and for preserving peace and friendship with them.[21]

The ordinance also provided that as soon as there were five thousand free male inhabitants, representatives could be elected to a general assembly. It allowed for three to five states, with a right to statehood once the population reached sixty thousand free inhabitants. The long-term intent to acquire land for an expanding white population is evident. Such population growth would no doubt come at the cost of Indian homes, hunting grounds, and the forest that covered most of the land.

How could those provisions be reconciled with the one that the Indians' land would never be taken without their consent? How could they be reconciled with Indian property, rights, and liberty never being invaded or disturbed, except in just and lawful wars authorized by Congress? De facto, American "utmost good faith" would prove only to mean that consent must be sought for taking land; not that a refusal to consent had to be accepted. The meaning of "just and lawful wars" would prove to depend on who decided what was just and what was lawful. The nod to legality and Indian rights would prove hollow. They were never intended to impede American land acquisition.

The federal government was unwilling to accept the Native American Confederation's insistence that only it could negotiate issues of land. Instead, the government pursued a contrary strategy. Not long after he was appointed, Governor St. Clair was instructed that "every exertion must be made to defeat all confederations and combinations among the tribes."[22] If not divide and conquer, government strategy was to divide, threaten, and purchase.

Large Ohio land transactions drove settlement efforts, which in turn triggered continued Indian attacks. In 1787, the Ohio Company purchased land between the Muskingum and Hocking Rivers. The result was the establishment of Marietta, Ohio. The Miami Land Company and John Cleves Symmes obtained three hundred thousand acres between the Little Miami and the Great Miami Rivers. The government set aside more than four million acres to fulfill its promise of land for war veterans. In 1788, Congress passed a law authorizing land grants in Ohio to Revolutionary War veterans. The parcels were assignable. Most were sold by veterans to land speculators.

On orders from General Harmar, troops observed boat traffic on the Ohio River. From October 19, 1786, to May 12, 1787, they counted 179 boats, carrying 2,689 settlers with 1,333 horses and 102 wagons, plus cattle, sheep, and hogs, westbound for Kentucky. From June 1 to December 9, 1787, they counted 143 boats, 3,196 settlers, 1,381 horses, and 165 wagons, plus cattle, sheep, and hogs, traveling to Kentucky.[23]

Boats on the Ohio River were prime targets for attack. At times, an ambush was set using a white to lure boats to the north riverbank. The white might be a prisoner coerced to cooperate, or possibly a boy or a young man who had been adopted. If the ambush was successful, everyone on board was killed or captured, everything on board was taken or destroyed. The Indians were keenly aware that the river traffic meant more settlers.

In January 1788, St. Clair advised Secretary of War Knox that additional land sales in Ohio "for the discharge of the public debt" depended on somehow securing "solid peace with the Indians." Then he warned Knox that a lasting peace was impossible "unless the inhabitants of the States that border upon them can be restrained from acts of violence and injustice" toward the Indians.[24] St. Clair closed by opining that an Indian war would put thousands at risk and be far too expensive.

That summer, Governor St. Clair reported that "[o]ur settlements are extending themselves so fast on every quarter where they can be extended; our pretensions to [Indian country] have been made known . . . in so unequivocal a manner, and the consequences are so certain and dreadful [to the Indians], that there is little probability of there ever being any cordiality between us."[25] St. Clair closed pessimistically, concluding that the United States was not prepared for the war that was likely to come.

Instead of a great council to negotiate an overall agreement, St. Clair was only able to bring Iroquois, without the Mohawk, and some Wyandot, Delaware, Potawatomi, Ojibwe, and Sac, who did not fully represent their tribes, to Fort Harmar. The result was two more treaties in January 1789. One was with the Iroquois, setting the bounds of their now-shrunken lands. The other purported to be with the Wyandot, Delaware, Ottawa, and Chippewa (Ojibwe) nations. It set a boundary running from the mouth of the Cuyahoga upriver to the portage, to the Tuscarawas branch of the Muskingum, to the "forks at the crossing-place above fort Lawrence, thence westerly to the portage" on the Great Miami, then west to the Maumee, then downriver on the east side of the Maumee to Lake Erie, and back along the lakeshore to the mouth of the Cuyahoga.[26]

From 1785 to January 1789, the federal government had pressured tribal representatives to sign treaties for land in Ohio and eastern Indiana. These were treaties of acquisition, not treaties of peace. They were treaties made through coercion, not fair bargaining. Most importantly, the tribal representatives who agreed to sell did so without authority to act on behalf of all the tribes with an interest in the land, or even with authority to act on behalf of all of their own tribe. By the end of the decade, the US government could not continue to ignore the Confederation's influence and its unwavering position that the treaties of the 1780s were invalid.

In May 1789, in correspondence to President Washington, Knox assessed the 1784, 1785, 1786, and 1789 treaties of Fort Stanwix, Fort McIntosh, Fort Finney, and Fort Harmar. He noted that "Indians are greatly tenacious of their lands and generally do not relinquish their right, excepting on the principle of a specific consideration for [their] purchase" and that it was "the practice of the late english Colonies and Government in purchasing" Indian land to "firmly" follow this policy. None of the treaties of the 1780s set forth specific consideration for the ceded land. Knox reported that the treaties continued to be "opposed and Complained of" because they were made with individual tribes; not with the Confederation on behalf of all affected tribes. Knox further noted that Congress had authorized negotiating a "general treaty" with the Indian tribes "inhabiting the country north west of the Ohio, and about Lake Erie," with $14,000 to purchase new land and $6,000 as compensation for land already ceded.[27] In effect, Knox informed the president that the earlier treaties had not achieved their purpose and that negotiations were needed with the Confederation to attempt to secure the expansionist goals of the United States, without resorting to seizing the land by force. Knox made no mention of the laws established by the Northwest Ordinance.

By late 1789, George Washington's perspective had become more nuanced. Now the president, he conditioned a just war in the Northwest on additional treaty efforts:

I would have it observed forcibly that a War with the Wabash Indians ought to be avoided by all means consistently with the security of the frontier inhabitants, the security of the troops and the national dignity—In the exercise of the present indiscriminate hostilities, it is extremely difficult if not impossible to say that a war without further measures would be just on the part of the United States.

But if after manifesting clearly to the Indians the dispositions of the general government for the preservation of peace, and the extension of a just protection to the said Indians, they should continue their incursions, the United States will be constran'd to punish them with severity.[28]

Despite Knox's conclusion that the treaties of the 1780s were of no value in dealing with the Confederation, no great peace council materialized. The Indian Confederation was split internally, divided on what its bottom-line position should be. Was the possibility of regaining Ohio land worth the price of war? Alternatively, was peace worth largely accepting the status quo of existing settlements?

Joseph Brant led the advocacy for compromise and diplomacy by accepting the Muskingum as a boundary line to the east as well as settlements that had been established west of the Muskingum and north of the Ohio. Brant and those who agreed with him were willing to concede existing American presence in return for no further white expansion into Indian land. Far more willing to fight, the Shawnee and other hardline leaders maintained that the Americans must leave Ohio and that the boundary must be the line established in the 1768 first Fort Stanwix Treaty.[29] In that treaty, the Iroquois had conceded Kentucky to white settlement. Now, even the Shawnee were willing to accept that. Significantly, neither of the Confederation's competing policies contemplated ceding more land in return for peace.

Even without the split within the Confederation, it is unlikely that a grand council with the United States would have been successful. The United States probably would not have agreed to stop extending white settlements. The Confederation probably would not have agreed to more land concessions. In the language of negotiation, there was no zone of agreement.[30] Each side would have judged war, despite attendant costs and risks, to be preferable to the terms offered by the other side. However, we cannot be certain of what a grand peace council might have achieved. Perhaps if such a council had been held, the dynamics of the negotiation might have altered positions enough for a meaningful agreement to have been reached. Perhaps, but it seems improbable. Another possibility is that a less meaningful agreement might have been reached if the government privately viewed it only as a temporary expedient. History teaches that the United States never maintained treaty lines once it was ready to push farther west.

Conflict between the ever-increasing flow of settlers and the Native Americans whose land was threatened sometimes waned but never ceased from the close of the Revolutionary War through the 1780s. As the decade closed and into 1790, raids by Indians and Kentuckians escalated. St. Clair wrote to Washington of "constant hostilities between the Indians who live upon the river Wabash and the people of Kentucky."[31] Blue Jacket, Little Turtle, and the Wyandot sachem, Tarhe, were the key speakers at a council in the latter 1780s.[32] The Shawnee told of how after that, in the summers, "war bands camped along the Great Se-pe."[33]

As 1790 began, Knox informed the president that "[t]he various tribes seated on the Wabash River, extending up to the Miami village [at the Maumee] and the several branches of that river, were the Indians" primarily responsible for attacks in Kentucky that he deemed "unprovoked aggressions." But Knox also reported that Kentuckians were retaliating with their own attacks, killing any Indians they found. Without finding "the actual perpetrators" of the Indian raids, "whites frequently make incursions into the Wabash country, northwest of the Ohio, and it is probable that indiscriminate revenge is wreaked on all bearing the name of Indians." Knox was troubled that the violence being done by Indians and whites was such that it was "uncertain who are right, or who are wrong." Yet there was no policy recommendation to treat the Indians and the Kentuckians equivalently. Instead, Knox advised that justice "forbid the idea of attempting to extirpate the Wabash Indians" until they first had a chance to agree to a treaty "on reasonable terms."[34] The disconnect, of course, was that "reasonable terms" had entirely different meanings to the government, to the Indians, and to many Kentuckians.

The term "Wabash Indians" was used frequently. Knox's description encompassed not only Indian villages in the Wabash River Valley but also along the Maumee and its sources, the St. Joseph and the St. Marys. Those rivers were outside the Wabash River Valley, though not far from its northeast edge. With the Wabash flowing almost 500 meandering miles and the

Maumee stretching 137 miles from present-day Fort Wayne to present-day Toledo, "Wabash Indians" denoted villages over a large part of Indiana and northwest Ohio. In 1790, the largest and most important were the cluster of Maumee towns at and near its headwaters. Geographical accuracy aside, they would be the primary targets of the coming campaigns against "the Wabash Indians."

Internecine raids continued unabated in early 1790. In April, three Kentucky counties complained to the secretary of war of almost daily "accounts of . . . horrid murders on our defenseless frontiers," of horses and other property being taken, and of several boats on the Ohio being attacked with "their unhappy crews murdered or carried into captivity."[35] When boats on the Ohio were taken, the number of victims could be substantial. In late March, news reached Miamitown that two Shawnee war parties had returned. Each had overwhelmed a boat on the Ohio. They took more than twenty prisoners and killed more than twenty others.[36] Among the prisoners were John Witherington, his pregnant wife, and their seven children. Kentuckian attacks on Indians were less documented.

Encouraging settlement and facilitating opportunities for land speculation acted like a strong wind whipping up the waves of an oncoming tide of violent conflict. Hostilities between Native Americans and settlers along the Ohio and in Kentucky were about to escalate into war between the United States and a Maumee Confederation, the militant portion of the larger 1780s Indian Confederation. This new confederation would comprise those the government called the "Wabash Indians" plus those who were willing to join them in the coming war. Years of raids had been bloody and damaging to both sides, yet inconclusive. In the 1790s, raids would be overshadowed by full-scale battles. At its most elemental, this was a clash between two diverse societies, both accustomed to war and to warring with each other. The more-populous people determined to migrate, take control of the land, and alter its fundamental nature; the smaller, indigenous population equally determined to maintain their homes and way of life in the woodlands of the Old Northwest.

Chapter Four

False Victory

T HE YEAR 1790 SAW THE FIRST SESSION of the Supreme Court, the first annual presidential address to Congress (now known as the State of the Union), and the first census. And in 1790, the United States went to war for the first time.

The new republic's first war was against the Indians of the Wabash and Maumee River Valleys. At issue was control of Ohio and eastern Indiana. This first war was undertaken by presidential order, without a congressional declaration of war, setting a precedent still followed today.[1]

President Washington's order for a military offensive against the Indians came on June 7, 1790. It was transmitted by Secretary of War Henry Knox to General Josiah Harmar, commander of US troops in the Northwest Territory. The army's senior ranking officer since 1784, Harmar had been.

breveted to brigadier general in 1787. Starting as a militia captain when he was only eighteen, five years later he was commissioned a captain in the Continental army. Harmar served in the unsuccessful invasion of Canada and under Washington, including during the difficult days at Valley Forge. He finished the war as a well-known lieutenant colonel and adjutant to General Nathanael Greene, the American commander in the south.

Knox's order for the offensive was couched in the justification of self-defense. It blamed the Shawnee and "banditti from several tribes associated with them" numbering perhaps only "two hundred fighting men, yet they seem sufficient to alarm the whole frontier lying along the Ohio, and, in a considerable degree, injure the reputation of the Government." With the premise that the frontier was too large to be defended against raiding parties, the "remedy" was to "extirpate, utterly, if possible, the said banditti. The President of the United States, therefore, directs that you, and the Governor of the Western Territory, consult together about the most practicable mode of effecting this object, in such manner as to not interfere with any treaties he may be about forming with any of the regular tribes of Indians on the Wabash."[2] In this initial directive, Harmar's troops were to be one hundred regulars and three hundred Kentucky militia, plus officers. Knox authorized the force to be mounted and provisioned for thirty days. He expected that they could reach their target after riding 135 miles in four days.

Knox advised Harmar that "[t]he Shawanese, and the banditti associated with them, are supposed to reside on the eastern branches of the Wabash River, towards its head." This was simply wrong. The Shawnee and their allies were in the Maumee villages, more than fifty miles from the headwaters of the Wabash. Looking back, it was an eerie mistake, for seventeen months later, St. Clair's army would be attacked on the eastern branch of the Wabash, close to its headwaters. Knox reiterated that until the "banditti" were "extirpated," the military offensive was to continue. The directive ended by emphasizing that "friendly, or even neutral tribes" should not be injured and that those tribes should be assured of the "just and pacific dispositions of the United Stated, at the same time, of their firm intentions of inflicting severe punishment upon all those of a contrary nature."[3]

Kekionga, known to the Miami as Kiihkayonki, was the largest of the Miami towns. It was situated at the headwaters of the Maumee, on the east bank of the St. Joseph, between the St. Joseph and the Maumee.[4] It is the largest village on a map drawn by Lieutenant Ebenezer Denny in 1790. The portage between Kekionga and the Wabash, the land path over which canoes could be carried to link water travel, was about eight miles. The portage between the Maumee and the Wabash provided a route between the Great Lakes, or even the St. Lawrence, and the Ohio, and from the Ohio to the Mississippi. It had long been controlled by the Miami. The portage had been known to Europeans, first the French, then the British, for over one hundred years, and, of course, far longer than that to the First Peoples.

The Miami tribe was centered at Kekionga and other Maumee towns. The Miami tribe was the most powerful branch of the Miami nation, which included the Wea, Piankashaw, and Eel River tribes.

Kekionga's chief was Pacanne, who was often gone on extended trips. During these times, his nephew, Jean Baptist Richerville (Peshawah) took over his responsibilities. Richerville's mother was Pacanne's sister, and Richerville's father was a French-Canadian trader. After first maintaining neutrality, Pacanne became a British ally during the Revolution. After America's victory, he was peaceful and cooperative until 1788, when Virginia "Big Knives" attacked a Piankashaw village and went unpunished.

Across the St. Joseph and slightly north of Kekionga was Miamitown, the village of Le Gris (Nagohquangogh). Rendering the nomenclature confusing, contemporaneous Americans sometimes referred to Kekionga as Miamitown and sometimes used either name to refer to the group of towns situated near the Maumee headwaters.[5] Notwithstanding Pacanne's status, Le Gris and Little Turtle were the two most influential Miami chiefs.

Frequently, Indians of different villages and of different tribes, as well as white and biracial traders, came to Kekionga and to Miamitown. Both villages were a mixture of indigenous and British culture, of war and of trade. Guests might be served coffee or tea, a social gathering might be enlivened by John Kinzie's fiddle playing, and raiding parties might return with captives and scalps. French-Canadiens held Mass on Sunday. A returning war party might tell of a prisoner being killed by a warrior intent on slaking a desire to avenge recently slain relatives, though his captor wanted to let him live. Some captives were put to work and lived in relative freedom, yet the dried heart of a prisoner who had been killed was displayed as a trophy. Henry Hay, a visiting trader, observed all of this, and all in his first week at Miamitown.[6]

Little Turtle was the war chief of the Miami. He was about thirty-nine and had a town that referenced his name, Turtle Town, northwest of Kekionga and Miamitown. Little Turtle has been described as being close to six feet tall. A lost portrait depicted him with a high forehead and hair that hung down simply, nearly to his shoulders.[7]

Allied with the British during the Revolutionary War, he gained fame in 1780 by defeating a force of French settlers organized by Augustin de La

Balme. La Balme had come to America with Lafayette several years earlier. Little Turtle was known for leading raids into Kentucky. While he rose to leadership as a war chief, in later life Little Turtle proved to have the instincts of a politician.

After his move from the headwaters of the Mad River, Blue Jacket maintained a home in Miamitown, by the river. This placed him near the center of trading and of the complex of villages. Blue Jacket's Town was reestablished, about forty-seven miles northeast of Kekionga, in the Glaize, at the confluence of the Maumee and the Auglaize.

About two miles downstream on the Maumee, northeast of Kekionga, was the Shawnee village of Chillicothe. It was the latest in a series of Chillicothe villages, denoting the clan of that name. Across the Maumee from Chillicothe was another Shawnee village. Delaware war chief Buckongahelas placed his village not far from those Shawnee villages, about three miles from Kekionga on the St. Joseph. Another Delaware village was about two miles south of Kekionga on the St. Marys.[8]

Firmly allied to fight with the Shawnee, the Miami, and the Maumee Delaware were Seneca-Cayuga and Chickamauga Cherokee. Both had migrated from the main body of their tribes. The Seneca and the Cayuga were two of the Iroquois nations of upper New York. A small number of Chickamauga Cherokee had moved from Tennessee to Ohio and then to the Maumee. They lived with, or close to, the Shawnee. The warriors of these five allies probably totaled about seven hundred to eight hundred. If the Wea, Piankashaw, and Eel River, the other tribes of the Miami nation, were added in, the number of warriors rose to about one thousand. Near the Wea and Piankashaw in the Wabash River Valley, and also inclined to fight, were the Kickapoo.

A visitor to Maumee towns would have seen wigwams, cabins, and a large, wooden house. The latter was the council house where people gathered for meetings and ceremonies. A majority of homes were bark-covered wigwams. A typical wigwam had frames of small poles supporting ridge poles and eve bearers. Thongs of hickory bark secured connections. Large pieces of dried elm bark were secured to the poles with bark thongs to form weather boarding and the roof. The doorway could be closed with a piece of bark or a blanket. An aperture in the center of the roof vented smoke from the cooking fire. Other homes in the Maumee towns were cabins, evidence of European influence. These might have doors and chimneys.

Blue Jacket's home in Miamitown was a cabin within five yards of the river. He may still have had the curtained bed he and his wife had slept in,

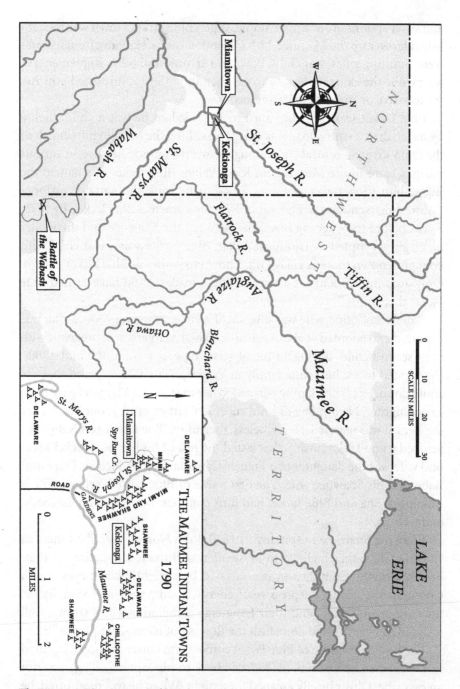

The Maumee River system, Kekionga, Miamitown, and Maumee Indian Towns, 1790.

and silver spoons, from a prior home. When Blue Jacket's town was reestablished farther up the Maumee, he had another cabin. Hanging from its walls were "hunting rifles, war clubs, bows and arrows, and other implements of war; while the skins of deer, bear, panther and otter . . . furnished pouches for tobacco, or mats for seats and beds."[9]

Blue Jacket was probably born in 1743. When he was a child, then a teenager, then a young man, his village was along the Muskingum, north of the Ohio River, in central Ohio. Roughly one thousand Shawnee, in various villages, were in the Muskingum River Valley. Blue Jacket was named the Big Rabbit (Sepettekenathe). As an adult he took the name Whirlpool (Wawcyapiersenwaw). Yet he was universally known as Blue Jacket. By 1773, a year before the ongoing hostilities between the Shawnee and the whites of Virginia erupted in Dunmore's War, Blue Jacket was a war chief with enough renown that his village was known to whites as Blue Jacket's Town. Only accomplishments as a warrior and a leader could have earned Blue Jacket that status.[10]

Blue Jacket's first wife was a white Shawnee, Margaret Moore. She was captured and adopted at about age nine. When Margaret was pregnant with their second child, during a time of relative peace around the mid-1760s, she wanted to see her white family in Virginia. Blue Jacket agreed that she could do so. Her white family persuaded her to stay, and Margaret gave birth to a daughter, Nancy. She did not meet her father until about 1804, after she herself was married. Nevertheless, thereafter, Blue Jacket and Nancy developed a good relationship that lasted the rest of his life. Blue Jacket's second wife was the daughter of a French-Canadian trader, Jacques Duperont Baby, and his Shawnee wife. The first name of Blue Jacket's second wife is unknown. She and Blue Jacket had four children: Jim, Mary Louise, Sally, and George.[11]

Enjoying Shawnee hospitality in 1810, John Norton described them as "mostly tall; rather inclined to be slender, well made and active . . . their brown swarthy Complexion is enlivened by sprightly black eyes, and a Countenance strongly expressive of energy, good nature and Vivacity . . . they are great Talkers and their Language is melodious and strong, well adapted to beautify and embellish the flowing of natural eloquence."[12]

The best description of Blue Jacket comes from Oliver Spencer. Captured in 1792, when he was ten, his journey back to his captors' village was not an easy one. Oliver briefly escaped for a night. When he was recaptured, he was beaten with switches from nearby sassafras bushes. Oliver was taken to a village at the Glaize. Once they arrived, he was placed in the care of Cooh-coo-cheeh, a widow, and a Mohawk medicine woman. Her two sons lived nearby in Blue Jacket's Town. She was already caring for two grandchildren, a girl about thirteen and boy about ten. The boy's father was said to be Simon Girty.

After first visiting the home of the warrior who had turned Oliver over to her, they "went to pay [their] respects to the ... celebrated Blue Jacket." Girty and another Shawnee chief, the Snake, were also visiting, which may account for Blue Jacket's attire. Blue Jacket clearly made a strong and favorable impression on Oliver, who wrote:

The chief was the most noble in appearance of any Indian I ever saw. His person, about six feet high, was finely proportioned ... strong and muscular; his eyes large, bright and piercing; his forehead high and broad; his nose aquiline; his mouth rather wide, and his countenance open and intelligent, expressive of firmness and decision. .... [H]e was dressed in a scarlet frock coat, richly laced with gold, and confined around the waist with a party-colored sash, and in red leggings and moccasins ornamented in the highest style of Indian fashion. On his shoulders he wore a pair of gold epaulets, and on his arms broad silver bracelets, while from his neck hung a massive silver gorget and a large medallion of His Majesty, George III.[13]

Given Oliver's detailed description, apparently unlike many Shawnee, Blue Jacket did not wear a nose ornament, nor did he have distended ears with large earrings.[14] When Oliver saw him, Blue Jacket was about forty-nine. A Quaker who met him the following year described him as "richly dressed ... lofty and masculine," with a "friendly" demeanor.[15] Oliver described the Snake as "a plain, grave chief, of sage appearance."[16]

Oliver was also impressed with Blue Jacket's family: "His wife was a remarkably fine looking woman. His daughters, much fairer than the generality of Indian women, were quite handsome, and his two sons, about eighteen and twenty years old, educated by the British, were very intelligent."[17]

The American frontier's horrific opinion of Simon Girty is reflected in Oliver acknowledging that his description of Girty might be prejudiced, as Girty was a "renegade" and a "murderer of his own countrymen, racking his diabolical invention to inflict new and more excruciating tortures." Through that lens of self-aware bias, Oliver saw a man with "dark shaggy hair ..., [a] low forehead ... brows contracted, and meeting above his short flat nose ... grey sunken eyes ... lips thin and compressed, and the dark and sinister expression of his countenance." To Oliver, Girty was "the very picture of a villain."[18] Girty was dressed Indian style, though plainly and without ornaments. A silk handkerchief covered his head, and he had a substantial scar high on his forehead. Stuck inside Girty's belt were two pistols. A short, broad dirk hung on his left side.

During the visit, Girty removed the handkerchief, revealing his scar. Girty told the boy how the blade of an officer's sword had opened his head, a wound that would have disabled most men. "With an oath," Girty said "he had 'sent the hated Yankee officer' that gave it 'to death.'" Perhaps Girty spun this tale to amuse himself, for it was a tale. The truth was certainly known to Blue Jacket and to many others. In a drunken rage, Joseph Brant had delivered the near-fatal blow after an argument over whether Brant or Girty's brother, George, deserved the most credit for a successful ambush. Girty also told Oliver that he would never return home, but that if he was "'a good hunter, and a brave warrior, [he] might one day be a chief.'"[19]

Simon Girty and his family were taken prisoner early in the French and Indian War when he was fourteen. Simon was adopted by the Seneca-Cayuga. His younger brothers were also adopted, James and John by the Shawnee, and George by the Delaware. Simon, James, and George lived as Indians for eight years, and John for nine, before being repatriated under the terms that ended Pontiac's War. During the Revolution, Simon, James, and George joined the British as Indian agents and interpreters, sometimes accompanying Indians on raids and into battle. James married a Shawnee and Simon Girty married a young woman who had been a Shawnee captive for four years while she was a teenager.[20]

From an American perspective, Simon Girty was a renegade and murderer. From British and Indian perspectives, he was a valued loyalist and ally. The reputation for torturing was undeserved. It dated back eleven years to when Girty witnessed the Delaware take revenge for the Moravian Massacre by torturing and burning Colonel Crawford at the stake.

Traders were an essential part of the greater Kekionga community. For some of the traders, there was genuine friendship with their Indian neighbors. For some, there was genuine loyalty to Britain. For all, self-interest dictated their support for maintaining the Native American way of life and independence from the United States. With some justification, the United States blamed the traders for encouraging Indian opposition to settlement and even for encouraging attacks. But while traders might supply guns and ammunition, like other trade goods, most favored peace and the compromise advocated by Brant and the moderates, as that was also in their self-interest. That was certainly the position of the Montreal merchants who wanted peace to ensure that their business continued smoothly.

For the traders, business, family, social life, and political allegiance were naturally interconnected. Often, they might have breakfast or dinner with Indian leaders, such as Le Gris, Blue Jacket, Little Turtle, or Richerville. Prominent traders with British roots included Alexander McKee, Matthew Elliott, George Ironside, and John Kinzie. While McKee and Elliott did not live in the Kekionga towns, they were frequent visitors. Ironside and Kinzie did make their homes in Kekionga.

McKee—White Elk to the Shawnee—held the rank of colonel and was the senior agent for the British Indian Department. McKee's father was Scots-Irish, and his mother was Shawnee. Born between 1735 and 1738, he grew up the product of both his parents' cultures.[21] Like his father before him, McKee became an Indian trader. His knowledge of Native American culture, his relationship with the Shawnee, and his language skills made it natural for him to also be employed by the Indian Department. He had been since 1760.[22] Before the Revolution, McKee and Richard Butler were friends. He and St. Clair also knew each other from pre-Revolution Pennsylvania.

Elliott, McKee's deputy, held the rank of captain. Elliott was born in Ireland and immigrated to Pennsylvania.[23] He also knew St. Clair and Butler. Ironside was born in Scotland and came to America after graduating from King's College in Aberdeen with an MA. He became an agent for the British Indian Department in 1792. Kinzie was probably also Scots-Irish. At this time, he was married to his first wife, an adopted white Shawnee. McKee, Elliott, and Ironside were all married to Native American women.

A letter dated February 16, 1787, from Ironside to David Gray, another trader, reflects the business, social life, and political turmoil of the Maumee towns:

Goods . . . will be very scarce here this summer [because the winter was too mild for good hunting with not more than eight days of snow on the ground]. We have had a sort of Dance here once a Week during the winter, which has made us pass our time pretty agreeably.—The Different Nations have sent an Emissary to Congress to desire them to rest on the other side of the Ohio and upon these terms they would make peace w[ith] them, which terms if they dont accept, the Indians are no[w] holding Council Chez les Chats to advertise all the different nations upon the Mississippi to hold themselves in readiness early in the Spring to fall upon them & force them into a Compliance.[24]

French Canadians still made up an important part of the trading community. No family was more important than the Lasselles, now in their second generation as traders. Jacques and Antoine Lasselles traded with the Miami before the American Revolution. With family and business connections throughout the Wabash/Greater Kekionga community, their relationship with the Indians was unsurpassed. Another of the French-Canadian traders was Toussaint Antoine Adhemar. Often called Anthony or Martin, he usually signed his name as Adhemar Saint-Martin.[25]

The already existing friendship between the Lasselles and Blue Jacket deepened when Jacques Lasselles Jr., commonly known as Coco, married Mary Louise Blue-Jacket. Not unusual for the frontier, when she gave birth to their first child in 1791, Mary Louise was about sixteen years old. Coco was about twenty-four.

While maintaining the communal ethos of providing food and care for those villagers who needed it, with trade well-established, some Native American private enterprise had begun. Everyone having enough, if enough existed, was not inconsistent with some having more, if more than enough existed. By the latter 1780s, Blue Jacket was operating as a trader himself, obtaining pelts and fur from Indian hunters to sell to the Montreal merchants and bartering manufactured goods to his fellow Shawnee and other Indians in exchange for those pelts and skins. Though atypical, in some ways, Blue Jacket exemplified the influence of white culture while still maintaining the Shawnee culture and fighting for Ohio to remain Indian country. How he lived demonstrated that attributes from each society could be valued and chosen. Simultaneously, Blue Jacket was a war chief, a diplomat, and a businessman.

On the recommendations of General Harmar and Governor St. Clair, the scope of Harmar's mission expanded exponentially. By the time he marched from Fort Washington, he was leading 320 regulars, with artillery, and 1,133 Kentucky and Pennsylvania militia. Additionally, there were "spies" (scouts), "guides," and "pioneers" (engineers).[26] Major John Hamtramck was to lead a separate force of thirty regulars and three hundred Kentucky militia from Fort Knox (at Vincennes, Indiana) in a secondary, diversionary strike.

The target had broadened from the Shawnee and associated "banditi" to "the Wabash Indians."[27] In Knox's words, the goal of the mission was to demonstrate "our power to punish [the Wabash Indians] for their depredations, for their conniving at the depredation of others, and for their refusing to treat with the United States when invited thereto."[28] Thus, the rationale for the attack was not just retaliation for Indian raids but also retribution for declining to come to treaty councils—treaty councils where only "yes" was an acceptable answer to American land demands.

The primary American targets were Kekionga, Miamitown, and the other Maumee towns. American power was to "be demonstrated by a sudden stroke, by which their towns and crops may be destroyed." As Harmar and Hamtramck prepared to depart, St. Clair reported that "[t]he depredations along the Ohio and the Wabash still continue. Every day, almost, brings an account of some murder or robbery."[29]

With the British still in their forts, Washington was intent on avoiding an accidental military conflict. Thus, he insisted that the British be notified before any attack could proceed. Accordingly, on September 19, 1790, St. Clair sent a letter to the British commander at Detroit. Recognizing that the British might already be aware of American military preparations, St. Clair wrote:

I am commanded by the President of the United States to give you the fullest assurances of the pacific disposition entertained towards Great Britain and all her possessions, and to inform you explicitly that the expedition about to be undertaken is not intended against the post . . . nor any other place . . . in the possession of the troops of his Britannic majesty, but is . . . with the sole design of humbling and chastising some of the savage tribes whose depredations are become intolerable; and whose cruelties have of late become an outrage. . . . After this candid explanation Sir, there is every reason to expect, both from your own personal character, and from the regard you have for that of your nation, that those tribes will meet with neither countenance nor assistance from any under your command, and that you will do what in your power lies to restrain the trading people from whose instigations, there is too good reason to believe much of the injuries committed by the savages has proceeded.[30]

With the goal of letting other tribes know they were not being targeted and should remain neutral, messages were also sent to the Delaware and to the Seneca-Cayuga living on the Sandusky, in accord with the treaties, as well as to the tribes living along the Great Lakes. The latter included the Ottawa, Ojibwe, and Potawatomi.

Hamtramck struck well southwest of Kekionga. He destroyed an abandoned Piankashaw village and its crops. Hamtramck encountered no resistance before returning to Fort Knox, though he might well have if he had ventured farther. While Hamtramck achieved a limited, tactical success, he failed to divert attention from Harmar's advance.

That advance began on September 26, when the militia under Colonel John Hardin moved out from Fort Washington. They were followed by Harmar with his federal troops on the twenty-ninth. Some six hundred packhorses carried the expedition's supplies. Cattle were herded along to supply fresh meat.

Harmar's route followed what the Shawnee called "the old salt trail," which war parties and hunting parties had used for generations to cross into Kentucky.[31] Moving in the reverse direction, Harmar proceeded along the Little Miami River, then the Great Miami River, across to the St. Marys, and along the St. Marys to the Maumee.

Slowed by the packhorses and cattle, Harmar's force averaged only ten miles a day. Not wanting his initial strike to wait for his whole force to be in position, on October 14, Harmar sent Colonel Hardin ahead with six hundred men, mostly Kentucky militia. Hardin reached Kekionga and Miamitown on the sixteenth, twenty days after leaving Fort Washington.

Indian scouts had discovered the advance of Harmar's *shemagane* (soldiers in Shawnee), eight days earlier.[32] Once again, the Indians were hampered by many men being away for the fall hunting season. Unable to gather enough warriors to mount a defense, villages in the area were evacuated. To deny the Americans lodging, much of Kekionga and Miamitown were burned before Hardin reached them. Messages were sent out asking for help from other villages. Traders removed as much of their goods as possible.[33] When the news reached Alexander McKee, he reported that the Indians of the Maumee towns were "too few to make much opposition, however I understand they are determined to attempt it and have asked the assistance of other Nations, who seem to be too far dispersed to be able to collect in such a short time."[34]

Harmar arrived with the main force the next day. In addition to Kekionga and Le Gris's village, three or four other towns were looted and burned without resistance.[35] More important than homes that could be rebuilt, needed food supplies of corn and other vegetables were eaten or destroyed. Some twenty thousand bushels that would have provided sustenance until next year's harvest were gone. The Indians of the Maumee would face hunger. Up to this point, Harmar's mission to inflict damage on the Maumee villages was successful.

Not satisfied and looking for a fight, Harmar dispatched a reconnaissance in force of three hundred men under Colonel Robert Trotter. Trotter accomplished virtually nothing. Two Indians were spotted and killed at the cost of one soldier wounded. That same day, uncontrolled plundering became so problematic that Harmar issued an order that it must immediately stop and that everything taken must to be turned in, to be fairly distributed among the army. Dissatisfied with Trotter, the next day Harmar sent out the same troops, this time led by Colonel Hardin. It was one time too many.

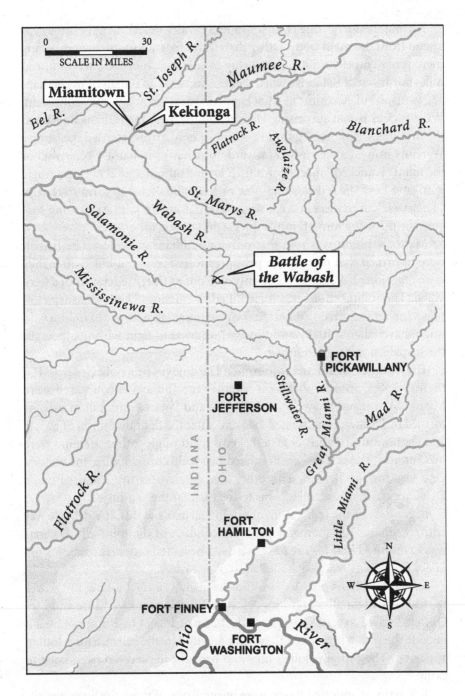

Fort Washington to Kekionga and Miamitown.

During the sortie, one company and a cavalry detachment became separated from the main body. Other than thirty federal troops, the remaining men were Kentucky militia. Advancing in columns, they were ten to fifteen miles northwest of Kekionga when they encountered an Indian camp, perhaps 150 yards ahead. Accounts of what happened next are not entirely consistent. What is clear is that surprising Hardin and his men, the Indians unleashed the first volley. A burst of gunfire and a shower of arrows startled the troops. Warriors immediately rushed forward, tomahawks in hand.[36] Nearly all of the militia panicked, "threw down their arms, without scarcely firing a single gun," and ran. The federals and nine or ten militia tried to form to charge. "They were cut to pieces except six or seven." Captain John Armstrong survived by throwing himself into a thicket and hiding for hours.[37]

Matthew Elliott was told that only one Indian was killed. The British were informed that one or two prisoners were taken and killed after they were questioned. A staggering twenty-five out of thirty federal troops were killed. The militia count was forty killed or missing. There was suspicion that many of the missing deserted.[38] Given the small number of militia who might have fallen initially and those who stayed to fight with the federals, the suspicion was well founded.

The number of Indians who routed Hardin was probably closer to 100 than to 150.[39] Sources differ on whether the Indians encountered were Miami, Miami and Shawnee, or Shawnee and Potawatomi. Elliott was informed by Delaware messengers two days after the fight that it was Shawnee and Potawatomi who defeated Hardin, though other details were inaccurate.[40] Those messengers carried two scalps to symbolize the victory. One was for the British. The other was carried on to Captain Pipe, a Delaware chief, whose village was to the east, on the Sandusky.

Regardless of the tribe(s) involved, in Harmar's words, the debacle was entirely due to "the shameful cowardly conduct of the militia."[41] Harmar was so incensed that for the next two days, he issued orders threatening artillery fire on any troops who failed to obey orders.

At night, Indians prowled around the army's camp, looking for horses to steal. The night after Hardin's defeat, militia Captains McClure and Mc-Quircy decided to set a trap. They attached a bell to a horse and hobbled it outside the picket line. Then they waited. Lured by the horse, a lone Indian appeared. The captains killed him and brought his severed head back to camp.[42]

Two more abandoned towns were burned, one of them the Shawnee village of Chillicothe. While it was being burned, there was a brief exchange of gunfire in which two Indians were killed.

Harmar withdrew on the twenty-first, heading back to Fort Washington. That evening, a scout returned and reported that about 120 Miami had returned to Kekionga. Harmar was persuaded by Hardin and other senior officers to allow a detachment to return and engage the Indians. The official goal, as later described, was to prevent the Indians from harassing the army as it withdrew. But certainly, the officers were motivated by a desire not to leave having suffered an ignominious defeat. Major John Wyllys, a federal officer, apparently shared the command with Colonel Hardin. Wyllys directly led sixty federal troops. Hardin commanded the Kentucky militia, three hundred infantry under Colonel Horatio Hall and Major James McMullen, plus forty dragoons under Major James Fontaine. They moved out late that night.

The plan was to have Wyllys, Fontaine, and McMullen ford the Maumee, then launch an early morning attack to drive the Indians toward the St. Joseph. Across the St. Joseph, waiting in ambush on the west bank would be Hardin and Hall.

Splitting forces to attack an Indian village had been used before and would be used for years to come. The tactic's success largely depended on two factors. Surprise was one. The other was not encountering too many warriors. Without surprise, or if too many warriors were encountered, the plan could be fatally defective. Custer's defeat is the prime example.

Hardin and Hall made a wide swing to ford the St. Marys and approach the St. Joseph from the west. Wyllys prepared to ford the Maumee from the east.[43]

Before the attack was ready to begin, surprise failed. Hardin's troops were spotted, and shots rang through the air. Little Turtle's Miami, Blue Jacket's Shawnee, as well as Delaware and Ottawa were ready to fight.[44] Under fire, Wyllys, Fontaine, and McMullen forded the Maumee to the west side of the river. Fontaine's dragoons were between Wyllys's regulars on their left and McMullen's infantry on their right. McMullen, however, veered off from Fontaine's flank to chase a small group of Indians.

Across a small prairie, Wyllys and Fontaine saw warriors concentrated in a thicket of trees. What they saw was not the complete picture. Fontaine began a charge across the prairie. His mounted militia followed him less than enthusiastically. Wyllys and his infantry charged behind them. In the lead, Fontaine was shot off his horse, killed or mortally wounded. With Fontaine down, the tentative cavalry charge quickly dissolved. Bravely, but foolishly, continuing to advance on foot, Wyllys's men were hit by a volley of gunfire at close range. It came not only from their front but also, unexpectedly, from their exposed right flank.[45] They had charged into an ambush. Miami, Shawnee, and others closed, and the combat become one of tomahawk, spear, knife, and bayonet. Wyllys died early in this melee. The husband of Cooh-coo-cheeh, the widow who took in Oliver Spencer, was tomahawking a soldier when he was mortally wounded by a bayonet thrust. He was one of the few Indians killed. Wyllys's regulars were nearly wiped out.

On the west bank of the St. Joseph, the troops were split, with Hardin south of Le Gris's village, a detachment under Major Stephen Ormsby just north of the village, and Hall farthest north.[46] They exchanged fire with Indians on both sides of the St. Joseph.

McMullen's men remained apart, on the periphery of the fight. Wyllys's and Fontaine's survivors tried to reach the other detachments. An increasing number of Indians engaged Hardin, Ormsby, and Hall. Ormsby had to rally his men to maintain the fight. The plan to drive the Indians into their guns had failed. Concerned at being outflanked, Hardin ordered a retreat. The battle was over.

After regrouping, the remaining Americans retreated back across the Maumee and began their march to Harmar's camp. Harmar complimented Hardin, Hall, McMullen, and their militia for "bravery" and Ormsby for "cool and gallant behavior."[47] He apparently failed to understand that Mc-Mullen had been useless.

Of the federal troops, Wyllys; his second in command, Lieutenant Ebenezer Frothingham; and fifty-two of their men were dead. Only seven survived. Of the militia, the dead and missing numbered sixty-four. While Harmar praised their bravery, since they were not in the worst of the battle, some may have deserted.

More Indian warriors arrived. That night, seven hundred gathered. Blue Jacket wanted to pursue Harmar and attack, separate, and scatter the Americans. But his plan was stymied by a lunar eclipse and Ottawa shamans. "[T]he Ottawa, through the superstition of their conjurors, were persuaded that if another action took place," many of their men would be lost, and they left in the night, "without consulting the other nations."[48] Seeing the Ottawa leave, many others did the same. Little Turtle and Blue Jacket could think strategically, and their warriors remained, but they could not rally enough others to execute Blue Jacket's plan. They were left with too few men to follow and further damage, or destroy, their withdrawing enemy.

Matthew Elliott arrived the next day. He learned that the Indians estimated that they had killed five hundred soldiers in the two fights, more than twice the actual number. Elliott saw what he took to be more than 150

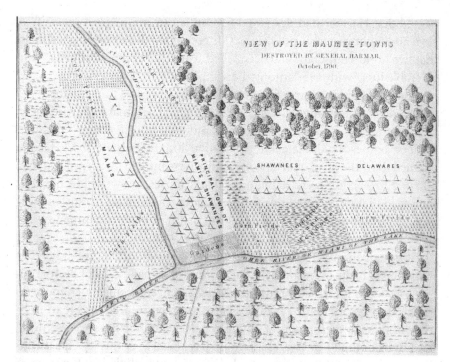

"View of the Maumee Towns Destroyed by General Harmar, October 1790," sketch by Lt. Ebenezer Denny. From the *Military Journal of Major Ebenezer Denny, an Officer in the Revolutionary and Indian Wars* (1859). (*Boston Public Library*)

scalps. Three prisoners were taken in the second fight. Elliott was told that "in both actions . . . the number of Indians killed . . . does not exceed Ten, and of wounded Fifteen most of them slightly.[49] Apart from the two engagements, about five Indians had been killed by Harmar's men.

For the American army, the total number of dead and missing in the campaign was 183. Of ninety-one federal officers and men in the two engagements, seventy-nine were dead. Of approximately six hundred soldiers in the two engagements, more than a fourth had been left behind dead and scalped.[50] Half of the packhorses were gone, either lost or captured.

Harmar's army returned to Fort Washington nine days later. It had taken almost twice that long for them to reach Kekionga. The date of their return was November 3, 1790. Exactly one year later, St. Clair's army would camp on the banks of the Wabash.

The first information to reach Governor St. Clair claimed victory. Thus, he initially reported to Knox "of the entire success of General Harmar at the Indian towns on the [Maumee] and the St. Joseph Rivers." St. Clair reported that Harmar had destroyed five Indian towns, a "great quantity of corn and other vegetable provisions." He recounted the absurd overestimate that two hundred Indians had been killed. The report acknowledged a "considerable loss," with 155 "among the slain."[51]

The day after his return, Harmar wrote a brief report to the secretary of war, enclosing his written orders for the campaign. Harmar expressed regret that "the Miami villages" had been abandoned and that the "villainous traders" had escaped. He acknowledged a "loss [of] about 180." Harmar claimed that "the head quarters of iniquity were broken up ... not less than 100 or 120 warriors were slain and 300 log-houses and wigwams burned." He added that "[t]he remainder of the Indians will be ill off for sustenance," as twenty thousand bushels of ears of corn had been consumed or destroyed, as were "vegetables in abundance."[52]

Although about half the number that St. Clair reported six days earlier, Harmar still badly overestimated the number of Indians killed. Elliott's contemporaneous information from Indian messengers seems much more reliable. Reports of enemy casualties based only on impressions tend to be overestimates, either in good faith or to protect and further careers. Moreover, one hundred dead warriors would have been a serious loss for the Indians, and ensuing events are entirely inconsistent with their suffering such consequential casualties. Despite the destruction of their homes, property, and food, they clearly saw this as a victory. Indian morale and support for the Confederation surged.

Three days after Harmar returned and two days after his report to Knox, St. Clair still claimed "success." "One thing, however, is certain, that the savages have got a most terrible stroke, of which nothing can be a greater proof than that they have not attempted to harrass [sic] the army on its return."[53] But the lack of harassment was not due to Indian casualties. St. Clair's reasoning was flawed. While a lunar eclipse that Ottawa shamans saw as a bad omen was beyond what St. Clair could be expected to imagine, any number of factors, other than heavy casualties, could have accounted for the lack of harassment.

Neither Harmar nor St. Clair convinced anyone with their claims of success. The facts of American losses—being routed from one battlefield and retreating from the other, leaving their dead to be scalped—spoke for themselves. With Harmar's agreement, a court of inquiry convened to consider his conduct during the campaign. The army officers who testified consistently faulted the militia's abysmal first performance and inadequate second performance. The court exonerated Harmar.[54]

Blue Jacket, understanding that repulsing the army had boosted the Confederation's credibility, quickly sought to turn military success into political gain. The day after Harmar returned to Fort Washington, Blue Jacket was addressing the commander of Fort Detroit, Major John Smith of the British 5th Regiment. Blue Jacket stressed past promises and current mutual interests.

Blue Jacket began by referring to "fend[ing] off the hatchet of our enemy" and the "successes in the effort to protect everything dear to us, our country, our families and our honor." He spoke of how the Indians had "accepted the hatchet" against the Americans when the king had asked, and how the hatchet was buried when the king "commanded peace." Now Blue Jacket asked the king, their "Father," and the English, their "Brethren," for "young men" (soldiers), for trade, for corn to plant, and for food, and clothing to replace what had been lost. He emphasized the Indians' dire needs, their justification, and what was at stake for the tribes and the British. Without the Shawnee, the Miami, and their allies, the British would have no fur trade, no forts, and no buffer between themselves and the Americans.

Lend us your aid. . . . Lend it to us effectively, or we must divide like a cloud separated by a Whirlwind and scatter away to the . . . waters of the Great Mississippi, and be no more seen among you. Protect the Barter between the White People and Red People, and forsake not the trade, that Links us together in amity and Interest. . . . The steps we have been obliged to take have reduced our families to want, even to Distress. We crave your interference to feed and clothe them; We have burned our Houses to retard the progress and prevent the Lodgement of our Enemies. Enemies who . . . secretly aim at the destruction of your Trading Posts. We have not ceded our Country . . . to the Americans by Deed, Treaty, or other ways . . . and we have always been led to understand that, when our Great Father over the wide waters gave peace to his disobedient children [the Americans], he did not give away our Country to them. . . . Some of our naughty young men have made war on the frontiers of America, because of their encroachments beyond the Ohio, they have done it without our nation's sanction; we as a People have made no war but as a People are determined to meet the approaches of an Enemy, who came not to check the insolence of Individuals, but with a premeditated design to root us out of our Land, which we and our forefathers and our children, were and are bound as men and Indians to defend, and which we are determined to do. Satisfied that we are acting in the Cause of Justice, and that the lands we hunt on and inhabit are ours.[55]

Referring to the war of "naughty young men . . . on the frontiers" because of American "encroachments" north of the Ohio, and distinguishing that from a nationally sanctioned war, might be seen as a diplomatic lie. Actually, however, it was rooted in a true distinction of tribal governance. Individual chiefs and warriors might choose to go, or not go, on raids against enemies. For the Shawnee, the Miami, and others, that was what had occurred along the frontier. In contrast to that, a national war required everyone to unite.[56] To the Maumee chiefs, they were now engaged in a national war.

Blue Jacket's speech epitomizes the quality of Indian rhetoric. He argued his case for British aid based on reason, appealing to British self-interest; justice, framing the issue as a war of self-defense against an American invasion of Native American land; and emotion, triggering feelings of sympathy for Indian hunger and of obligation to repay Indian loyalty. In classical terms, Blue Jacket had employed the three means of Aristotelian persuasion: logos, ethos, and pathos.

Trade and support would continue. Traders and British agents would continue to encourage and supply the Confederation's resistance. But neither Blue Jacket's rhetoric nor his reasoned arguments nor loyalty nor past promises would induce Britain to risk war with the United States by intervening militarily.

The Native American warriors of the Maumee Confederation were military surrogates, simultaneously acting in their interests and in English interests. But the calculus changes when it is the surrogate who needs active military assistance. Then, history teaches that surrogates should beware. Ask the Shawnee of the 1790s. Ask the Kurds of 2019. No British soldiers would fight alongside the Maumee Confederation against the American army.

Eager to follow up not just politically but also militarily, Little Turtle, Blue Jacket, and probably Buckongahelas led hundreds of warriors into southeast Ohio at the end of December. Gathering so many warriors was unusual in the midst of winter. On January 2, they surprised a civilian blockhouse, killing fourteen settlers. Then they headed for Dunlap's Station. At the same time, a second large war party was traveling farther east to attack Baker's Station.

Dunlap's Station was on the east bank of the Great Miami River, only about seventeen miles from Fort Washington. Covering more than an acre, it comprised three blockhouses in a roughly triangular shape, with ten cabins in between them. Inside the station were Lieutenant Jacob Kingsbury with twelve soldiers and about twenty-two male civilians, plus women and children.

The opportunity to surprise Dunlap's Station was lost when Indian scouts came upon three or four of the civilians out surveying less than a mile from the station. One was quickly killed, another was captured, but the other(s) escaped back to the station. Two days later, around sunrise, Confederation warriors surrounded the station. Their captive, Abner Hunt, was ordered to demand that Lieutenant Kingsbury surrender. The threat to Hunt if there was no surrender, whether explicit or implicit, was clear. Kingsbury refused, and the attack began. Gunfire was exchanged, and fire arrows flew into the station's wooden structures. Despite being struck, the wood failed to ignite. Had it been summer and dry, the result would have been different. As it was, the defenders were protected inside the blockhouse and cabin walls, which the attackers had no way to penetrate. Some warriors dared to come so close that two of their dead were left behind, to be scalped by the defenders when their bodies could not be retrieved. That night, whether out of frustration or as revenge for their dead, Hunt was brought within two hundred yards of the station and killed.[57] The next morning, Blue Jacket, Little Turtle, and their warriors began the journey back to the Maumee.

Baker's Station was on the south bank of the Ohio, about a dozen miles downriver of what is now Wheeling, West Virginia. Here too, the Confederation force failed to surprise the station and a demand for surrender was refused. For two days, gunfire was exchanged with little effect. Then the attackers withdrew.[58]

Notwithstanding these setbacks, the Confederation remained confident. Raids, especially against Ohio River traffic, resumed in March as the winter weather improved.

At the end of 1790, Secretary Knox documented two surprisingly candid admissions. "[I]t is a well known fact, that unless [the Indians can] be civilized, and learn the arts of agriculture, the taking away of their lands *for the usual pitiful considerations*, is taking away the means of supporting their lives."[59] (Emphasis added.) So American leadership knew that the amounts paid for most of Ohio in the 1780s treaties were pitifully small. Even more important, it was understood that the large-scale taking of Indian lands deprived them of necessary hunting grounds. With the loss of these hunting grounds, the Indians would not be able to meet their needs for food and for furs to trade.

Just days into 1791, Knox bluntly warned, "There is reason to fear the defeat of the army on the frontiers will be severely felt, as there is no doubt but the Indians will, in their turn, flushed with victory, invade the settlements." Knox had predicted that Harmar's "expedition will either incline the Indians to treat for peace, or it will induce them to wage open war in the coming spring."[60]

In January, his assessment to President Washington was that Harmar's campaign would not cause the Indians to "sue for peace," but instead "their own opinion of their success, and the number of trophies they possess, will, probably . . . encourage them to a continuance of hostilities."[61] Knox warned that Harmar's failure might result in the Indians at the Maumee "obtaining considerable assistance from the neighboring tribes," as well as receiving "all possible assistance in the power of certain malignant whites, who reside among them." "Trophies" referred to scalps and to the muskets and rifles of dead soldiers. "Malignant whites" meant McKee, Elliott, Girty, and the traders.

Knox's letter reveals several motives for subduing the "Wabash Indians" and taking their lands. He noted that securing "the territory northwest of the Ohio . . . would assist in the reduction of the national debt" because the government could then sell the land to settlers. He also noted that the number of settlers was "rapidly" increasing and they demanded protection. He suggested that without such protection, "seeds of disgust will be sown" that might lead to the government losing control of the frontier, not to the Indians but to disgruntled Americans or to foreign interests. Thus, the motivation involved economic, political, and national security interests.

At the same time, Knox recognized that "the encroaching settlements and rapid population of the frontiers" were causes of Indian "hostilities." So it was understood that expanding settlements and peace were antithetical.

Knox's January 1791 report to the president ended with specific recommendations. None suggested the possibility of limiting settlements or of not securing more Indian land. Such a radical, conceptual change would have been as alien to Washington as living in a wigwam. What Knox strongly recommended was another expedition against the "Wabash Indians." He thought they might have 1,100 warriors and might potentially add 1,000 more from other tribes. He suggested that 3,000 troops, plus commissioned officers, might be needed, consisting of 1,200 regulars, a regiment of 500 rangers, and 1,300 levies who would have to be recruited and trained. He noted that if fewer regulars were available, or if rangers were not used, then proportionately more levies would be needed. When Knox proposed this, neither a ranger regiment nor levies existed, nor did the regular army have 1,200 troops.

The 1790 offensive against the "Wabash Indians" had been costly to both sides, albeit by very different measures. For the Indian towns, the loss of tens of thousands of bushels of corn and other vegetables left a serious food shortage. But the army had been repelled with heavy losses, while the Indians had regained their villages with few casualties. The scalped bodies of soldiers overshadowed the destruction of food and homes, for it bolstered the Indians' will to fight, their spirits, and their numbers. For the federal government, the situation in the Northwest was worse in January 1791 than it had been a year earlier.

Chapter Five

St. Clair's Army Forms

I N 1791, THE BILL OF RIGHTS WAS RATIFIED. Treasury Secretary Alexander Hamilton saw his proposal for a national bank effectuated when the First National Bank of the United States was established. The District of Columbia was created. Washington, DC, was named for the president. Vermont became the fourteenth state.

And by March 3, Congress had passed, and President Washington had signed, An Act for Raising a Second Regiment to the Military Establishment of the United States and for Making Further Provision for the Protection of the Frontiers. The act authorized both the creation of the 2nd US Regiment of Infantry and the recruitment of two thousand additional soldiers on six-month enlistments. These short-term soldiers were known as "levies" and would form the 1st and 2nd Regiments of Levies. The new law also provided for payment, albeit low, of militia to further supplement the army's numbers. The law was deemed necessary to raise a force large enough to mount an offensive against the so-called Wabash Indians. Somewhere in the process, Knox's idea for a regiment of rangers was lost or discarded.

Counting the levies, an army consisting of one infantry regiment was being expanded to four regiments. There was obviously much recruiting to be done, many officers to be chosen and commissioned, and a great deal of arms, ammunition, clothing, tents, and other equipment to be obtained. Large numbers of packhorses would be needed to carry equipment and supplies. Efficacious plans for obtaining and supplying food to thousands of soldiers as they marched through the frontier wilderness toward the Maumee were also needed. To say there was much to be done understates the scope of the enterprise.

The president immediately appointed Governor St. Clair a major general, making him the highest ranking officer in the army, and placed him in command of the Northwest frontier forces. Despite his immense new responsibilities, St. Clair remained governor of the Northwest Territory. Washington later wrote to St. Clair that he had been appointed based on his "knowledge of the country north-west of the Ohio, and of the resources for an army in its vicinity, added to a full confidence in your military character, founded on mature experience."[1]

With the news of his appointment, St. Clair received lengthy instructions from the secretary of war. Knox had fought from Bunker Hill through Yorktown and had commanded Washington's artillery. Knox informed St. Clair that he was delivering the instructions "as authorized and commanded, by the President of the United States." The instructions were qualified as "general principles," with the expectation that St. Clair would "exercise [his] talents" and "judgment" in the event that unforeseen circumstances required "material deviations." Knox made it clear that peace was still preferred, as "the great mass of the people of the United States" believed that the cost in "blood and treasure" would exceed any benefit of war. Knox wrote of possible boundaries St. Clair could agree to in negotiations. These included the Wabash to the Maumee to Lake Erie, lines the government had sought in treaties for years. Yet Knox also observed that peace "is of more value than millions of uncultivated acres, the right to which may be conceded by some, and disputed by others." No consideration was given to obtaining peace by leaving Ohio to the Indians. If peace was not secured, then "coercive means" were to be used.[2]

Most new troops would be recruited in the east. Then they would march to Fort Pitt to be transported on the Ohio River some 470 miles to Fort

Washington. The fort was located on high ground in what is now downtown Cincinnati. It was "contemplated that the mass of the regulars and the levies may be recruited and rendezvous at [F]ort Washington, by the 10th of July."[3] This was premised on swift recruiting, effective supply lines, and efficient troop movements. Events proved all of these presumptions to be false. While the efficiencies of supply and movement might be unknown, to presume that all recruiting would be quickly accomplished was far too optimistic.

Knox's instructions briefly considered the possibility of unforeseen circumstances delaying some of the troops. "In this event, the expedition must not languish. . . . [T]o supply the numbers essential for the expedition, you must call forth, in the name of the President of the United States, the militia of Pennsylvania, Virginia, or the district of Kentucky."[4]

If peace was not achieved by May 10, General Charles Scott was authorized to take up to 750 mounted Kentuckians to strike Wea towns in the Wabash. A goal of the mission was to capture as many women and children as possible, to exert pressure on the Indians to agree to terms. Knox stressed that prisoners should be treated humanely. Authorizing any additional raids was left to St. Clair's discretion, though those were to be limited to five hundred men.

Absent a peace agreement, the highest priority was for St. Clair to establish a fort at "the Miami town" on the Maumee "for the purpose of awing and curbing the Indians." The fort was to be garrisoned with enough troops not only to defend it but also to have five hundred to six hundred additional soldiers available to "chastise any of the Wabash, or other Indians, or to secure any convoy of provisions." Knox suggested that the total garrison should therefore be between 1,000 and 1,200 enlisted men, plus officers. In the event of continued hostilities, St. Clair was to secure a defensible position at the Miami village, with artillery, before seeking out the hostiles to "strike them with great severity."[5]

A secondary goal was to establish small military posts between Fort Washington and the new fort at the Maumee.

Strongly suggested, but ultimately left to St. Clair's discretion, was whether to seek fifty Iroquois and fifty Chickasaw (or other southern tribe) scouts. There is no record that St. Clair did much to obtain them. Late in the campaign though, twenty Chickasaws did arrive, prepared to scout for the army. No Iroquois came. Most, like Brant, sympathized with their Native American brothers on the Maumee, even if they disagreed on what peace terms were acceptable. Furthermore, Iroquois would have been extremely reluctant to fight against Seneca-Cayuga.

Then came a statement that revealed a critical belief ingrained in the American military and political leadership. "[I]t is to be presumed that disciplined valour will triumph over the undisciplined Indians."[6] Not that victory would depend on superior tactics or superior numbers. Not that having artillery would be a decisive advantage. Just a presumption that disciplined valor would triumph over undisciplined Indians. Unspecified by Knox was how disciplined valor was to translate into action. Was it a line of troops continuing to fire volleys on command, despite taking enemy fire? Was it bayonet charges to force the enemy to abandon their positions? And how much discipline could be expected of an army largely comprised of barely trained new recruits? In time, answers would come.

Knox sent a message to the Indians of the Maumee and the Wabash in March. Separate messages were sent to the Seneca, Wyandot, and Delaware living east of the Maumee. The Shawnee, Miami, and others in the Maumee and Wabash River Valleys were told:

The President of the United States is anxious that you should understand your true situation, and the consequences of your persisting any longer in . . . hostilities. The United States are powerful, and able to send forth such number of warriors as would drive you entirely out of the country. It is true, this conduct would occasion some trouble for us, but it would be absolute destruction to you, your women, and your children. The United States require nothing of you but peace. Nay, they are desirous of making you understand the cultivation of the earth, and teaching you how much better it is for human kind to have comfortable houses, to have plenty to eat and drink, and to be well clothed, than to be exposed to all the calamities belonging to a savage life. The offer of peace now made to you is for your good, and the Great Spirit above will approve it. Reflect that this is the last offer that can be made; that, if you do not embrace it now, your doom must be sealed forever.

The message then said the Indians should come to Fort Washington to make "a firm peace" with General St. Clair, and they would "find the terms he shall dictate will be full of justice, moderation, and humanity."[7]

Thus, the message was at once conciliatory, threatening, and paternalistic. It offered peace on apparently nonnegotiable, undisclosed terms that were promised to be just, moderate, and humane. It ignored various facts. Women of these tribes cultivated tens of thousands of bushels of corn, squash, beans, melons, and pumpkins. Their homes were probably as comfortable as the average white home on the frontier. When their villages were not being destroyed, they typically had enough food. Implicit in Knox's message was that the forest must give way and farming must be paramount. Not surprisingly, neither demanding trust in the government's unspecified peace terms nor promoting an alternate way of life that emulated whites while deracinating Indian culture were persuasive.

The messages to the Seneca, Wyandot, and Delaware spoke of why the United States wanted only what was good and how it was the victim of the hostile Shawnee and Miami. It asked these tribes to help persuade the Shawnee and the Miami to accept American peace terms. There was an implication that it would be wise to cooperate with the winning side, the United States. Knox's diplomatic efforts to keep these tribes away from the Maumee and to politically separate them from the Miami and the Shawnee had mixed results. Some Delaware, Wyandot, and Seneca-Cayuga were ready to fight. Others stayed neutral.

On March 10, Richard Butler was commissioned brigadier general of the levies. Twenty-two days later, he turned forty-eight. Breveted to major general, he was appointed second in command to Major General St. Clair. Once muscular, by now he was "somewhat corpulent."[8]

Winthrop Sargent was St. Clair's adjutant general. He had been an artillery officer throughout the Revolutionary War and served under Henry Knox. As the governor was now also a major general, Sargent, the secretary of the Northwest Territory, was now a colonel. Serving as St. Clair's aide was twenty-two-year-old Vicomte de Malartic (Malartie), a volunteer from France. The count had served in Louis XVI's French Guards. Early in the French Revolution, American land speculators, including William Duer, induced five hundred French to immigrate to the new settlement of Gallipolis, Ohio. Among them was Count Malartic.[9]

On paper, each regular regiment was to have 912 men, plus officers, organized into three battalions, with four companies in each battalion. The levy regiments were supposed to be slightly larger, with 1,000 men, plus officers, also organized into three battalions of four companies each. The artillery battalion was to have 304 men, plus officers.[10]

While that was the regimental strength on paper, recruitment did not provide the designated numbers. The challenge of recruiting regulars was compounded by a recent severe cut in army pay. Consequently, many soldiers whose enlistments were up in the 1st Regiment chose not to reenlist, thereby creating the need for even more recruits. In the levy regiments, the largest shortfall was in the battalion recruited from Tennessee. It was more than 30 percent short of its allotted manpower when it began its march to Fort Washington in late June or early July. Recruiting to bring a Pennsylvania battalion up to full strength continued well into July.[11]

Since the 1st and 2nd Regiments were the army's only infantry regiments, not every man of every unit could be assigned to St. Clair's expedition. As a result of that and of recruiting shortfalls, each regiment of regulars with St. Clair amounted to a reinforced battalion.

Major John Hamtramck commanded the 1st Regiment, and Major Jonathan Heart commanded the 2nd. Hamtramck had more than six years of experience as a captain in the Continental army. He returned to the army in 1785 and had been assigned to the Northwest Territory since October 1786. In Harmar's campaign, Hamtramck commanded the diversionary move into the Wabash. Major Heart was a Yale graduate, class of 1768. He served throughout the Revolutionary War. Enlisting as a private, he was promoted through the ranks to major. Heart rejoined the army in 1785 and had been stationed on the frontier since then.[12]

Secretary Knox selected most of the officers to be commissioned for the regiments of regulars. The captains served in the Revolutionary War, in Harmar's campaign, or both. Most notable among them was Robert Kirkwood. He was reputed to have fought in sixty engagements, including Washington's successes at Trenton and Princeton, Horatio Gates's disaster at Camden, and Daniel Morgan's triumph at Cowpens. Possibly unique among the officers of the regulars, Kirkwood had fought off an Indian attack. Many of the lieutenants also had experience in the Revolutionary War or in Harmar's campaign.[13]

The other regular army unit was the Battalion of Artillery, commanded by Major William Ferguson. A Pennsylvanian, he entered the Continental army in 1777 as a captain lieutenant of the 4th Continental Artillery Regiment. Just a month later, he was captured. After eighteen months, he was freed in a prisoner exchange and returned to his unit as a captain. In 1785, Ferguson returned to the army as an artillery captain. Captains James Bradford and Mahlon Ford also served in the Revolutionary War and had been artillery officers since 1786. The junior artillery officer was Lieutenant Edward Spear. Though junior in rank, he was forty-six, had served five years during the Revolution, and had been an artillery officer since 1787.[14] One of the artillery's civilian wagon drivers, Thomas Irwin, called the artillery officers "as good as any that ever carried a gun."[15]

George Washington took a particular interest in who would command the 1st Levy Regiment. He asked a fellow Virginian, William Darke, to take command, after it had been offered to two others, including Henry "Light Horse Harry" Lee. Regardless of whether Darke accepted, Washington authorized him to select a major to command the Virginia battalion of the regiment and to select four captains, four lieutenants, and four ensigns for the battalion.[16]

Darke accepted the command. He was about to turn fifty-five. Darke had known Washington since 1755, serving under him in the Virginia militia during the French and Indian War. Darke began the Revolutionary War as a captain in February 1776 and was promoted to major before being captured in October 1777 at Germantown. Held for thirty-seven months, he was freed in a prisoner exchange. He finished the war as a lieutenant colonel and was discharged in 1782. After the war, Darke returned to Berkeley County, Virginia. He was awarded 6,666.66 acres of western land for his military service. In March 1790, Darke received a warrant for an additional 1,111.5 acres of the Northwest Territory.[17] His land holdings gave him a substantial financial interest in the control of Ohio.

George Gibson commanded the 2nd Levy Regiment. Forty-three years old, he had commanded the 1st Virginia State Regiment on the frontier from June 1777 to January 1782. For sixteen months prior to that, Gibson was an officer in the Continental army.[18] Like Darke, he had been out of the military for almost nine years. Being out of the military for years was typical for the levy officers.

The battalion commanders of the 1st Levy Regiment were Majors George Bedinger, Henry Gaither, and Matthew Rhea. As a young man, Bedinger immigrated to Kentucky. For him, the frontier was home. In the Revolutionary War, he captained a scout company for more than five years. After that, he was a major in the Virginia militia, fighting in Kentucky. Gaither joined a Maryland regiment as an ensign in 1776 and finished the war as a captain. Rhea joined a Virginia regiment in 1777 as a quartermaster and became a first lieutenant.[19]

In the 2nd Levy Regiment, the battalion commanders were Majors John Clark, Thomas Patterson, and Thomas Butler. Born in Pennsylvania, Clark likely had experience on the Pennsylvania frontier. He was a captain in the Continental army when he was discharged in 1781. During the Revolution, Patterson was a captain in a New Jersey regiment for two and a half years. For unstated reasons, Winthrop Sargent deemed Major Patterson to be "a damned bad soldier . . . and a very scoundrely character."[20]

Richard Butler appointed his brother, Thomas, as a major commanding the East Pennsylvania Battalion of the 2nd Levy Regiment. Thomas Butler entered the Revolutionary War as a first lieutenant in 1776. Nine months later, he was promoted to captain. He won praise from Washington for his bravery at Brandywine. At Monmouth, he distinguished himself for holding a narrow gorge under heavy British fire, giving Richard Butler time to withdraw their regiment.[21]

In the levy regiments, the battalion commanders were largely allowed to select their company commanders and more junior officers. Most captains of the levy regiments served in the Continental army. Not so many had frontier experience. One of the captains, Edward Butler, was appointed by his brother, Richard Butler. Nineteen years younger than Richard and almost fourteen years younger than Thomas, Edward began his military service as a sixteen-year-old ensign in 1778. The next year he was promoted to lieutenant. Edward Butler commanded a company in Clark's West Pennsylvania Battalion.[22]

For the Butlers, like the Custers eighty-five years later at the Little Big Horn, the campaign would be a family affair.

Other officers also had familial relations. Lieutenant Colonel Darke appointed his youngest son, Joseph, as a captain commanding a company in the Virginia Battalion. Joseph was thirty-two and lacked military experience. Captain William Purdy commanded a company in which his brother, Hugh Purdy, was an ensign. Lieutenant Russell Bissell and his brother, Cadet Daniel Bissell, were in the 2nd US Regiment. James Rhea served as the quartermaster and then as the adjutant in his father's battalion. Captain Jacob Slough, a company commander in the 2nd Levy Regiment, was Lieutenant Colonel Gibson's nephew.[23]

In the battle to come, there would be additional family connections, relationships that spanned the two armies.

Several officers whose sons were too young to be in the army brought them along on the expedition. One of these was Captain Joseph Shaylor, whose wife had died in 1790. Presumably, his wife's death led Shaylor to bring Joseph Jr. with him. Joseph Jr. was probably about eleven, though he may have been a few years older. Captain Samuel Newman brought his son, who was probably about the same age as Shaylor's son. Newman's reason for bringing his son is unknown. Perhaps he thought the expedition would be a great adventure and an education in military life. Although Major Heart reportedly "brought his twelve-year old son with him from Connecticut," the better evidence is that the boy was younger and did not accompany him.[24] These fathers must have been confident that if their sons did as they were told and did not stray from camp, the danger was minimal. After all, this was an army of more than two thousand troops. Coincidentally, Heart, Shaylor, and Newman were all from New England, and all were in the 2nd US Regiment.

Two cavalry units were organized under Captain Alexander Truman of the 1st US Regiment and Captain Jonathan Snowdon of the 2nd Levy Regiment. Starting as an ensign, Truman finished the Revolutionary War as a captain. He received an appointment as an army captain in June 1790. Snowdon also began the Revolutionary War as an ensign; he finished as a first lieutenant. His appointment as a captain in the levies came in April 1791. The men of the cavalry were levy volunteers.[25]

The regulars and levies of the army were supplemented by militia. From Pennsylvania, there was a rifle company led by Captain William Faulkner. His company comprised a lieutenant and sixty-one men. As hoped for, Faulkner's men were accustomed to living on the frontier under the threat of Indian raids.

For the additional troops, in early September, St. Clair exercised his authority to call for Kentucky militia. He sought 1,050. He received at least 453, plus officers.[26] They were commanded by Lieutenant Colonel William Oldham, an early Kentucky settler. After brief service as a captain in the Continental army, he resigned to move to the Falls of Ohio (at what is now Clarksville, Indiana). Returning to Kentucky, he served as a sheriff before accepting command of the militia.[27]

A vestige of the British army was that many officers, from general to captain, had enlisted men assigned to them as servants, sometimes referred to as waiters. At least eighty enlisted men were assigned to provide this luxury. It depleted the army's combat effectiveness, since men assigned as servants were not normally expected to fight.

The chief scout and the surveyors were civilians. In the eighteenth century, a common meaning of "scout" was one who spies out the enemy. Hence, "scout" and "spy" were often used interchangeably. St. Clair's chief scout was George Adams. He had a reputation as an experienced frontiersman and had fought, and suffered multiple wounds, in Harmar's campaign. Despite being designated chief scout, Adams seems have done virtually no meaningful scouting and never sought to spy out the enemy Indians.

Nor was Adams useful as a guide. Although he had reached the Maumee in Harmar's campaign, the chief scout was not competent to guide the army back to Kekionga. No effort was made to retrace Harmar's route, although in addition to Adams, St. Clair had other veterans of Harmar's campaign. These included Major Heart; Captain Armstrong, who had barely survived Harmar's campaign; and Captains David Strong, John Smith, Thomas Doyle, John Pratt, William Kersey, and Jacob Kingsbury. Apparently, none had the woodsmanship skills to retrace Harmar's route. Seemingly disregarding his Harmar veterans, St. Clair wrote, "Not a single person being found in the country who had ever been through it . . . both the geography and topography were utterly unknown; *the march was, therefore, made upon a compass-course.*"[28] (Emphasis added.)

Harmar had guides and scouts designated in his order of march.[29] Unlike Harmar, St. Clair marched without a guide. The glaring organizational failure of proceeding without a competent guide would profoundly affect the campaign.[30]

The expedition's head surveyor was Captain John S. Gano. The assistant surveyor was Jacob Fowler. Lacking a guide, the surveyors' responsibilities included charting the army's course through the unmapped wilderness using a compass. Without the benefit of a map, a compass did not enable the surveyors to plot an accurate course to their destination. At best, they could lead the army in the general direction of the Maumee towns. As St. Clair acknowledged, relying on charting a "compass-course" was "conjectural indeed."[31] Unless the St. Marys River was reached, recognized, and then followed to the Maumee, eventually scouts would need to locate St. Clair's targets.

Numerous other civilians were also with the army. This was partially due to the limited number of troops, partially to the government's supply system, and partially to another vestige of British influence. Civilians with the army were known as camp followers. They had official status, supplementing the troops to perform numerous jobs, from laundress to packhorse handler, from waggoneer to cattle herder.

The army's procurement and supply systems were operated by civilians, with responsibilities split between the quartermaster general, Samuel Hodgdon, and the War Department's general contractor, William Duer. The quartermaster general was tasked with procuring and transporting supplies and equipment for military units, such as kettles and axes for each company. While the quartermaster general provided equipment on a unit basis, the general contractor was responsible for procuring and delivering equipment and supplies for individual soldiers, such as uniforms, knapsacks, and tents. He was also responsible for purchasing and delivering food to the troops, wherever they might be.

Food essentially meant flour and beef. Beef would be transported on the hoof, with cattle being driven along on the army's march, to be butchered as needed. Civilians hired by the general contractor herded the cattle. It was impossible for the army to transport more than a fraction of the flour it needed. Thousands of pounds of flour would have to be delivered on convoys of packhorses, wherever the army was, on its march or at the Maumee. The packhorse handlers for these convoys were civilians, as were the packhorse handlers traveling with the army. The latter were needed for transporting equipment too heavy or too cumbersome for the troops to carry but not so heavy that it needed to be transported in wagons. The army's waggoneers were also civilians. Six wagons were needed for the artillery battalion's equipment and ammunition. Though fewer in number, civilians employed by the quartermaster general also accompanied the army.

Each company had a civilian artificer. Their job was to maintain and repair the company's equipment. Each company was authorized to have four women working jobs such as laundress, seamstress, and cook. Some were soldiers' wives. They drew daily rations and were subject to military orders. Another category of camp follower was family members accompanying an officer or an enlisted man. They were referred to as retainers. Some of the retainers were wives, some children.

The total number of civilian camp followers at the outset of the campaign—men, women, and children—is thought to have exceeded two hundred. Women probably numbered well over a hundred. Like its two generals, the army—with its servants, retainers, laundresses, wagons, artillery, and cattle—had grown fat.

From early May to early June, General Butler repeatedly complained, in St. Clair's words, of "fatal mismanagements and neglects in the quarter master's and military stores departments, particularly as to tents, knapsacks, camp kettles, cartridge boxes, pack saddles, &c. all of which articles were deficient in quantity, and bad in quality." Inefficiencies delayed troops from assembling at Fort Washington, as they were forced to wait for equipment or detour to obtain it when it could not be delivered. A congressional investigation concluded that there were "gross and various mismanagements and neglects in the quarter master's and the contractor's departments."[32]

Neither Hodgdon nor Duer had an easy task. Supplying the newly expanded army in a timely manner would have challenged an honest, efficient system. In 1791, the procurement system was neither. But both Hodgdon and Duer exacerbated what was already difficult. Probably some dishonesty and certainly substantial incompetence resulted in inferior and unsuitable equipment.

A major shortcoming was the army's tents. The lightweight tents provided for the troops failed to protect them from the rain and from the cold weather of October and November. The explanation given was that a summer campaign, not a fall campaign, had been expected. Lightweight tents, though, were cheaper to buy and perhaps more profitable to sell to the government.

One of the major deficiencies was a lack of packhorses. Hundreds were required, but Duer and his agent on the frontier, Israel Ludlow, failed to obtain them. Thoroughly dissatisfied, St. Clair bypassed the War Department's contractor and issued an order to purchase eight hundred horses.

Concomitant with Duer and Ludlow not procuring horses, there was a failure to provide the hobbles and bells needed for the horses. Since the horses would have to be allowed to graze at night, hobbles were needed to prevent them from wandering too far. Horse bells were needed so they could be readily located in the morning.

Beyond horses, there were other extensive shortfalls in supplying the equipment needed for the campaign. As they waited for the rest of the army to arrive at Fort Washington, those troops and civilians with the necessary skills worked to manufacture much of what was lacking. This included harnesses, wheels, kegs, and kettles, as well as the horse hobbles and bells. Gun carriages for the cannons and leather splints for the wounded arrived from Philadelphia but were defective, so new ones had to be made. Some of the knapsacks that were supplied split open and needed to be repaired.[33]

Various other problems arose over the summer, as efforts continued to organize, supply, and move troops to Fort Washington. Dispatches were thrown overboard when the boat carrying them was attacked on the Ohio River. Whiskey was so available at Fort Washington that St. Clair moved many of the troops six miles north to Ludlow's Station.

Besides inadequate equipment, the overriding concern was that the army was falling further and further behind schedule. As of late July, General Butler, the levy regiments, and some of the 2nd US Regiment had not reached Fort Washington. St. Clair wrote to Treasury Secretary Hamilton, "I am at my Wits end about it . . . and the Season is passing-from every appearance it will be September at Soonest before it will be possible to move, and then there is not much time left for the operations of the Campaign."[34]

That same day, Knox wrote to St. Clair, stressing that Washington considered their mission of the utmost priority and was dissatisfied at the delays. Knox closed:

The President of the United States has commanded me to urge, that as soon as your troops are assembled or such portion thereof as you may judge proper, that you commence the establishment of such of your posts of communication, to which your force may be adequate.

He is greatly anxious, that the campaign be distinguished by decisive measure so that the expence incurred may be manifestly useful and important.[35]

Both St. Clair and Butler were under pressure to do whatever was necessary to embark on the campaign, a campaign now more than six weeks behind schedule. In August, Knox wrote to Butler. If he was still at Fort Pitt, the president wanted him to proceed to Fort Washington "with all possible dispatch" with all of the "troops, officers and stores" for the campaign. Dissatisfied with the delays, it was the president's opinion "that unless the highest exertions be made . . . to repair the loss of the season, that the expenses which have been made for the campaign will be altogether lost, and that the measures from which so much has been expected will issue in disgrace."[36] From August 4 through September 1, Knox wrote to St. Clair: "The president still continues anxious that you should, at the earliest moment commence your operations"; "The president is persuaded you will brace to exertion every nerve under your command"; and "[The president] therefore enjoins you, by every principle that is sacred, to stimulate your operations, in the highest degree, and to move as rapidly as the lateness of the season, and the nature of the case will possibly admit."[37]

Colonel Darke grew dissatisfied and resentful of General Butler. Taking advantage of his relationship with Washington, Darke wrote to accuse Butler of inactivity and delay in moving the troops. He also accused Butler, a Pennsylvanian, of being prejudiced against Virginians. In response, Washington first emphasized that the interest of the country was paramount, "[t]o that interest all inferior considerations must yield." Perhaps remembering his years as a general, Washington then wrote, "As an apology for the seeming inattention of a commanding Officer it should be considered that the variety of objects, which engage him, may produce an appearance of neglect, by no means intended—In General Butler's particular instance some allowance should be made for the effects of bodily indisposition, combined with the cares of his station." Closing on a positive note, Washington expressed his confidence that no one "will more cheerfully make this allowance than [Darke]."[38]

Whether or not the claim of prejudice was true, there was acrimony in Butler's history with Virginia. In late summer 1774, as Dunmore's War was imminent, Butler was arrested by Virginia for violating an ordinance that prohibited transporting goods to the Shawnee. At the time, Butler was a leading Pennsylvania Indian trader, and Pennsylvania was at peace with the Shawnee. Butler's goods were confiscated, and he was jailed for several weeks before Governor Dunmore ordered his release, conditioned on Butler's posting bond and promising never to bring charges against the Virginians responsible for his arrest.

General Butler was delayed by his responsibility to get lagging units to Fort Pitt and to a lesser extent by his health. One of those lagging units was Captain Newman's company. Newman's journal details the travails his company of new recruits experienced in reaching Fort Washington. Recruiting his company in Massachusetts for the new 2nd US Regiment consumed April, May, and June. On July 1, they were transported by ship from Connecticut to Perth Amboy, New Jersey. From there they marched seventy-three miles to a barracks at Philadelphia. On July 30, they marched to Fort Pitt. It was not a smooth journey. When he started, Newman had eighty-one men, five of whom were prisoners, confined for desertion, and four female camp followers. At least two of the women were married to soldiers in the company. Even Newman's early journal entries recount desertions and other crimes. Compounding these problems, two days into the march, he ordered a halt for the day after fourteen miles because the men were "fatigued, and unused to Traveling." That night, Newman was disturbed to receive an order from the secretary of war directing him to allow Mary Hastings to join his company. His private reaction: "this Casualty increased my provision return to Eighty Eight, she's a d - - - - d Bitch & I intend to Drum her out the first time she gets drunk."[39] In the four weeks it took to reach Fort Pitt, Newman's journal documents floggings for desertion, drinking, and disobedience. Privately, Newman expressed both regret and indignant justification for ordering the punishments. He dismissed two of the women for bringing rum to the men and another woman for insolence. He also allowed one woman, with her infant, to join the company.

In late August, the water level on the Ohio was too low for passage from Fort Pitt. Then, rain and a rising river blocked departing for two more days. Finally, in the first week of September, Butler and the remaining troops, including Newman's company, gathered at Fort Pitt and were able to embark and proceed down the Ohio.

Knox and Washington presumed that recruiting would be accomplished and that, within a few months, new battalions would reach Fort Washington from as far away as New England and Maryland. Their presumption rested on eager recruits and highly efficient recruiters. That thinking proved to be wildly unrealistic. Recruitment and troop movements took too many months for the intended summer campaign. Instead of July 10, the expedition's forces were not assembled at Fort Washington until the second week of September. Moreover, there had been little time for military training. The training the levies and the new 2nd US Regiment received ranged from little to virtually none.

Chapter Six

The Allies

AFTER BEING IN WINTER CAMPS, Kekionga, Miamitown, and other villages were rebuilt in the spring. Some Shawnee and Delaware rebuilt downriver at the Glaize. Another Delaware village moved south to the White River. Maumee villagers were sure they would be the target of another major attack in 1791. Having not been ready to protect their villages, Confederation leaders knew that better preparation was needed.

They had endured a harsh winter. After Harmar's destruction, food was in short supply. The shortage was exacerbated as warriors from other villages gathered at the Maumee in spring and summer. Confederation leaders stressed their continuing need for the British to provide substantial amounts of food.

The British had established a supply base downriver from Kekionga at the Maumee Rapids. Thomas Rhea was a prisoner there in late May and early June. Rhea was captured in western Pennsylvania by five Delaware and over the next few weeks was moved to the Maumee Rapids. There he observed hundreds of Indians coming to meet with the prominent trader and senior British Indian agent, Colonel Alexander McKee. Rhea could see the British providing guns, ammunition, clothing, and provisions of corn, pork, peas, and more, all of it very much needed to defend and maintain the Maumee towns. After being moved to Detroit, Rhea saw a party of French Canadiens leaving to bring supplies to Kekionga. After his captivity ended, Rhea reported these and other details in an affidavit given to a judge in Pittsburgh, on July 2, to document his experience. General Butler promptly transmitted Rhea's affidavit by express to Secretary Knox. Knox, in turn, quickly sent the affidavit on to Tobias Lear, Washington's personal secretary, for delivery to the president.[1]

As recently as 1788, the Wyandots had urged Little Turtle and the Miami to accept a wampum belt signifying an agreement for peace. As late as summer 1790, Egushawa (also given as Egushwa, Augooshaway, Agashawa, and Negushwa), the principal chief of the Ottawa, advocated that they "sit still . . . and not trouble ourselves about the Shawnees, who alone are out in war."[2] Now, the attitude of many, including Egushawa, had shifted. Increasingly aware that the American desire for expansion might never abate, and encouraged by the victories against Harmar, they were ready to join to defend the Maumee against the army's anticipated 1791 campaign. Those among the intertribal Confederation who were ready to fight had grown significantly. In effect, they composed a Maumee Confederation of Shawnee, Miami, Delaware, Wyandot, Seneca-Cayuga, Ottawa, Ojibwe, Potawatomi, Chickamauga Cherokee, and Kickapoo.

Nevertheless, intratribal divisions still existed. There were those Shawnee who had migrated across the Mississippi and south to Tennessee. More significantly in terms of numbers, a substantial portion of the Wyandot and Delaware remained neutral, though sympathetic to those at the Maumee. Almost all of the Chickamauga naturally remained in the south, engaged in their own struggle against white settlement.

Even more significantly, while the Seneca-Cayuga (or Mingos) were willing to fight, the Senecas and Cayugas who remained with the Six Nations of the Iroquois were not. Many of the Six Nations followed the influential Mohawk Joseph Brant's insistence that there must be compromise. Some thought the Maumee Confederation should capitulate and accept the peace terms available from the United States.

Two communications early in the 1790s reflect the tribal extremes exemplified by the Shawnee and the Seneca.

In April 1790, Antoine Gamelin, an American emissary, was at Kekionga. His goal was to separate the Miami from the Shawnee. The night before Gamelin was going to leave, Blue Jacket invited him to have dinner at his cabin. Blue Jacket bluntly told Gamelin that the Shawnee did not trust the Big Knives. As recorded by Gamelin, Blue Jacket told him the Big Knives "had first destroyed their lands, put out their fire, and sent away their young men, being a hunting, without a mouthful of meat; also had taken away their women." Blue Jacket was suspicious that offers of peace would lead to the loss of land "by degrees" and that "a certain proof that they intend to encroach on our lands, is their new settlement on the Ohio."[3] Destroying Shawnee lands appears to refer to the deforestation that followed white settlement.

In January 1791, three Seneca chiefs—Cornplanter, Half-Town, and Big-Tree—went to Philadelphia to negotiate with President Washington. Through translators, the chiefs sent written messages to him, and his written messages were read to the chiefs. Their message of January 10 concluded:

Father: You have given us leave to speak our minds concerning the tilling of the ground. We ask you teach us to plough and to grind corn; *to assist us in building saw mills*, and to supply us with broad axes, saws, augers, and other tools, so as that we may make our houses more comfortable and more durable; that you will send smiths among us, and, above all, that you will teach our children to read and write, and our women to spin and weave. The manner of your doing these things for us we leave to you, who understand them; but we assure you that we will follow your advice as far as we are able.[4] (Emphasis added.)

The Seneca had been growing corn and other vegetables since before whites first appeared. The message reflected George Washington's vision of converting Indians to a predominantly agrarian culture. The announced desire to build sawmills fit Washington's goal of deforestation and his view of trees as a commodity. A generation earlier, the Seneca chiefs' message would have been unthinkable.

Eleven weeks later, the Seneca chiefs' message to Washington was quite different. They complained that three Indian men and one woman who had been trading at Big Beaver Creek in Pennsylvania had been murdered by a raiding party from Virginia led by a noted frontiersman, Samuel Brady. Brady and his men had also taken nine horses and trade goods. The victims were Delaware. Brady and his men were retaliating for a Delaware raid in

Virginia. Knox transmitted the message to Washington along with letters from Fort Pitt expressing the concern of Pennsylvanians.[5]

Knox opined that this and other similar incidents "will have the most pernicious consequences. . . . It appears to have been an atrocious murder." Knox advised that after verifying the complaint, St. Clair should "disavow and disapprove the murder in the strongest terms," assure the Indians that everything would be done "to bring the accused to punishment," and indemnify the families of the victims for the loss of the horses and trade goods. Knox's private assessment to the president was blunt: "the accused will either not be apprehended, or if apprehended, will not be convicted, yet nothing farther."[6] That assessment proved to be correct. Two years later, Brady was acquitted. Then he was appointed chief of the army's scout company.

Unlike the years when raiding parties formed and operated autonomously, the Maumee Confederation was now engaged in a national war, so strategy and tactics were determined by the leading chiefs, and everyone was expected to support the tribe's efforts.[7] Blue Jacket, Little Turtle, and Buckongahelas were the most renowned of their war chiefs.

In the Miami language, the Maumee River was the Taawaawa Siipiiiwi . The Americans were Mihši-Maalhsaki.[8] In this time of national war, Little Turtle's authority as war chief now surpassed that of the Miami civil chiefs.

As their principal war chief, Blue Jacket led the Shawnee. For years, they had been the most active tribe fighting the Big Knives and settlers, with Blue Jacket at the forefront of that struggle. Born into the Pekowi clan, his influence and following had long extended across clan lines. As with Little Turtle, in this time of national war, Blue Jacket's authority now exceeded that of the Shawnee civil chiefs.

Buckongahelas led the Delaware. He may have been as old as seventy-one. Like Little Turtle and Blue Jacket, he had a well-earned reputation for his prowess in combat, as well as for his wisdom in council. He was said to be "esteemed as one of the greatest warriors . . . among all the Indians." Ebenezer Denny described Buckongahelas as "a very large stout man."[9]

The people who became known as the Delaware were the Lenape, the People. Once they lived primarily along a river coursing through eastern New York, Pennsylvania, and New Jersey. In 1610, the English named that river the Delaware after Lord de la Warr III, the governor of Virginia. The name Delaware was eventually accepted by the Lenape.[10] Regardless of their name, their tribal history was one of being forced west across the Alleghenies, then west out of Pennsylvania. Now, the westward pressure had come to Ohio. No other tribe in the Confederation had been pushed west so many miles. It was far enough for Buckongahelas and the Delaware who followed him.

In the mid-1600s, several small tribes, one of whom had been an original member of the now destroyed Huron Confederation, joined together to form the Wyandot Nation. The Wyandot were led by Tarhe. It is often translated as "the Crane," but according to the Wyandot, the English meaning is unknown. Tarhe was six feet four and about fifty years old. He is said to have fought and gained repute as a young warrior in Pontiac's War and to have been with the Shawnee at Point Pleasant. Tarhe had long been a chief, though not a war chief. In 1788, he became the sachem, the paramount chief of the Wyandot Nation.[11]

A confederation within the Maumee Confederation was the Three Fires, comprising the Ottawa, Potawatomi, and Ojibwe. The Potawatomi lived in northern Illinois and southern Wisconsin. The Ottawa were centered in lower Michigan, although there was an Ottawa village along the Maumee. The Ojibwe were the farthest away, in upper Michigan, northern Wisconsin, and Minnesota.

Egushawa, an Ottawa, was the Three Fires' most noted chief. Egushawa and the Ottawa fought against the British in the French and Indian War and in Pontiac's War. Before becoming the principal chief of the Ottawa, he was a war chief. About fifty-one years old, his influence extended beyond the Ottawa to the Potawatomi, the Ojibwe, and, to a lesser extent, the Wyandot.[12]

Only infrequently did the Three Fires torture prisoners. But ritual cannibalism, such as eating the heart of a brave enemy, was sometimes practiced.[13]

The Seneca and Cayuga, with the Mohawk, Onondaga, and Oneida were the original five nations of the Iroquois (Haudenosaunee, meaning "They Made the House") Confederation. The Seneca-Cayuga (Mingo, as they were known to whites) had split off from the main branch of their tribes to move west to Ohio. They had been aligned with the Shawnee in fighting white settlement since the 1770s. In 1791, eleven Haudenosaunee led by Du Quania, probably Mohawks, came to the Maumee to join the fight.[14]

The Chickamauga Cherokee were the branch of the Cherokee Nation most aggressively resisting white settlement. Because of this, a natural affinity had developed between the Chickamauga and the Shawnee. It was the Chickamauga that Cheeseekau's band of Shawnee had joined a year or two earlier. Cheeseekau's move south paralleled a small number of Chickamaugas who came north in the 1780s to live and fight with the Shawnee. In April

1791, anticipating the coming American offensive, the Shawnee sent messengers in all directions asking for warriors to join them. This brought a small number of additional Chickamauga to help. It may have been one of these messages that prompted Tecumseh to return north that summer.

While St. Clair's main force struggled to begin its part in the campaign, American military action commenced in June when Charles Scott's Kentucky militia launched their strike into the Wabash. Once again, Colonel John Hardin led the advance party. They attacked and burned Wea and Kickapoo villages in the mid-Wabash River Valley. A number of the inhabitants were French, with ties to the British in Detroit. Many of the warriors had gone to the Maumee. Heavily outnumbering those who had remained at home, Scott claimed to have killed thirty-two, mostly men, while suffering only five wounded. The Miami remember Scott killing thirty-eight. They also remember finding the badly mutilated body of a village war leader, Keekaanwikania.[15] Fifty-eight women and children were taken prisoner.

After Scott's attack, Alexander McKee wrote to his superior, Sir John Johnson, the British superintendent of Indian affairs, that the "continual alarms of hostile intentions and preparations of America" made it impractical to convene a grand council of chiefs to discuss what peace terms would be acceptable. Referring to Scott's attack, McKee was concerned that "little attention will be paid to any Proposals for a Termination of the Calamities of War, while the Indians are heated by the recollections of Injuries so fresh on their minds."[16]

Sir John Johnson was born in 1741, the son of Sir William Johnson and Catherine Weisenberg.[17] Johnson, in turn, reported to Sir Guy Carleton, Lord Dorchester, the governor of British North America.

Shawnee oral history remembered that through the summer, "the Ohio and the settlements of Virginia and Kentucky swarmed with war parties and the Villages daily swarmed with the victorious shouts of returning warriors."[18] In those raids, it was whites, often defenseless, men, women, and children, who suffered. In these months, the British still hoped for a diplomatic solution. Peace that preserved the Indians' status quo was in Britain's self-interest. Peace would avoid conflict with the United States. Peace would maintain their forts and the fur trade.

Joseph Brant also sought a compromise. He accepted that eastern Ohio was already too populated with white settlements to expect to regain it. He was convinced that accepting the status quo of settlement there, in return for peace, was the best, most realistic option for the Native American people.

For Brant and those who agreed with him, that choice was superior to war, with its attendant losses, cost, and risk of defeat. But like the rest of the Confederation, they were not willing to concede all the tens of thousands of additional square miles west of the Muskingum that the government claimed through the Fort McIntosh, Fort Finney, and Fort Harmar treaties.

On June 23, Brant opined to John Johnson that only the Miami and the Shawnee seemed "unreasonable," refusing to agree to his compromise, in contrast to the "Lake Indians" (Potawatomi, Ottawa, and Ojibwe), the Delaware, and the "Hurons" (Wyandot), whom Brant found to be "reasonable."[19]

Days later, an American emissary, Timothy Pickering, met with Indian leaders who had not joined the Shawnee and Miami. His primary mission was to secure their continued neutrality. A secondary goal was to enlist their help in opening peace talks. One of the leaders was Captain Hendrick, a Stockbridge chief. Not only had the Stockbridge been part of Rogers' Rangers in the French and Indian War, they had fought for American independence against the British. On June 27, Hendrick asked Pickering if the United States would require land concessions as a condition of peace with the Western Indians. Pickering answered:

"The United States will require no such condition. The Western Indians will retain all of their lands, agreeably to the treaties of peace subsisting between them and the United States, until of their own will and choice, they shall fairly sell them, unless they should obstinately persevere in their hostilities until the United States shall drive them from their Country; and in that case their Lands will never be restored to them."[20]

The treaties of Fort McIntosh, Fort Finney, and Fort Harmar had purportedly been with the Wyandot, Delaware, Ottawa, Ojibwe, and Shawnee, but the Confederation rejected the authority of the treaties signatories and hence the treaties' validity. The difference between the boundaries set out in those treaties and the Confederation position was tens of thousands of square miles, more than twelve million acres.

Pickering's answer to Hendrick left ambiguities. Did the United States insist that all past treaties were valid? Did the United States maintain that the Miami were bound by those treaties, though no Miami had agreed to them? Pickering made no secret that the government would continue to seek more Indian land. Why did he speak of future land sales in the context of peace terms? In light of past coercive demands, did his reference to the Indians' "own will and choice" and to fair sales mean that a refusal to sell would be accepted? Would the government only recognize a Confederation agreement to sell, or would it accept a land sale from any convenient chief, as it had done in the past?

Four days after Pickering responded to Hendrick, McKee was able to convene a "General Council." McKee reported that speeches had arrived from the "American States" to the Mohawk, Delaware, and "Hurons" (Wyandot), "calculated to divide them," but that they had "resolved on a General Confederacy of all the Nations of their Colour to defend their Country to the last." McKee further reported that the council contended that the boundary line should be the Ohio on the south, east to the Muskingum, then north to the portage crossing to the Cuyahoga, to Venango (now Franklin, Pennsylvania), then to Lake Erie.[21] This adopted the more moderate position espoused by Brant, though maintaining the Ohio as the boundary line west of the Muskingum would require Fort Washington, Cincinnati, and other settlements to be abandoned. Following the council, a delegation of chiefs, including Brant, traveled to meet with Johnson.

Neither the government nor the Confederation had taken a position that induced either a truce or negotiations.

St. Clair authorized a second militia strike in August. James Wilkinson commanded. This time the Kentuckians attacked an Eel River village. Like the Wea and the eponymous Miami, the Eel River were a tribe of the Miami Nation. The village chief was the Porcupine (Gaviahatte). He had an adopted white son, Black Snake, the once and future William Wells. Over seven years earlier, in March 1784, Wells was captured when he was about fourteen. With his red hair, he was given the name Wild Carrot (usually given in sources as Apekonit, but to the Miami, Eepikihkaanit).[22] As he became a warrior, Wild Carrot became Black Snake.[23]

Wells took to Indian life. Probably in his late teens, he married an Eel River girl. By early 1791, they had a child. According to Wells's family history, William's older brothers, first Carty, then Sam, traveled to meet with him to urge him to leave the Miami. As a result of talking to Sam, William returned to Kentucky to see his birth family. Then, after a few days, he chose to go back to his Miami family.[24]

Wilkinson's attack on the village came while the Porcupine, Black Snake, and most of the men were at Kekionga and Miamitown. Six warriors were killed. Among thirty-four women and children taken prisoner were Black Snake's wife and child.

St. Clair mistakenly believed that the damage done by Scott and Wilkinson detached the Wabash Valley Indians from the Confederation force gathered at the Maumee. While the attacks lessened the number of Wabash warriors, some remained, or returned, after checking on their villages. One of them was Black Snake. Though young and of the Eel River, he was a trusted protege of Little Turtle. In late 1791 or early 1792, Wells would marry Little Turtle's daughter, Sweet Breeze (Manwangopath). Eventually, they would have five children together.

Many at the Maumee suspected that the raids by Scott and Wilkinson were originally intended for their villages, but hearing that they "were too strong & prepared," the Big Knives veered off, "ransacked . . . unprotected villages, massacred . . . old men, and carried off . . . women & children."[25]

Over decades of trade, many of the Maumee Confederation had acquired guns, principally light muskets known as fusils or fusees. The years of frontier raids, as well as the two Harmar fights, had provided a variety of additional muskets, as well as rifles, from fallen Americans. The British supplied significant numbers of "Brown Bess" muskets to their Native American allies during the Revolution and now were doing so again. The Brown Bess was the musket used by most of the Maumee Confederation.

Beginning in 1722 and continuing for more than a century, the Brown Bess musket was the standard gun of British infantry. Brown Bess was a nickname with several different origin stories. The most plausible is that in the early 1700s, when the nickname came into use, Bess was slang for a woman and Brown Bess was lower-class slang for a prostitute.[26]

The Brown Bess was just over five feet long. The Long Land Pattern had a barrel length of forty-six inches, while the Short Land Pattern's barrel was forty-two inches long. They were muzzle-loading, smoothbore, .75-caliber flintlocks that fired a paper cartridge containing a musket ball. Sometimes several pellets of buckshot were added on top of the cartridge. This was referred to as buck and ball. It was intended to be fired into a concentrated mass of enemy soldiers.

The effective range, where muskets were reasonably accurate and the musket balls maintained lethal velocity, is generally said to be one hundred yards. Aiming upward increased range but decreased accuracy. At maximum range, the velocity of musket balls diminished enough that they might no longer strike hard enough to kill.

Muskets lacked sights to help aim. The aerodynamics of musket balls also impeded their accuracy. When fired while the gun was held level at a height of about four feet, a musket ball initially rose more than an inch, but less than two inches, in the first thirty to thirty-five yards. The trajectory then started to fall. At one hundred yards a musket ball might be two and a half feet above the ground, depending on the exact muzzle velocity and assuming level ground. Beyond 150 yards, a musket ball would probably hit the ground.[27]

The rifles some Confederation warriors acquired were typically "long rifles," also known as Pennsylvania or Kentucky rifles. In contrast to smoothbore muskets, rifles had rifling, spiral grooves inside the barrel. At a distance, long rifles were considerably more accurate than muskets, at least in the hands of a capable rifleman. A marksman with a long rifle might be able to aim and hit a target two hundred or more yards away. Opinions differ on how much more. Three hundred yards has been described as "a formidable distance even for a skilled rifleman."[28] But it has also been claimed that four hundred to five hundred yards is the maximum range for an expert who takes into account varying conditions, including the gunpowder load, the wind, and elevation changes.[29] At closer ranges, the advantage of distance became moot and rifles' slow reloading time gained importance. It was more difficult to ram a ball down the grooved barrel of a rifle than down the smooth barrel of a musket. Although some more-skilled riflemen were faster, the average rifleman often took one to two minutes to reload a rifle.[30]

Almost all Confederation warriors carried a knife and a tomahawk. A few preferred a war club to a tomahawk. Unlike the British, Native Americans did not attach bayonets to their muskets when charging the enemy; tomahawks and war clubs were preferred. Some warriors carried a bow and arrows, either because they lacked a gun or to use if they ran out of ammunition.

The European style of warfare, with lines of infantry standing in the open, exchanging volleys of musket fire, then reloading and firing again on command, was often used by the Continental army during the Revolutionary War. Such methods were anathema to Native Americans. Tribes lacked the numbers to sustain major losses, which meant individual lives were prized, not treated as expendable. If there was to be an exchange of gunfire, Woodland Indians sought to shoot from positions of cover, simultaneously trying to inflict casualties while avoiding casualties of their own. Lacking the advantage of cover, Indians would lay prone to exchange fire.[31]

Woodland warriors were trained to advance and retreat with control and coordination, alternately moving under covering fire, then in turn providing covering fire for others to move, then reloading and starting the cycle again.[32] After Point Pleasant, a Virginia officer described how the Indians "beat back slowly and killed and wounded our men at every advance."[33]

From their training, they also knew to avoid the impact of an enemy charge by giving ground, but not truly retreating. Their goal was to melt into the forest, then outflank and, in effect, ambush those who had charged them.[34] Alternatively, they might come back to attack whatever soft target their charging enemy had left behind. This was tactical mobility combined with flexible opportunism. It was not "hit and run." Rather, it was a tactic of first run, then hit.

That Indian warriors did not blindly follow orders, or stand in forma-tion, or wait for commands to load, fire, and reload, was true. But focusing only on that overlooked their combat proficiency. They were skilled in ma-neuvering to outflank their enemy, to advance and retreat with coordinated covering fire, and to turn enemy charges to their advantage. All of this re-quired the warriors to follow their training, to follow their plan of attack, and to follow battlefield directions. This was Indian discipline.[35]

Chapter Seven

Bland, Bouquet, and Bayonets

ALL OF ST. CLAIR'S REGULARS AND LEVIES, except for Rhea's Frontier Battalion, were equipped with French 1766 and 1774 Charleville muskets. France had supplied them to the Continental army during the Revolutionary War. Charleville muskets were generally comparable to the Brown Bess, although they were somewhat lighter and .69 caliber not .75 caliber.

With competent skill, a musket could be reloaded and fired three to four times a minute. The reloading process might take longer to say than to do:

Bite the cartridge.

Pull the hammer back to half-cock and push the frizzen forward to open the pan and pour a small amount of powder into the flash pan.

Snap the frizzen back to position, covering the flash pan.

Hold the musket vertically with the muzzle up.

Pour the remaining powder down the barrel.

Insert a lead ball into the barrel.

Push cartridge paper into the barrel.

Remove the ramrod from under the barrel and use it to push the wadding and the bullet down the barrel.

Replace the ramrod.

Pull back the hammer to fully cock.

Raise the musket to firing position with the gun butt against the shoulder.

Aim and fire.[1]

When gunpowder ignited to propel a musket ball out of a barrel, a small cloud of white smoke was also emitted. When many guns were fired simultaneously, the small cloud became a much larger cloud. Naturally, this affected what the combatants could see.

Like the British and other Europeans, the army's muskets were equipped with bayonets. When a bayonet was attached to a musket, the time required to reload increased. For American and European armies, it was axiomatic that this disadvantage was more than offset by the ability to charge the enemy with bayonets fixed to their muskets. Bayonet charges were a favored tactic. They were potentially devastating, if properly executed against an enemy who lacked an effective countermeasure.

Rhea's battalion was recruited from the Southwest Territory (now Tennessee). Both Rhea's battalion and Faulkner's Pennsylvania militia company carried rifles. The Kentucky militia were armed with a mix of muskets and rifles. As bayonets did not fit on rifles, riflemen carried hatchets.

Officers and some noncommissioned officers were issued swords. Many officers were issued fusils. Sergeants and corporals carried the same muskets, or rifles, as the rest of their unit.

A leading military publication of the eighteenth century was General Humphrey Bland's *A Treatise of Military Discipline; In Which Is Laid Down and Explained the Duty of the Officer and Soldier Thro' the Several Branches of the Service.*[2] As a young officer in the mid-1750s, George Washington trained Virginia colonial troops using Bland's *Treatise.*[3] One of the myriad military maneuvers and procedures Bland detailed was how to properly pursue the enemy:

When any of the Battalions have forced those attacked to give way, great Care must be taken by the Officers to prevent their Men from Breaking after them; neither must they pursue them faster than the line advances; For if a Battalion advances out of the Line it may be attacked on the Flanks. . . . The commanding officers must therefore remain satisfied with the Advantage of having obliged the Enemy to give way, and not break the Line by advancing before it in the Pursuit.

Bland warned against being "too elated" and chasing the enemy "too fast without Reflecting on the Danger . . . [for] if they should separate in pursuing those they beat, the enemy may destroy them one after another."[4]

As a British officer in the French and Indian War, St. Clair must have known of Bland. Indeed, St. Clair maintained that he had "joined theory to practice, by an attentive perusal of the best military books, in most languages."[5]

From the French and Indian War, St. Clair also must have known of Robert Rogers and Rogers' Rangers, famed for their scouting, raids, and Indian fighting. Rogers had written of his accomplishments and methods, including his "Rules of Ranging." Like Bland, he cautioned about maintaining cohesion when advancing against an enemy who had been repulsed. In his seventh rule, Rogers advised that the flanks and the center should have "equal force," maintain "a due distance from each other, and advance from tree to tree, with half of the party before the other [half every] ten or twelve yards." Chances are that St. Clair did not study Rogers' methods.[6]

Two victories over the Indians influenced conventional American military thinking: Bushy Run and Point Pleasant.

In August 1763, as part of widespread attacks masterminded by Pontiac, Fort Pitt was besieged. Colonel Henry Bouquet led about 450 soldiers, mostly Scottish Highlanders, to relieve the fort. About the same number of Delaware, Wyandot, Seneca-Cayuga, and Shawnee left Fort Pitt and moved to intercept them. Bushy Run began with an ambush. While some Indians blocked the British line of march, others were positioned on the British flanks. Maintaining their composure, the English and Scots fixed bayonets and repeatedly charged, dislodging their attackers. Over two days, multiple bayonet charges forced the Indians from the positions they had taken. The battle ended with the Indians giving up the fight. It was a decisive British victory. Most British and American military leaders concluded that Indians lacked discipline and could not withstand bayonet charges by disciplined troops. These became twin tenets of American military thinking.

But this was flawed, post hoc ergo propter hoc reasoning. The conclusions were based on the end result rather than on a thorough analysis of what happened. To avoid casualties trying to hold meaningless positions, the Indians did not seriously resist the British charges. Instead, they gave

way while continuously seeking to outflank the British and renew their attack. After one seemingly successful charge, Indians were firing from high
ground along the British flanks. Another charge was ordered. Once again,
it dislodged the Indians from their position, but not from the battlefield.
This time the charge left the main British force separated from its supply
convoy. Seizing the opportunity, Indians attacked the convoy. Others continued shifting to outflank the British troops. By nightfall, Bouquet had suffered significant casualties. He and his men had taken a defensive position
on a hill, where they were surrounded and lacked water. Despite their apparently successful bayonet charges, they were in mortal danger.

The next day, two companies pulled back from the British line. Thinking
that the time had come to close in and annihilate the remaining soldiers,
the Indians charged. Rushing past where the British had been, they ran into
musket volleys from the companies that had pulled back. Outflanked and
ambushed, the Indians were now routed by a bayonet charge. Strategically
and psychologically, it was a British victory.

Bouquet did not draw any broad conclusions about the value of bayonet
charges. In letters to Governor James Hamilton and Lieutenant James Mc-
Donald, he recognized the bravery of the Highlanders and of the Indians.[7]
In both letters, Bouquet described his success as a "lucky blow."[8] Lost on
most British and Americans was that the first day at Bushy Run "show[ed]
the core of Ohio Valley 18th Century Indian battlefield tactical expertise in
large-scale wars: the flanking movements accompanying the half-moon for-
mations and the maintenance of that formation through an ability to charge
or retreat according to battlefield circumstances."[9] Bouquet's fifty killed and
sixty wounded probably exceeded the Indians' casualties. By 1763, when
Bushy Run was fought, St. Clair had immigrated to Pennsylvania and apparently was at least acquainted with Bouquet.[10]

Eleven years after Bushy Run and one year before the Revolution began
at Lexington and Concord, Virginia battled an Indian coalition at Point
Pleasant in the brief Dunmore's War. St. Clair, Richard Butler, and the president were well aware that the Indians had attacked Virginia's army and had
been forced to retreat back across the Ohio River. Knowing that outcome
may have inflated their confidence and further solidified their belief that
Indians lacked the discipline needed in battle. Had they lived through the
bloody experience at Point Pleasant, their memory of how the battle ended
might not have inspired as much confidence.

About nine hundred Virginians camped at Point Pleasant, preparing to
join other Virginia units in an offensive against the Shawnee and the
"Mingo." Virginia Colonel William Fleming was sure that for a force of

mostly well-armed "Woodsmen . . . the Shawnese and the Mingoes [would] be [no] more than a Breakfast." Under Cornstalk, the leading Shawnee chief, Shawnee, Seneca-Cayuga, and their allies crossed the Ohio during the night, positioning themselves to attack before dawn. Estimates vary, but Cornstalk probably had seven hundred to eight hundred men.[11]

The fight began prematurely for both sides when Indian scouts collided with Virginia hunters. Initially, three hundred Virginians advanced as a reconnaissance in force. Meeting heavy fire, they were pushed back. Under intense pressure, the Virginians sought to stabilize a defensive line. A Virginian later recalled Indians "[d]isputing the Ground with the Greatest Obstinacy, often Running up to the Very Muzels of our Gunes where the[y] as often fell Victims to their rage." Reinforcing their positions, the Virginians continued to be on the defensive. Despite "repeated and desperate attacks to break the Virginia line," it held.[12]

After some hours, the Virginians launched a counterattack. Heeding Bland's cautionary note, Virginia commanders maintained their hard-won advantage and avoided potential disaster.[13] When they were finally able to push the Indians back, the Virginians moved forward with cohesion, not allowing their advance to degenerate into a wild pursuit. Even with that, the Indians inflicted casualties as they slowly gave ground, remaining alert for an opportunity to turn back and outflank the Big Knives. By no means beaten, Cornstalk stopped moving back and deployed his warriors in a defensive position along a wooded ridge. The fight raged on through the day, until Cornstalk ordered a withdrawal back across the Ohio. It was a Virginia victory, but it had been difficult and costly. Some fifty Virginians were killed and ninety wounded, about twenty mortally. The overconfident Colonel Fleming barely survived three wounds. Major Ingles reported that the Virginians took twenty scalps. Native American warriors carried off an unknown number of their dead and mortally wounded.[14] The dead included Tecumseh's father, Pukeshinwau. Their number of wounded is also unknown.

Dismissing the Indians as undisciplined "savages" who could be readily beaten with discipline and bayonet charges dangerously underestimated the lethal prowess of the Confederation warriors.

Chapter Eight

The Slow Trek
through the Forest

HE FIRST STAGE OF ST. CLAIR'S PLAN was to erect a small fort, primarily as a supply depot. The site chosen was some thirty miles northwest of Fort Washington, on the banks of the Great Miami.[1] Construction began on September 10, as General Butler and the last of the army's units were reaching Fort Washington. The new post was named Fort Hamilton, in honor of Treasury Secretary Alexander Hamilton. From there, the entire force, less the new post's garrison, would move on toward the Maumee.

The late arriving units, including Captain Samuel Newman's company, moved out to rendezvous with the main force on September 15. The weather was rainy, the road muddy, and thick morning fog was a regular occurrence. For four days, they were beset by rain. In his journal, Newman "d - - - - d" the cheapness of the contractor who provided such thin tents that the rain ran through them as if through a "Sieve! This is the Country cheated, and the Soldier imposed on."[2]

During these rainy days, Newman's son returned from the hospital at Fort Washington. According to his father, he was dispirited but not thinking about the danger and difficulties that lay ahead. By late September, Newman believed that hostile Indians watched their every move. Close to one hundred horses were already gone, either lost, stolen by Indians, or as Darke suspected, by whites leaving false Indian signs. On September 26, three of Newman's men disappeared after being given permission to go to the river to wash. Suspected of desertion, they were never found. Two days later, two more of Newman's men disappeared, again after going to the river to wash. When they appeared at Dunlap's Station, despite claiming to have been lost, they were confined on suspicion of desertion.[3]

During September and continuing into October, the army's problems began to multiply. The delays in reaching Fort Washington were compounded by the slow pace of construction at Fort Hamilton. As the timeline stretched out, morale was already dropping, worsened by the rainstorms, leaking tents, and related illnesses. By October 3, Newman had a "Violent Cold in [his] head & limbs." Yet he was the only captain in the regiment "well [enough] to [be on] duty."[4]

Recruiting deficiencies, desertions, illness, and injuries took a toll on the number of troops actually available. As of September 27, not counting officers, 1,634 regulars and 1,674 levies were in service, 820 men short of what was authorized. Outside of Ohio, 219 were in Georgia, 17 were at West Point, and 373 were marching to the frontier. Of the 2,699 "troops on the Ohio," 699 were sick, assigned to garrisons, craftsmen, or otherwise "non-effectives."[5] This left St. Clair with 2,000 regulars and levies fit and available "for the expedition," plus officers.[6] Knox's projection that St. Clair would have 3,000 troops had been too optimistic.

Knox explained to the president: "Had the operation commenced two months earlier, it would have been more comfortable for the troops, and have given greater time to have improved all advantages. But the extreme field from which the troops have been collected, the lowness of the waters on the Ohio, and the tedious delays of some of the agents in the business, have rendered an earlier campaign impracticable."[7]

It was not until October 1 that Fort Hamilton was essentially finished. The walls were 150-feet long, with a diamond-shaped bastion at each corner. A three-foot trench, filled with pointed stakes, ran around the walls. Two cannons were left for its defense. Captain John Armstrong of the 1st

US Regiment was placed in command. Approximately sixty sick men from among the regiments were assigned to garrison the fort.

It was also October 1 when Lieutenant Ebenezer Denny joined General St. Clair's staff as his aide-de-camp. Denny, another Pennsylvanian, began three years of Revolutionary War service as a nineteen-year-old ensign. Less than a year after being discharged, he rejoined the army in 1784. Now thirty, he had been with a detachment of the 1st US Regiment in Harmar's campaign, though he had not seen combat. In his words, he joined the general's "family" of Colonel Winthrop Sargent, the adjutant general, and the young Count Malartic, St. Clair's volunteer aide.[8]

Before Denny left to join St. Clair, General Harmar told him the expedition was doomed to defeat. Harmar's assessment was based on the poor quality of many of the men, compounded by their lack of training, with officers "*totally unacquainted with the business*" of fighting Indians, and with "both quartermaster and contractors extremely deficient." (Emphasis added.) Harmar was astonished that St. Clair would "think of hazarding, with such people, and under such circumstances, his reputation and life, and the lives of so many others, knowing too . . . the enemy with whom he was going to contend; an enemy brought up from infancy to war, and perhaps superior to an equal number of the best men that could be taken against them." Denny ruefully journaled, "I had hopes that the noise and show which the army made on their march might possibly deter the enemy from attempting a serious and general attack."[9]

As to St. Clair hazarding his reputation, Harmar overlooked or was unaware of the presidential pressure to proceed with the campaign. Refusing to proceed would likely have cost St. Clair his governorship, his political standing, and his reputation. St. Clair explained his decision to proceed. "[T]he body of the troops was raised for six months only; that the public expectations were up in an extraordinary degree; and that the secretary of war had written, in the name of the president, in the most positive terms, to press forward the operations; it will be evident that no officer could have taken it upon himself to decline it."[10]

That night, word reached St. Clair that the Kentucky militia were expected to arrive at Fort Washington the next day. St. Clair decided that he and Lieutenant Denny should ride back to ensure that the militia proceeded onward, while General Butler began the army's march toward Kekionga. The army's path and deployments were to follow orders for march, battle, and encampment that St. Clair had issued a few days earlier.

The expectation was that the Kentucky militia would bring their own rifles. But many were not frontiersmen and did not have a rifle. Some brought a rifle, some brought a musket, others came unarmed. Ensign Piercy Pope of the militia observed that many of the men were "old," and many were not "woodsmen."[11] After some difficulty in getting them properly equipped, Colonel William Oldham was ordered to march from Fort Washington on October 6. With them was a herd of several hundred head of cattle to provide beef. St. Clair and Denny remained at Fort Washington until the next morning.

During that first week of October, two miles from camp, Indians killed a soldier and captured another, along with six horses. Then they disappeared into the wilderness. Twenty-six soldiers and ten of the Kentucky militia also disappeared, deserting into the night.

Despite the delays and complications, stage two of the campaign began as the army forded the Great Miami and advanced in the late morning of October 4. Not all those listed as sick were left behind, so the four army regiments totaled more than two thousand, plus officers. They marched out in their blue coats, with red trim on the lapels and cuffs. Under their blue coats, they wore white waistcoats. The regulars had white crossed belts and white trousers. The levies were both brown. Neck stocks and shoes were black, as were hats and helmets. Some hats and helmets were adorned with red feathers.[12] These were the uniforms of European warfare, such as Washington's army wore during the Revolution. They were not the browns and greens that could blend into the colors of the forest. The sound of fifes and drums accompanied the army as it marched away from Fort Hamilton.

Some of the women and children who had accompanied the army stayed at Fort Hamilton, waiting for an opportunity to safely return to Fort Washington. Most continued on with the army, as thus far, the journey had not been long. Also continuing with the army were its contracted employees. The total number of civilians at this point may well have still been around two hundred.

Daily rations for enlisted men were supposed to be a pound of flour or bread, a pound of beef, and one gill (about a half cup) of rum.[13] Officers were to receive more, the amount increasing with rank. Authorized civilians also received army rations. With over two thousand mouths to feed, that meant more than a ton of flour and of meat being consumed daily.

In St. Clair's order of march, first came the surveyor, with his compass, and a small party of riflemen, charting the path and marking the way for the road that would have to be built through the woods. Then came the road cutters with an armed escort, followed by an advance guard. The main body of the army followed, marching in two columns, designated as the right wing and the left wing. A cannon pulled by oxen was positioned in the front, middle, and rear of each column. Between the two columns was the remaining artillery, plus the wagons, packhorses, and camp followers. Behind them came the cattle herd. About a hundred yards outside of each column, a file of cavalry and a party of riflemen were deployed. Scouts paralleled the march outside of the cavalry. Finally came the rear guard.

The artillery battalion now had eight brass cannons, three-pounders and six-pounders, as well as two light 5.5-inch Coehorn iron mortars.[14] Three-pounders and six-pounders referred to the weight of the cannon balls each could fire. A 5.5-inch mortar referred to the diameter of the barrel. Cannon balls were solid and were also known as round shot or solid shot. Their destructive power came from smashing into their targets. Against massed infantry, cannon balls might bounce along the ground, creating swathes of destruction. Alternatively, the cannons could fire canisters that unleashed cones of small lead balls. To fire at a level angle, a cannon barrel was at zero degrees. The barrel could be elevated to increase the cannon's range up to a maximum of forty-five degrees. Mortars always fired upward at a forty-five degree angle, though their range could be adjusted by increasing or decreasing the amount of gunpowder used to propel the shell. A mortar shell might be solid shot, or it could be fused to explode. Traditionally, mortars were used against enemy fortifications, infantry massed in line(s), or infantry marching forward. Once positioned on a battlefield, neither cannons nor mortars could be readily repositioned.[15]

The army's route began by following a generations-old Indian path through the woods. But that was a path for people, or horses, in single file. No more than eighteen inches wide, it was not nearly enough for an army with oxen hauling artillery and pulling wagons, thus, the need for the path to be widened into a road. Bushes had to be cleared. Trees had to be cut down. It was hard, slow work. St. Clair's marching order was for two parallel tracks to be cleared, two hundred to three hundred yards apart. A column was to proceed along each track. General Butler was to lead the right wing and Lieutenant Colonel Darke the left wing. After the first day out, when the army advanced all of three miles, Butler altered St. Clair's order. Butler had one track cut instead of two. He had an infantry column march single file through the woods, about one hundred yards on each side of the road. Nevertheless, still slowed by the thick woods and frequently needing to bridge creeks and ravines, after five days, the army had only progressed about twenty-two miles.[16]

St. Clair and Denny rode into camp that night. St. Clair was highly displeased to learn that Butler had altered his marching order. They had known each other for close to twenty years. They had prospered on the Pennsylvania frontier, enhanced their reputations as Revolutionary War officers, and emerged on the national stage. Throughout their careers, St. Clair always occupied a position senior to that of Butler. Three years earlier, while Butler was the superintendent for Indian affairs, Congress had removed much of his authority and given it to Governor St. Clair. One year earlier, Harmar, not Butler, was picked to lead the army against the Indians. Butler may have thought from the start that he was the better soldier and should have been given command of the army, not St. Clair. It was a possible source of resentment.

When St. Clair expressed his displeasure, his criticism of Butler was not private. What Richard Butler heard sounded blunt, impolite, and arrogant. Darke later accused St. Clair of treating Butler improperly and of having "a supercilious behavior to the officers in general."[17] St. Clair flatly denied that such conduct was within his character. As to the criticism of his attitude toward his officers in general, St. Clair deflected that toward Adjutant General Sargent. St. Clair praised Sargent for insisting on strict adherence to orders and that officers complete their paperwork, such as accounting for provisions. St. Clair also suggested that this engendered resentment among the officers that extended to him, as Sargent was acting on his behalf.

In St. Clair's account, after he and Denny returned to the army, Butler apologized for changing the order of march and gave his reasons for doing so. That sounds not so much like an apology but merely showing respect to the commanding officer. St. Clair proceeded to tell Butler he was wrong for several reasons. Wrong because one road made it more difficult to shift into battle formation if attacked. Wrong because the width of only one road actually increased "the quantity of big timber to be cut down." Wrong because one officer should not alter another officer's order. St. Clair claimed he spoke "without the least heat." Whatever the tone, Butler took the rebuke as an insult and deeply resented St. Clair thereafter. According to St. Clair, in their first conversation at Fort Washington, Butler was already "soured and disgusted." Now, he described how Butler's "coolness and distance increased, and he seldom came near."[18]

On October 7, the weather turned dry, giving the army a respite from rain for five days. Colonel Oldham's militia reached the army on the tenth. Winthrop Sargent's assessment of the militiamen was unsparing:

Picked up and recruited from the offscourings of large towns and cities; enervated by idleness, debaucheries and every species of vice, it was impossible they could have been made competent to the arduous duties of Indian warfare. An extraordinary aversion to service was also conspicuous amongst them. . . . The late period at which they had been brought to the field left no [time] to attempt to discipline them. They were, moreover, badly clothed, badly paid and badly fed.[19]

Sargent's disdain for Oldham's militia mirrored British General James Wolfe's opinion of American colonial troops thirty-two years earlier. They "are in general the dirtiest, most contemptible, cowardly dogs that you can conceive. There is no depending upon 'em in action. . . . Such rascals as those are rather an incumbrance than any real strength to the army."[20]

On October 12, near a swamp that had blocked the army's advance, a sergeant with five riflemen spotted an Indian. Shooting from sixty yards, they wounded him. Closing the distance to thirty yards, they shot and appeared to hit him again. Having dropped to "all fours," the wounded Indian gave a "war whoop" and managed to scramble into the swamp. At that point, fearing that other Indians might be near and that pursuit might lead them into an ambush, the sergeant prudently ordered his men to return to camp. Their "prize" was the Indian's rifle.[21]

That same day, though they saw no Indians, a patrol discovered an Indian cabin with fresh meat, some roasting over a fire. The patrol shared it with others, including Newman, who enjoyed both bear and venison. But unseen Indians took two army horses.

The rains returned the night of the twelfth and continued for much of the next six days. Journaling that his tent leaked "as usual," Newman sarcastically added "Contractor got his Benediction."[22]

When it camped on October 13, the army was about forty-four miles northwest of Fort Hamilton. St. Clair determined that about a mile from camp was the site for a second supply depot. So the army remained in place constructing this second fort, which was named Fort Jefferson for Secretary of State Thomas Jefferson. Smaller than Fort Hamilton, its four walls were approximately one hundred feet long, with a bastion at each corner.

Newman learned that the army was pausing to build this second fort when he and his work detail were called back to camp. They had been cutting the road, six and a half miles ahead of the army's encampment. The road had become known as St. Clair's trace. In the parlance of the time, trace meant the path or course being followed. That night Newman "supp'd with Lieut. Melcher" of the First Regulars and relished that the Lieutenant served "coffee with milk in it!!"[23]

Construction consumed another ten days, though the work detail consisted of two hundred men, plus their officers. But only eighty axes, one frow (an axe with the blade and handle forming an "L"), and one saw were available. Had the army been fully equipped, they would have had more tools, and construction could have proceeded at a faster pace.

Whether or not he thought about it from the start, as the days passed, Butler certainly concluded that he should have been given command of the army. While Fort Jefferson was under construction, he went to see St. Clair. Butler expressed doubt that the campaign's objectives could still be accomplished unless a bold new strategy was adopted. He proposed that he take the best thousand men they had and move on the Maumee villages as quickly as possible. Presumably, that meant marching unencumbered by wagons, artillery, and camp followers. Butler's strike force would seize the villages, defeat any Indian opposition, then hold their position until St. Clair and the rest of the army could join them. St. Clair may have suspected that Butler wanted to shunt him to the side while Butler seized the glory of taking Kekionga. St. Clair sarcastically described how Butler would have had him wait until the fort was constructed before bringing the "remainder" of the army forward "at [St. Clair's] leisure." St. Clair explained his reaction was "astonishment" which "was depicted on my countenance, and, in truth, had liked to have laughed in [Butler's face], which he probably discovered." Controlling his words, if not his nonverbal reaction, St. Clair replied that the proposal deserved consideration and that he would think about it and give Butler his answer in the morning. The next morning, St. Clair officially rejected Butler's plan. According to St. Clair, after this, Butler's "distance and reserve increased still more."[24] The rejection of his plan and St. Clair's expression upon hearing it must have cemented Butler's disgust with his commander. Based on what happened in the coming days, it is safe to conclude that Butler never let go of his resentment and deemed St. Clair unfit to command.

Butler's proposal came not only amid the army's halt and worsening weather, it also was made in the context of St. Clair's health problems. In addition to his preexisting gout, St. Clair had developed a bilious colic, as well as "rheumatic asthma" with a bad cough.[25] Bilious colic comes from a blockage of the bile duct. The symptoms often occur after fatty meals, with pain in the upper right or central abdomen, and may include nausea and vomiting.[26] The likeliest medical explanation is that St. Clair developed gallstones. At times during the campaign, the pain was debilitating.

On the seventeenth, while construction proceeded, two soldiers were out hunting when one was suddenly shot in the upper thigh or hip. His companion concealed them in bushes throughout the night. The next morning, they were able to return to camp.[27] That day, "[s]everal Indians [were] discovered in [the] vicinity, and five or six men are missing but whether by desertion, or to the enemy, [was] uncertain."[28]

Since the first day out of Fort Hamilton, when five men deserted, sporadic desertions had continued to occur. These desertions did not amount to a significant loss, but as October wore on, levies started to reach the end of their six-month enlistments. By the twentieth, close to one hundred men, including an entire company were discharged.

During this time, increasing the army's discomfort, the weather went from "chilly" on the seventeenth to "cold" on the eighteenth."[29] With the drop in temperatures, frost was occurring. This was more serious than just discomfort for the troops. Frost was ruining the grazing the horses needed. Packhorses started to starve and die for lack of food, despite half of the troops otherwise off duty being sent out every afternoon to "bring grass from the prairie to serve [the horses and cattle] overnight."[30]

Incessant rain turned a bad road into a bad road of mud, slowing down the packhorse convoys. Though the men were not starving, insufficient food was increasingly problematic. Not much flour remained when a packhorse convoy arrived with six thousand more pounds. With the convoy was a herd of 240 bullocks. But the new flour was only enough for three more days. Faced with the mud and the lack of grass, the packhorse master swore to Captain Joseph Shaylor that he would not come back again. Sargent was concerned that the situation would soon be critical, unless Duer and his agents obtained new packhorses.

Faced with the reality of a food shortage, on the nineteenth, St. Clair issued a series of orders. First, the army's packhorses, some three hundred, were turned over to the contractor so they could bring back desperately needed supplies, especially flour. The number of packhorses left suggests that many had already died, been lost, or been stolen. Second, the contractor was ordered to immediately proceed to Fort Washington and return with supplies. St. Clair intended to have Kentucky militia escort the supply train back. That changed when Oldham warned him that once they reached Fort Washington, his men would never return. Taking Oldham's warning seriously, St. Clair assigned most of Faulkner's Pennsylvania rifle company to be the escort. St. Clair also ordered that officers no longer receive extra rations. He reduced the daily flour ration to half a pound and increased the daily beef ration to one and a half pounds. But offsetting the loss of flour with more beef lasted only two days. Then the beef ration returned to one pound per day.

The nineteenth brought more bad news. Three officers' servants stole their horses to desert to the Indians and the British. All three, however, were captured and brought back under arrest. Their cases were added to the courts-martial that had been ongoing before a tribunal of officers for the past five days. The tribunal finished hearing the courts-martial on the twenty-first.

The night after the beef ration returned to its original one pound with nothing to compensate for the flour shortage, twenty Kentucky militia deserted. The next morning, five more followed, though they ran into troops to the south and were brought back.[31] Many of the remaining Kentucky militia were threatening to leave if rations were not increased.

St. Clair had been making plans to resume the march toward the Maumee and hoped to do so at a faster pace. With the army no longer having packhorses, most of the baggage needed to be left behind. Newman, for one, planned to stuff extra shirts and whatever else he could into a knapsack. At the same time, he was concerned that he might be assigned to garrison Fort Jefferson. He wanted no such thing. Despite the tents, the weather, and the food shortage, Newman did not want to miss the action when it came. Thus, he journaled his relief when it was Captain Shaylor and Lieutenant Daniel Bradley who were assigned to stay at Fort Jefferson with more than one hundred men too sick to march.[32] As at Fort Hamilton, two cannons were left for Fort Jefferson's defense. The oxen were faring much better than the horses, and Sargent observed that "the great burden of transportation . . . should rest upon oxen."[33]

The night of the twenty-first, the frost was severe and ice on the nearby stream was "near a half inch thick."[34] A supply train of packhorses with flour, along with a small number of cattle, reached the army on the twenty-second. While helpful, more was needed.[35] Quartermaster Hodgdon was ordered to Fort Washington "to make some more certain arrangement with regard to supplies of provisions-the contractor not to be depended on."[36]

Though St. Clair's bilious cholic, rheumatic asthma, and cough eased, as if in exchange, pain from gout returned to his left arm and hand.

All troops were summoned the afternoon of October 23. The message that St. Clair delivered was not one of perseverance, patriotism, or duty. At three o'clock he hanged three of the men who had been court-martialed and found guilty. Two of the three deserting servants were hanged, as was a levy who murdered a soldier and threatened to shoot an officer. The third captured deserter testified that the others had persuaded him to desert, though the condemned men's officers believed the opposite was true. Instead of being hanged, the third deserter was sentenced to five hundred lashes, with one hundred to be administered on five different days.

The ten days spent erecting Fort Jefferson not only meant ten days closer to the weather worsening as November approached but also ten more days of rations consumed, ten days closer to the end of levy enlistments, and ten more days for discontent to fester.

Many of the civilians who had gotten this far either chose or were ordered to stay behind when the army marched from Fort Jefferson. Without them and without packhorse handlers until a convoy returned, the number of civilians leaving with the army was probably one hundred or less. This included about thirty-five women, at least one infant, and possibly several other children.[37]

The day after the executions, the army resumed its march, following an Indian path north through woods of white oak, walnut, hickory, and ash. Evidence of many Indian camps were seen, some of them old, some new enough for campfire ashes to still be warm. They progressed for six miles before halting. Even though he was on a horse, St. Clair was so ill that he had trouble keeping pace. That night there was heavy rain again. After only a day, the march stalled. The army remained encamped waiting for supplies, though the deputy surveyor and an escort were dispatched to reconnoiter ahead.

While the army remained encamped on the twenty-fifth, President Washington delivered his third annual address to Congress. The longest portion of the speech concerned Indian troubles on the frontier. Washington's frustration is evident from the first lines:[38]

"Fellow-Citizens of the Senate and House of Representatives:

In vain may we expect peace with the Indians on our frontiers so long as a lawless set of unprincipled wretches can violate the rights of hospitality, or infringe the most solemn treaties, without receiving the punishment they so justly merit."

Thus, the president informed Congress that frontier conflict stemmed from "lawless" Indians who failed to accord "hospitality" to white settlers taking their lands and who failed to abide by treaties to which they had not agreed; "unprincipled wretches" who needed "punishment." Washington's description served his political goals more than it did historical accuracy, however one might idealize "the rights of hospitality." After several paragraphs on the country's accomplishments and progress, Washington returned to Indian problems and policies.

Defending and securing "the western frontiers" was sought to be accomplished "on the most humane principles," by which Washington meant a combination of treaties, persuasion of "the wavering," and expressing "friendship" with "the well-disposed tribes." He said "effectual measures" had been taken "to make those of a hostile description sensible that a pacification was desired upon terms of moderation and justice." With "effectual measures" unsuccessful, Washington justified war and "offensive operations" to "punish [Indian] depredations." He referred to the success of Wilkinson's and Scott's attacks that summer and to other offensive operations not yet completed. Nothing was specified concerning St. Clair's mission. Washington said that "[o]vertures of peace are still continued to the deluded tribes." After expressing the hope that future "coercion" would not be needed, the president set forth his policies:

That Indians "should experience the benefits of an impartial dispensation of justice." (Yet neither Washington nor his successors took steps to effectuate impartial justice on the frontier.)

"That the mode of alienating [Indian] lands, the main source of discontent and war, should be so defined and regulated as to obviate imposition and as far as may be practicable controversy concerning the reality and extent of the alienations which are made." (This statement provides the most critical insight into Washington's thinking. The policy question was never whether Indian land could or should be taken. It was only a question of how to take it, minimizing trouble and expense to the extent practical.)

That regulations should promote fair commerce with the Indians "and that such rational experiments should be made for imparting to them the blessings of civilization as may from time to time suit their condition." (Washington was well aware of the economic benefits of the fur trade.)

That the executive should be empowered to deal with the Indians.

"And that efficacious provision should be made for inflicting adequate penalties upon all those who, by violating their rights, shall infringe the treaties and endanger the peace of the Union."

Washington concluded that following "the mild principles of religion and philanthropy toward" the "unenlightened" Indians would be both "honorable" and "sound policy."

The night of the president's address to Congress, Sargent's diary records that one of the militia in a small hunting party "is supposed to have fallen into the hands of the savages . . . he was observed by two of his companions . . . to be pursued by them."[39]

The morning after Washington addressed Congress, the army's muster roll shows that the artillery battalion, the US regiments, and the levy regiments totaled 1,851 "present for duty" and 73 "present sick." Of those present, 1,792 were categorized as enlisted men, those being sergeants, corporals, privates, and "Music" (fifers and drummers). Officers, from lieutenant colonel to ensign, including 7 assigned as quartermasters, numbered 110. Additional personnel were 5 surgeon's mates, 4 cadets, 5 quartermaster sergeants, 5 sergeant majors, and 3 "Senior Music." Surgeons were a category on the muster roll, but none were present. Thus, references in the literature to doctors are references to "surgeon's mates," not to "surgeons."

By unit, the muster roll shows the following were present:

Artillery Battalion: 4 officers, 86 enlisted men, a cadet and a "Senior Music."

First US Regiment: 17 officers (including Lieutenant Denny and General Butler's staff officer, Ensign John Morgan), 301 enlisted men (including 1 "Music" and 16 "present sick"), a quartermaster, 2 cadets, and 2 "Senior Music."

Second US Regiment: 14 officers (including 1 "present sick"), 378 enlisted men (including 13 "Music" and 5 "present sick"), a quartermaster, and a cadet.

First Levy Regiment: 33 officers, 521 enlisted men (including 8 "Music" and 19 "present sick"), 3 sergeant majors, 2 quartermasters, 3 quartermaster sergeants, and 3 surgeon's mates.

Second Levy Regiment: 35 officers (one "present sick"), 506 enlisted men (including 8 "Music" and 31 "present sick"), 2 sergeant majors, 3 quartermasters, 2 quartermaster sergeants, and 2 surgeon's mates.

"Faulkner's Independent Company": 3 officers and 64 enlisted men.

Colonel Oldham's regiment of Kentucky militia: 31 officers and 418 enlisted men, plus a quartermaster, a paymaster, 2 surgeon's mates, a sergeant major, and a quartermaster sergeant.

Other categories on the muster roll for the regulars and the levies were "sick absent," "confined," and "on command." The latter meant they were not present due to being detached and assigned elsewhere. One hundred seventeen were listed as "sick absent," 29 as "confined," and 716 as "on command."[40]

There are apparent mistakes on the muster roll. Lieutenant Colonel Darke and Lieutenant Colonel Gibson of the levy regiments are listed as "on command" though both were present in camp. Although Captain Shaylor had been left in command of Fort Jefferson, none of the captains of the 2nd US Regiment is listed as "on command."

Counting Faulkner's company and the Kentucky militia, according to the muster roll, the total military personnel present on the morning of October 24 was 2,446. The muster roll did not include General St. Clair, General Butler, Adjutant General Sargent, or Vicomte Malartic.

Within hours, that number decreased as Colonel Darke had to discharge thirteen more men from the Virginia levy battalion because their six-month enlistments were up. The battalion was "melting down very fast," and there was "considerable dissatisfaction among the levies with their enlistments."[41]

At the same time these problems were occurring, Denny described St. Clair as so ill that he was "scarcely able to accompany the army."[42]

Also that day, a militia reconnaissance force of fifty men found five Indians camped. The Indians escaped, and St. Clair complained that the militia "suffered them to slip through their fingers."[43] In the Indian camp, in addition to what might be expected, more than twenty dollars was found.[44]

St. Clair and most other officers thought that the Indians and Indian signs that had been seen were merely from hunting parties, not from scouts sent to spy out the American army. Some, perhaps all, were from hunters. But it was likely that hunters had returned to alert the Confederation chiefs, who then dispatched scouts.

Seeing only hunters did not prove that the army had not been seen by Indian scouts. Ironically, a good reason to believe that the Indians and Indian signs the army observed were merely hunting parties was because for scouts, remaining unseen was a fundamental priority.[45] St. Clair should have known this. From his service in the French and Indian War, he had to know of Rogers' Rangers fame for scouting French forts without being detected. He himself would soon dispatch a long-range scouting party to the Maumee, knowing they would have to avoid discovery or face death. With its blue-and-white uniforms and its wagons, artillery, horses, oxen, and cattle, the army was easy to see. Indeed, St. Clair later maintained that of course the Indians knew of the army's advance and that to think otherwise was "ridiculous."[46]

Yet the farther the army advanced, the more St. Clair's expectation hardened into certitude that they would not be attacked before they neared the Maumee, if they were attacked at all. Confident that his order of march provided the best design to react to an attack, and equally satisfied that his order of encampment established the best defense to withstand an attack, it was easy for St. Clair to enjoy the comfort of certainty.

His confidence was consistent with the tenets that American discipline, courage, and bayonets must surely triumph over undisciplined Indians. The British at Bushy Run and the Virginians at Point Pleasant had done so, and unlike them, St. Clair had artillery. Confidence is good and often necessary. The self-deception of arrogant overconfidence can be fatal.

In fact, not long after St. Clair's expedition departed Fort Washington, it was discovered by far-ranging Indian scouts.[47] From that point on, scouting parties maintained their watch, sending messengers back to the Confederation leadership. These scouting reports were augmented by intelligence obtained from deserters and prisoners. Knowledge of the army's approach, of its progress, and its path enabled the strategic decisions the Confederation chiefs would make.

Desertion to the British had begun early in the army's march. Just twenty-five miles out of Fort Washington, five men deserted on October 4. One of them was John Wade. A British loyalist, he was defecting. Born in Ireland, Wade was a Tory who fled to Nova Scotia during the Revolution. Some years later, he returned to the United States on business. When he refused to take a loyalty oath, he was jailed. Wade secured his release by agreeing to enlist, which suggests how desperate some recruiters were to sign men up.

According to Wade's later declaration to the British, "to protect him and his companions from the Indians, [Wade] carried a flag for peace."[48] Taken by Indians, Wade was able to explain that he had information on the American army's march. By October 27, Wade and his written declaration were in the hands of Fort Detroit's commander, Major John Smith.[49] Wade informed the British that St. Clair had left Fort Washington with 1,500 regulars and 700 levies under six-month enlistments, 100 dragoons, 13 cannons, about 460 mules, and about 200 packhorses. One blockhouse had been built and another was to be built along the way. Some of the artillery was for one or both of the blockhouses. Two other deserters, John O'Neil and Maurice Gears, also gave declarations to the British.[50]

Given the supply line problems, and with thirteen more men of the Virginia battalion insisting their six months were up and they be discharged, Winthrop Sargent had grown pessimistic. In Sargent's mind, however, there was little choice about what to do. "[T]he General is compelled to move on, as the only chance of continuing our little army," he wrote. To Sargent, the "only prospect" of success meant "immediately marching the army so far into the enemy's country" that those whose enlistments were ending would be afraid to turn back on their own.[51]

Without knowing Sargent's thinking, Colonel Gibson shared his pessimism because of the levies' enlistments expiring. Unlike Sargent, he thought they should turn back. From the start, Gibson had been disgruntled that Colonel Darke was deemed to have seniority over him. Gibson had also grown dissatisfied with Sargent's demanding attitude. He shared his feelings with his nephew, Captain Slough.[52]

Chapter Nine

The Scout

AN EXPRESS RIDER FROM FORT WASHINGTON brought word to St. Clair that "the mountain leader" and a party of Chickasaw were coming.[1] The mountain leader was Piominko. Accompanied by nineteen Chickasaw warriors, he reached St. Clair's camp on October 27. Among them was another prominent Chickasaw leader, George Colbert, whose Scottish father lived among the Chickasaw for many years.[2]

Of the primary Chickasaw chiefs, Piominko was the most pro-American and had helped forge the Treaty of Hopewell in 1786 between the Chickasaw and the new American nation. Chickasaw territory encompassed northwest Alabama, northern Mississippi, far western Tennessee, and southwestern Kentucky. Piominko's home was probably in northern Mississippi. He was about forty-one.

For over two hundred years, the name was typically given as Piomingo. But in 2014, the Chickasaw nation issued an official correction, explaining that "Minko" means "leader" and "Piominko" means "Prophet Leader."[3] Thus, the name itself identifies a chief. Earlier in his life, Piominko had one or more other names, which changed with his accomplishments.

The Chickasaws arrived in Fort Washington on their way to Congress. There were ongoing issues of protecting Chickasaw land and of Chickasaw relations with the United States and Spain. The Chickasaws seem to have first learned that St. Clair needed scouts when they arrived at the fort and decided to alter their plans. Piominko likely concluded that scouting for St. Clair would benefit his people by building their credit as reliable friends of the Americans.[4] Not that he would have trusted the average settler to care, but what mattered was gaining the good will of President Washington and members of Congress.

Starting from Fort Washington, it was simple for the Chickasaws to follow St. Clair's trace through the forest. When they arrived at the army encampment, St. Clair welcomed them but was too ill to do more than that. Now that he had Indian scouts, how best to use them?

For a day, Piominko and his men rested. During that day, a much-needed ten thousand to twelve thousand pounds of flour, about a four-day supply, arrived loaded on seventy-four packhorses. Some clothing also arrived, inducing forty men to reenlist and receive new clothes. Also, twice that day, soldiers encountered Indians. In one incident, two soldiers were shot. One was killed and scalped. The other was badly wounded, but he escaped back to camp. Another two soldiers were surprised and could have been shot. Instead, the Indians raced toward the Americans trying to capture them. The soldiers ran, and the chase was on. One soldier escaped, the other did not.

By the next morning, St. Clair had a plan. He met with Piominko, as well as with Captain Richard Sparks, a levy company commander in Major Clark's West Pennsylvania Battalion.

Of all of St. Clair's officers, Richard Sparks was uniquely qualified for a scouting mission, for he had been raised by the Shawnee and trained to be a warrior from childhood until he was about fourteen. In the ensuing years, he had honed those skills fighting on the Pennsylvania frontier, during and after the Revolutionary War. That part of Sparks's life began in 1778, when he enlisted in a ranger company in the Pennsylvania regiment commanded by Colonel Richard Butler, now General Butler. Recognized for his skill, Sparks was promoted through the ranks.

Sparks was most likely born around 1757, although possibly as late as 1760. When he was three to five years old, he was taken by the Shawnee either in western Pennsylvania or western Virginia (now West Virginia). Named Shantunte (or Shawtunte) by the Shawnee, he was adopted, probably by Tecumseh's parents before Tecumseh was born.[5] Shantunte lived as a Shawnee until February 1775.[6] Then he, like many other whites, was returned under the peace terms that ended Dunmore's War. A teenager who no longer spoke English, Shantunte, against his will, was forced to return from the Shawnee.[7] For the teenager, it felt calamitous, and he thought about how he could escape back to his Shawnee family.[8]

Nevertheless, Sparks's life became one of scouting and fighting against the Shawnee and other tribes on the frontier. But had it not been for the terms that ended Dunmore's War, Sparks likely would have remained Shantunte and been a Shawnee warrior following Blue Jacket, instead of an army captain.

We can only wonder how much Sparks pondered that. Had he come to believe that the Indians had to be defeated to bring peace to the frontier? Did he choose the natural path for him to succeed in white, frontier society? Was he in the army simply because he married into a prominent, frontier family, the Seviers? Or did Sparks scout and fight because it allowed him to live as a warrior?

St. Clair told Piominko and Sparks that they were to conduct a long-range reconnaissance of Kekionga and the other Maumee towns. In the parlance of the day, they were to scout and spy out conditions at the Indian villages. Their mission was expected to last at least ten days, "unless they sooner succeed in taking prisoners and scalps."[9]

In addition to the Chickasaws, four or five soldiers were chosen to join the scout.[10] Sparks, Piominko, and their men set out that morning. Following the usual scouting methods, Piominko or George Colbert most likely took the lead in the "pilot" position, followed by Sparks as the commander. If Colbert piloted, Piominko was probably with Sparks in the commander position. Several Chickasaws would have been deployed on either side of the main body as flankers, each with a segment of the surrounding 360 degrees to watch. One of the most skillful Chickasaws would have been given the key position of "tail," responsible for covering the party's trail and for guarding against a threat from the rear.[11]

For concealment and silence, Sparks and the four riflemen would have worn dark-colored frontier garb, not uniforms, and preferably moccasins, not boots, with their powder horns and packs high and tight against their bodies.

Assuming that the scouting party proceeded on the same general line as the army, in approximately twenty-four miles they would have come to a small river flowing northwest. None of the scouts had been in this wilderness before. The St. Marys was known to flow northwest to the Maumee and Kekionga. Sparks and Piominko may have thought, as St. Clair and Butler did five days later, that this was the St. Marys, or they may not have been sure. Either way, it would have been natural to follow the river northwest. They would have moved parallel to the river, not along the bank, but inside the cover of the woods to avoid being seen. Security, silence, and concealment, not speed, are the paramount considerations of a scout.[12]

After some twenty-five to thirty miles, as the river became larger, it turned almost due west. By then, the scouts would have recognized that the river must be the Wabash, not the St. Marys. The two rivers are in different watersheds. After flowing west, the Wabash turns south on its five-hundred-mile course to the Ohio. The St. Marys goes north to the Maumee, which flows 137 miles northeast to Lake Erie. Sparks and the Chickasaws would have understood that "[h]ills and watersheds have a grain like wood."[13]

If Piominko and Sparks followed the Wabash, it should have been relatively simple for them to turn northeast, more or less along the portage that linked the Wabash to the Maumee. What is certain is that they located Kekionga. They had probably been out for close to a week.

Following the best scouting methods, they would have set up a base, as well as an alternative site to meet at, if their base was discovered. Then, most likely Sparks or Piominko would have quietly and cautiously moved close to the village to gather the needed intelligence. Possibly one to three others came along to provide cover or, if needed, a diversion to protect the observer.

Fulfilling their mission, they spied out conditions at Kekionga, Miamitown, and other villages nearby and downriver. What they found was ominous—not because the towns were well defended, but because almost all those they saw were women, children, and old men. Nearly all the warriors were gone—more than would be gone on hunting trips. The meaning was clear. The Miami, Shawnee, and their allies had left to confront St. Clair. What was unknown was when they had left.

How had the Confederation force not been seen by the scouts? A direct march from Kekionga toward St. Clair probably parallelled the St. Marys before turning south. If the scouts followed the Wabash and the Confederation force took a more direct route to intercept St. Clair, they would have bypassed each other, miles apart, unseen and unheard.

The scouts had completed their assigned mission to reconnoiter Kekionga, Miamitown, and other Maumee towns.[14] The mission was a tactical success but a strategic failure.

With arrogant unconcern for being confronted and attacked, St. Clair had thought only from an offensive perspective. No spies were dispatched to scout days ahead of the advance and warn of approaching Indian forces. Both offensive and defensive long-range scouting missions might have been ordered, even if it meant splitting up the Chickasaws, perhaps with Sparks and Colbert leading one group and Piominko the other. To reconnoiter the Maumee, a party of ten might actually have been better than a party of twenty-five or twenty-six. Fewer men were less likely to be spotted. If spotted, twenty-six were far too few to fight a village filled with warriors. As a scouting expert and Special Forces veteran explained: "How a [scouting] party avoids detection by the enemy is more important than their ability to fight their way out of trouble."[15] The advance patrols St. Clair did send out were militia until the end of October, when he began to use levies. Neither their skills nor how far they ranged was the equivalent of Sparks and the Chickasaws or what an experienced unit of rangers could have done. Denny's one criticism of St. Clair was both well justified and understated:

"But one most important object was wanting, can't say neglected, but more might have been done towards obtaining it; this was *a knowledge of the collected force and situation of the enemy; of this we were perfectly ignorant.* Some few scouts out but to no great distance."[16] (Emphasis in original.)

Chapter Ten

Mortal Stakes

AS ORIGINALLY PLANNED, ST. CLAIR'S EXPEDITION should have begun moving on the Maumee when the summer woods were a lush green. With its mid-September departure, verdant leaves soon started transforming into fall colors. Now, in late October, after too much cold rain and frost, most leaves had fallen from their branches.

The slow pace resulting from clearing the forest for artillery and wagons, from constructing two forts, and from waiting on needed supplies, had consumed enlistment time and food. Weeks of muscle-straining labor, inadequate rations, sun-obscuring clouds, damp and rain-sodden clothing, cold fall temperatures exacerbated by high humidity, and debilitating illnesses had taken their toll on morale and health.

Exemplary leadership might have pushed back against the sinking morale. Instead, neither General St. Clair nor General Butler nor any group of lesser-ranking officers provided the motivational lift their troops needed. The next crisis came four days after the scouting party left.

Since spring, messages had been sent to villages and tribes outside the Maumee asking for help to fight the expected American invasion. Many had heeded the call and come to the Maumee. While strengthening the Confederation, that added to the demand on food, exacerbating the shortage and increasing the need for British aid. A considerable number of men, about six hundred, were out on far-ranging fall hunts, which were important. So, despite the expectation that the American army would return, without knowing that St. Clair's approach had begun, some chose to hunt. The better evidence of Tecumseh's whereabouts is that he was among the hunters. He and the others would miss the coming battle.[1] But this year, unlike in 1790, most warriors stayed close enough to Kekionga to remain available to fight.

Last year, not being able to stop the Americans from burning their villages and destroying a bountiful harvest had left a desperate food shortage. No doubt the community did not want to evacuate and abandon thousands of bushels of needed food again. With reports of St. Clair's advance coming in from scouts, there was time for chiefs to hear from their followers, for the women's councils to meet and be heard, and for ongoing discussions in the Maumee villages. Villagers must have urged their chiefs and leading warriors to stop the army before it reached their homes. There was time for the Confederation war council to meet at Kekionga without being rushed.

The day the Chickasaws arrived in St. Clair's camp was probably the day the war council reached its strategic decisions. Some chiefs, Egushawa and Tarhe, were the principal chiefs of their tribes. Others, like Blue Jacket and Little Turtle, were war chiefs, their voices taking on more weight in this time of national war. Each council member had an opportunity to speak, put forth his ideas, and have his opinions heard.

Unlike Dwight Eisenhower's authority over western European operations in World War II, no supreme commander was making final decisions and issuing orders. That was not the Indians' way. Major decisions required consensus.[2] Imagine that whether and how to invade Normandy had required a consensus among American, British, Canadian, and French army, navy, and air chiefs.

If D-Day had required such a consensus of the chiefs, no doubt some would have been more influential than others. So it was at the Maumee war council. While Buckongahelas, Egushawa, and Tarhe were held in particularly high esteem, it was Little Turtle and Blue Jacket who were looked to above all others. Little Turtle's stature may have been enhanced by the

Miami having agreed to share their territory along the Maumee after Logan's Raid. As for Blue Jacket, everyone knew that the Shawnee had been at the forefront of the struggle against white settlements since the early 1770s and that Blue Jacket had been a war leader throughout those years. Like Tarhe, Blue Jacket's experience included Point Pleasant, to date the largest engagement any of the Confederation warriors had ever fought.

Simon Girty was also at Kekionga. On October 28, he reported to Alexander McKee that an American army of 2,200 was on its way to attack and that this intelligence was confirmed by "[d]eserters and prisoners that are daily brought in who also say that" the Americans had five cannons and two Coehorn mortars with "320 Kentucky Militia" and "100 Light Horse." The original intelligence reports came from Indians spying out the army's approach. Supplementing those reports were deserters and prisoners who must have been brought to Kekionga. The explanation given for the desertions was that "bad usage & scarcity of provisions obliged them daily to quit the army."[3] Even if "daily" was exaggerated, there must have been multiple prisoners and deserters providing information. The intelligence reports would have included descriptions of the army's configurations at its nightly camp and when it was on the move. Overall, the information from the scouts, deserters, and prisoners was quite accurate.

With the benefit of good intelligence, the needed consensus on what to do and how to do it was probably reached rather easily. Although they were substantially outnumbered, the answer to the first strategic question was: intercept and stop the American army, destroying as much of it as possible before St. Clair reached the Maumee.

Should their attack be an ambush while their enemies were on the march? Or should they attack while the Americans were encamped? The council chose the latter strategy, though it could be adjusted depending on when and where they intercepted St. Clair. Either way, they would attack from a half-moon formation. With sufficient numbers, the half-moon was the favored formation of Eastern Woodland tribes. Employing a crescent formation to achieve a double envelopment dates back to antiquity. It was how Hannibal destroyed a Roman army at Cannae in 216 BC.

The half-moon was flexible. Tactically, it could be utilized to set an ambush, as had been done at Bushy Run and Blue Licks. Alternatively, it could be used to launch an attack. The center advanced to confront the enemy, with the points sweeping around the quarry's flanks to achieve a double envelopment. Sometimes the enemy was encircled. Modern equivalents include the tank tactics of the Germans and the Allies in World War II and the Israelis in the Six-Day War.

The war council planned to use the half-moon to advance and envelop the American army. In the center of the crescent, left to right would be the Delaware, the Shawnee, and the Miami. With their ties to the Shawnee and being few in number, the Chickamauga Cherokees most likely joined the Shawnee. The Three Fires would form the left point of the crescent, while the Wyandot, the Seneca-Cayuga, and Du Quania's small Haudenosaunee band would form the right point. Once the battle began, each sector would operate relatively autonomously. Prominent tribal chiefs might try to give broader directions. If an overall command could be communicated, it would come from Blue Jacket or Little Turtle.

Experience had shown that while Kentucky militia typically included "good marksmen," they could be panicked. If charged early, like at the first Harmar fight, most could be expected to run. Thus, the preferred tactic was to come to "close quarters as soon as" practical against militia, knowing they "lacked the discipline to enable them to withstand the impetuosity" of an onslaught of rushing warriors.[4] Any militia who did not run would face Indian tomahawks and war clubs. American leaders were not the only ones to assess their enemies' lack of discipline as a weakness to be exploited.

Different tactics would be used against the regulars and the levies. When warriors reached their positions, guns already loaded, as naturally as breathing, each would find cover before beginning to fire. As with their way of life, Native American tactics were at one with nature. Trees, logs, and rocks were not obstacles. They were concealment and shields against enemy musket and rifle balls. The soldiers would not be rushed until their ranks were weakened. Blue Jacket and Tarhe remembered Point Pleasant well, where brave but reckless charges against an organized defensive line failed. Confederation leaders did not want to repeat that.[5]

The Confederation leaders knew that St. Clair had artillery and were aware of how devastating artillery blasts could be. Silencing the artillery by killing the gun crews was a priority. A group of Miami led by Black Snake were to concentrate their guns against the artillery crews in the army's front line. Similar directions were given to warriors who would face the artillery in the army's rear line. It is likely this responsibility went to Wyandots, as their crescent would face the rear line's artillery and because they were more numerous than the Seneca-Cayuga.

In addition to targeting the artillery crews, Confederation chiefs reminded their warriors to look for and target officers.

With the decision to intercept and attack the Americans made, the warriors prepared themselves. War dances were held. A typical war dance revolved around a post placed in the center of the dance ground. Usually, a chief would begin by calling the men to fight and striking the post with his war club or tomahawk. Warriors formed a circle, and the chief started his dance accompanied by music from drums and rattles. Then, striking the post and calling out their deeds or those of their ancestors, warriors joined the dance. As they danced, war cries rang out. High-pitched tones transitioned to lower tones. Musical phrases were often repeated, and dancers reiterated their accomplishments.[6]

Lieutenant Denny had seen Shawnee demonstrate a war dance. Naked except for breechclouts, the dancers' bodies and faces, in Denny's eyes, were painted "to have a horrid appearance." Armed with tomahawks and scalping knives, warriors formed a circle, dancing at a moderate pace "to a mournful kind of tune." Then giving a "war-whoop," they sat down. After a short silence, one after another they rose and resumed dancing. Recounting exploits and injuries, they "urg[ed] the others to be strong, and rise and revenge themselves upon their enemies." The dance ended with all of the warriors "yelling, jumping" and imitating "shooting, scalping and tomahawking . . . until" there was a signal for silence. With the dance concluded, "a short speech" was given.[7]

The army remained in camp on the twenty-eighth, with St. Clair in his tent, enervated with pain. That same day, the Confederation warriors began their march southeast to intercept the army. Simon Girty reported that there were 1,040 warriors. That same number was given by "a chief . . . who was in the action." In 1810, virtually the same number, 1,050, was related in Shawnee oral history.[8] In stark contrast to army morale, Girty reported, "The Indians were never in greater heart to meet their enemy, nor more sure of success, they are determined to drive them to the Ohio, and starve their little posts by taking all their Horses and Cattle."[9]

The warriors' enthusiasm and confidence was undiminished by the expectation of being outnumbered two to one. Singing their war songs, columns of tribes marched from Kekionga. For easier movement and hunting, soon the columns broke into groups of twenty to thirty, the size of a typical war party. Their pace was unhurried.

Simon Girty marched with the Wyandots.[10] It is likely that James Girty joined the Shawnee.[11]

In addition to William Wells, another white Indian warrior was George Ash. Taken and adopted by the Shawnee in 1780 when he was about ten, Ash was among Blue Jacket's warriors.[12] There were probably other adopted white Shawnee with Blue Jacket. When Stephen Ruddell told Tecumseh's story, he said Tecumseh missed the St. Clair battle but was silent as to whether he or his younger brother, Abraham, were there. His silence suggests they were. Anthony Shane's biographer concluded he was also at the battle with the Shawnee.[13] Shane grew up with Tecumseh and the Ruddells. He was born Antoine Chêne to a French-Canadian father and an Ottawa mother. In French, "Chene" means oak.

Upon receiving Girty's report, McKee forwarded it to John Johnson. McKee informed Johnson that he had sent an "Interpreter [Girty] . . . to observe the proceedings of the Indians as to gain intelligence of the movements of both parties." He also advised Johnson that it was probable that the next few days would determine the fate of the current campaign. McKee added that provisions, especially food, would need to be supplied to the Confederation "owing to their being continually collected together to watch their villages."[14]

When the Confederation force left the Maumee, the army was about seventy-five miles away. With information coming to them on an ongoing basis, Little Turtle, Blue Jacket, and the other chiefs were aware of that. They knew the country and knew the Indian path that the army was widening into its road. They could take a more direct route. There was no need to hurry.

By now, the levy battalion from Tennessee was so depleted it was combined with the Virginia battalion. With the consolidation, some of the officers, including Major Rhea, were allowed to go home.

The day Sparks and the Chickasaws were dispatched, a large work party began road construction in preparation for resuming the march. A bridge was "thrown across the creek" in front of the encampment.[15] Also that morning, with two junior officers, an ailing Major Bedinger led a detail of twenty-six enlisted men, who were being discharged, to escort packhorses back to Fort Hamilton or to Fort Washington to obtain more food. Two women who wanted to return to Fort Washington accompanied them. In Major Bedinger's absence, Captain Nicholas Hannah assumed command of his battalion.[16]

The army crossed the bridge the next morning, progressing seven miles through oak, hickory, maple, buckeye, and beech trees, before halting to make camp in the midst of thick woods. As it typically did, the militia bivouacked behind the army's rear line. St. Clair's illness was so severe that Denny and others "supposed he would not be able to proceed."[17] Two supply trains were due to be on their way from Fort Hamilton. The smaller one was thought to be close enough to arrive in a day.

That night the army suffered through a violent thunderstorm. Lightning flashed and high, gusty winds brought down entire trees. Perhaps pushed over the edge by the storm, in the morning sixty to seventy Kentucky militia ignored their officers and headed back down St. Clair's trace toward the Ohio River and home. Worse, they loudly declared they would stop the oncoming supply trains and take what they wanted. Colonel Oldham learned of the desertions on his way back from breakfasting with St. Clair.

For the general, this presented a crisis for two reasons. First and foremost, it was essential that the supply trains reach the army intact. Second, there was serious concern that the rest of the Kentucky militia might also desert. Additionally, St. Clair hoped that the deserters could be apprehended. How to protect the supply trains, discourage the remaining militia from deserting, and perhaps arrest the morning's deserters were the questions swirling through St. Clair's mind.

His answer was to order Major Hamtramck and the 1st US Regiment, some three hundred troops, to march back to meet and escort the second, larger supply train. St. Clair hoped this show of strength would intimidate the remaining militia from deserting, as the regiment would be on the road back to Kentucky. If possible, Hamtramck was to overtake and arrest the deserters. But that was only a hope, not an expectation, which dimmed as the regiment's departure was delayed for hours while cattle were slaughtered to provide them with beef.

The regulars of the 1st US Regiment were considered the best soldiers in the army. It would be at least several days before they returned. Depending on the second supply train's progress, it might be closer to a week. While securing the supply trains was critical, in dispatching hundreds of his best troops, St. Clair reacted as if the militia were a more dangerous threat than the Indians. Implicit in his decision was that the Indians did not pose a serious risk to the army. St. Clair was not alone in his dogmatic belief that the Indians would not attack, just as they had not attacked Harmar's main force.

When the regiment departed, three officers remained behind. Captain Thomas Doyle was on guard duty. Lieutenant Cornelius Sedam and Ensign Bartholomew Schaumburg were assigned to the regiment's baggage train, which remained with the army.[18]

Much-needed good news arrived that evening in the form of 212 packhorses. They bore almost thirty-two thousand pounds of flour, enough for full rations for more than two weeks.[19] With them was their escort, Captain William Faulkner, with half of his men. They had passed the deserters without incident. That might have suggested recalling one or two of Hamtramck's battalions. But St. Clair's thinking remained inflexible, and there was no change in his orders.

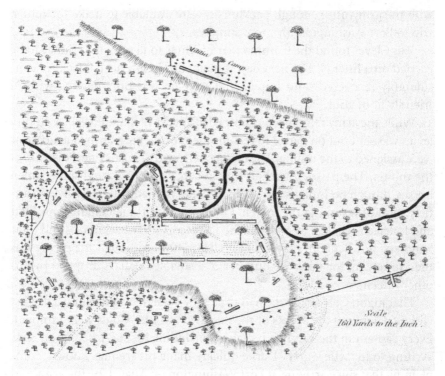

"A Plan of the Encampment and Sketch of the Action . . . Nov. 4th, 1791" by Winthrop Sargent, from *Diary of Col. Winthrop Sargent During the Campaign of 1791,* 1851. Key: a. Butler's Battalion, b. artillery, d. Patterson's Battalion, e. Faulkner's Company and Clark's Battalion, f. Cavalry, g. Second Regiment, h. Gaither's Battalion, j. Bedinger's Battalion, +++ Enemy. (*Boston Public Library*)

Led by Robert Benham, the packhorse handlers were civilian employees of the quartermaster general. During the Revolutionary War, Benham had been an officer on the frontier. In 1779, with sixty-three men, including Benham, Colonel David Rogers was bringing three keelboats back to Fort Pitt. Propelled by poles and oars, they moved upriver on the Ohio. Near the mouth of the Licking River, they were ambushed by Matthew Elliott, James and Simon Girty, and a war party of Wyandot, Seneca-Cayuga, Delaware, and Shawnee. Most of Rogers' command were killed. A handful were captured. Despite being wounded in both legs, Benham, with another wounded soldier, managed to hide on shore and escape.

Among Benham's packhorse handlers was his eighteen-year-old nephew, Benjamin Van Cleve. Another was Daniel Bonham. Benham had taken Bonham in as a boy and raised him. Benham and his men were ordered to stay with the army until enough packhorses were available to make the return trip to Fort Washington for more supplies.

Van Cleve "found the Commander in Chief so ill with the gout as to be carried on a litter."[20] The next day, though, St. Clair reported feeling "considerably recovered" and hoped that now he was only dealing with "a friendly fit of gout."[21]

While the army remained encamped, Captain William Powers with fifty levies was sent out on patrol to reconnoiter ahead. Previously, such patrols were assigned to the militia. The change reflected St. Clair's new distrust of the militia. The patrol found an Indian camp and recovered some stolen horses, though no Indians were seen. A detail of road cutters worked in anticipation of resuming the march. On November 1, Lieutenant John Platt and fourteen regulars were dispatched to escort forty packhorses and their handlers, not Benham's crew, to Fort Hamilton. Although the escort was then to return, for now, the number of available regulars dropped by another fifteen.[22]

That night, Colonel Darke had time to write letters and vent his disgust with St. Clair and the events of the past two months. Colds were rampant. Every captain in the Virginia battalion, including his son Joseph, was sick. Writing to his wife, Sarah, Darke quickly made his feelings known, complaining that since arriving at Fort Washington on August 29, the army had been "crawling through Indian Country, for an excuse for our Idleness . . . we have built two Forts, though in fact we have been very busy doing nothing." Darke described his "commander" as "so exceedingly afflicted with the Gout that all the men that can possibly get in reach of him are scarcely enough to help him on and off his horse and indeed, now a Litter is made to carry him like a corps[e] between two horses."[23]

In a letter to Colonel John Morrow, Darke sarcastically described "our Glorious campaign [in which] we have been better than two months marching rapidly into the Indian Country and have got 83 miles already and are going on Rapidly at the rate of one mile or a little better a day." Similar to what Butler had proposed weeks before, Darke made it clear that he thought the main force should have been sent ahead at a quick pace to reach the targeted Indian towns. He blamed "our Grate and Good Governor" for not being willing to allow the troops to do so until St. Clair was "able to" be at the "Head" of the advance. Not one to doubt his own abilities, Darke asserted that if he had been in command, the army would have been "six weeks forwarder than we are." Darke noted that more than three hundred horses had been lost or stolen, had died, or were weak from starvation. He expected the expedition would turn back in a month, unable to continue

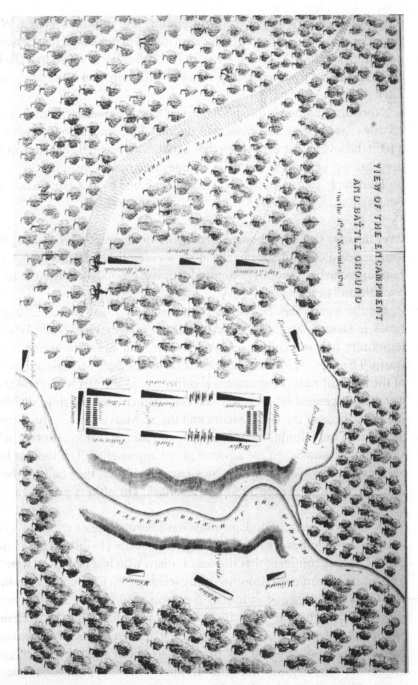

"View of the Encampment and Battle Ground on the 4th of November, 1791," from *Military Journal of Major Ebenezer Denny, an Officer in the Revolutionary and Indian Wars*, 1860. (*Boston Public Library*)

for lack of horses, levies' enlistments ending, and militia deserting. With the men wanting to be home, Darke anticipated that the march back would be far quicker than the march forward. In a "P.S.," Darke noted that the Indians had killed five men and he believed two more had been taken prisoner. [24]

Notwithstanding his disdain for St. Clair, Darke agreed with the general on one critical point. He envisioned reaching "the Indian Towns" without a fight, believing that even when they arrived, they would "not find an Indian, except" perhaps a "few" friendly ones who only wanted peace. [25]

The deeply rooted, optimistic arrogance shared by St. Clair, Darke, and others would soon be tested.

Over the next two days, the army was again on the march, progressing sixteen or seventeen miles, generally along an established Indian path. Cold rain turned to light snow. They moved over wet ground, through oak, hickory, ash, and beech.

On the second day, November 3, they started out at 9:00 AM. Several times, in Denny's words, "[f]resh signs of the savages were seen." [26] When a temporary halt was called, wagon drivers built a large fire, trying to get warm. The fire was inviting. Soon it attracted General St. Clair and some of the other officers. They chatted about where in the vast wilderness they were. Their general opinion was that they had crossed the ridge dividing the watersheds of the Great Miami and the St. Marys. Coming back from the front of the column, Colonel Sargent announced that four or five Indians had run away when the advance guard approached. The Indians had been camped, cooking venison. St. Clair opined that they had not been watching the army in preparation for an attack. The officers gathered at the fire concurred.

St. Clair believed the Indians must have been aware of the army's advance. It was significant to him that they had not tried to disturb the army's march. He was confident that the only Indians who had been seen were "a few straggling hunters [encountered] by accident." St. Clair considered that he had no intelligence of an Indian "force too great for [the army] to cope with" and thought that no such intelligence was obtainable. In St. Clair's mind, "in a calculation of probabilities . . . it appeared most probable that, as [the Indians] did not attempt to molest us in our advances, which they might have done to great effect, that they had been disappointed in collecting a sufficient force; that they either would desert their towns on the approach of the army, or sue for peace, which they had been informed they could have on proper terms; it was this last event that I most expected." [27]

The march resumed. After about two miles it was halted where Quartermaster Hodgdon thought they should make camp. St. Clair, however, was concerned that the ground was too low and would turn to mud if it rained. Captain Thomas Butler was sent ahead to search for a better campground. When he returned without success, still dissatisfied, St. Clair dispatched a Mr. Buntin to proceed farther than Captain Butler had gone.[28] Growing impatient waiting for Buntin to return, St. Clair decided that he and Richard Butler should look for themselves. Taking an advance guard with them, the generals rode about two miles before meeting Buntin. He was "returning with the information that he had found an excellent situation near a large creek . . . further on."[29] St. Clair and Butler rode forward another mile and a half or more to see the site for themselves. "[B]eing perfectly satisfied with it," they sent back orders for the army to move forward.[30] Wagon driver Thomas Irwin heard that the advance guard's message was "that they had got to a fine, running stream and good place to encamp at."[31]

The army reached the stream about 4:00 PM. It was later than usual for the army to make camp, and the light was starting to fade. St. Clair found it "impossible to examine the country so well as it ought to have been done."[32]

St. Clair and other officers believed they were at the St. Marys. Estimates of the water's width averaged about forty-five feet. The dark green water was shallow. The riverbanks rose steeply for thirty feet. East of the river was an area of high, dry ground. In Sargent's eyes it was "a very handsome piece of rising ground." To St. Clair it was "a commanding piece of ground."[33]

St. Clair directed the army to camp on the high ground. Setting up its usual defensive position, the front line ran along the length of the knoll, overlooking the creek and facing west. The rear line paralleled the front line. The front and rear lines were about 370 yards long, with 60 to 70 yards between them.

Opposite the left end of the front line, the river was as much as 150 to 200 yards away. Then, the water's path turned toward the rise before turning again to parallel most of the front line, a scant 25 to 50 yards away. Then, the meandering path of the water turned again, running in front of most of the northern width of the rise, before turning away to the northeast. South of the high ground was a small creek, now known as Buck Run. It flowed into the main stream. Wetlands bordered the north, east, and south sides of the rise. Dense woods, thick bushes, and old logs surrounded the knoll.

Denny assessed that "the men were much fatigued."[34] Setting up camp took hours, and it was dark before tents were pitched and fires kindled.

Thomas Irwin estimated that "it was near eight o'clock before the troops got fixed for lodging and cooking their scanty mess of provision."[35]

Excluding the Kentucky militia, the army numbered 1,380 enlisted men, 80 of whom were still assigned as officers' servants, plus approximately 95 officers (including 6 assigned as quartermasters), 2 cadets, 5 quartermaster sergeants, 5 sergeant majors, 5 surgeon's mates, and 1 senior music.[36] That totals 1,493, but it was 448 men and approximately 21 officers less than had been present when the army mustered the morning of October 26. Most of the difference resulted from detaching the 1st US Regiment. The rest came from discharging levies and dispatching troops to escort packhorse convoys.

Since mustering the morning of October 26, 2 officers and 129 enlisted men of the Kentucky militia had deserted. Despite the desertions, the Kentucky militia still had 29 officers and 289 enlisted men, plus a quartermaster, a paymaster, 2 surgeon's mates, a sergeant major, and a quartermaster sergeant.[37]

Thus, as they camped in the dusk on November 3, St. Clair's total force, not counting civilians, numbered approximately 1,817.

With General Butler commanding, Patterson's, Clark's, and Butler's battalions of the 1st Levy Regiment formed the front line from right to left. The three six-pounder cannons were placed between Clark and Butler. Major William Ferguson commanded this battery.

From left to right, the 2nd US Regiment, and Henry Gaither's and George Bedinger's battalions of the 2nd Levy Regiment, formed the rear line. Captain Nicholas Hannah still commanded Bedinger's battalion. As the senior regimental officer, Colonel Darke commanded the rear line. The other three cannons, the three-pounders, were positioned between the two levy battalions.[38] Captain Mahlon Ford commanded this battery.

Alexander Truman's cavalry and William Faulkner's riflemen were positioned on the right flank, at the north end of the rise. Jonathan Snowdon's cavalry were on the left flank between Butler's battalion to the west and Bedinger's to the east.

Wagons, civilians, regimental medical staffs, General St. Clair, and his staff were inside this defensive perimeter. The senior officers' tents were large marquees, accommodating themselves and their personal supplies, with room for meetings. Benham and his packhorse handlers pitched their tents behind the right side of the front line. They were due to depart the next morning so they could return with fresh provisions.

St. Clair and Major Ferguson discussed setting up knapsacks and other nonessential baggage around the artillery to create makeshift breastworks in case of an attack. But given the troops' fatigue and the increasing darkness, they decided it could wait until morning. There was a second, arguably even more important, omission. Despite Major Ferguson, Captain Ford, Captain Bradford, and Lieutenant Spear having almost twenty-four years of combined experience as artillery officers, no one calculated where the cannons could hit from their placements on the front and rear lines.

There was no room on the rise for Oldham's militia. They crossed the stream and some three hundred yards of bottomland. Then they climbed a sharp incline of almost ten yards, coming out to "a high extensive fine flat of open woods" where they made camp. The clearing stretched some four hundred yards before woods again covered the land.[39]

The militia could see many signs of Indian camps, both old and recent. Fresh tracks indicated that a party of fifteen Indians, some on horses, had left not long before the militia arrived. Colonel Oldham concluded that this was a scouting party. It was the first time in the campaign that Indians were thought to be something other than a hunting party.

St. Clair "judged [their position] to be about fifteen miles from the Miami village" and he intended to attack "as soon as the first regiment" returned.[40] Thus, St. Clair contemplated remaining in place for some days, waiting for the regulars of the 1st Regiment to return.

In reality, St. Clair and the army were on the Wabash, almost forty miles short of where they thought they were at the St. Marys. They were only about four miles from where the Wabash begins and the water was shallow, which is why the river was described as a creek and as a stream. It was forty-nine days and some ninety-seven miles since the march began; thirty days and seventy-four miles since departing Fort Hamilton; twenty-nine miles and ten days out of Fort Jefferson.

St. Clair went to bed that night more troubled by gout pain than by worry of being attacked. Despite the increasing evidence of Indian activity and the absence of hard intelligence, St. Clair continued to believe he was likely to reach the Maumee towns without encountering significant opposition. Nevertheless, upon hearing about the Indians whom Oldham took to be a scouting party, he ordered Oldham to send out four or five patrols, each comprising an officer with twenty men, "at least an hour before day . . . to take different directions, to make discoveries."[41]

Six outposts were set up between Buck Run to the south and the northeast bend of the river to the north. This positioned the outposts in front of the rear line and in front of the north and south ends of the camp. More than 15 percent of St. Clair's federal troops, 220 men, plus officers, were assigned to the outposts. On the south and southeast, Ensigns John McMickle and Hugh Purdy commanded.[42] East of the camp, from south to north, Captain Newman, Ensign Samuel Turner, and Captain Hannah commanded. Along the river, Ensign William Gray Cobb was in charge of the northeast outpost.[43]

As the Confederation force approached, their scouts brought back welcome news. Those they had come to kill were camping at the Wabash, Waapaahšiki to the Miami.[44] It was about two hours before sunset as they closed the distance to less than three miles. The Confederation force quietly camped about a mile and a half northwest of the army's position.[45] There was a ridge between the camps, approximately a mile from the Confederation's camp, a half mile from the army encampment, and a quarter mile from the militia.[46] The ridge was higher than the knoll where the army was camped and higher than the ground where the militia was camped.[47] From there, Confederation chiefs observed the army and the militia in the fading light. The chiefs took care not to be observed at the edge of the ridge. Farther back they were safely out of sight.

Now they knew the American positions and the terrain that would become their battleground. Now, Little Turtle, Blue Jacket, Buckongahelas, Tarhe, Egushawa, and other chiefs could confer and finalize the specifics of their plan of attack. Launching the assault in the late afternoon would mean a fight that stretched into the night. Preferable to that was an attack at first light. George Ash recalled, "We concluded to encamp; it was too late, they said, to begin the 'play.' They would defer the sport till next morning."[48]

Chiefs describing the coming battle as "play" and Ash referring to it as "sport" illuminate the Shawnee mindset. At the same time, the Shawnee, the Miami, the Delaware, and the others of the Maumee were fully aware that their land, homes, and food were at risk. At dawn, the work would very much be play for mortal stakes.[49]

Chapter Eleven

Night Patrol

T HE SUN SET AND, IN THE DARKNESS, SNOW BEGAN TO FALL. The army and militia campfires were easily seen from the ridge. Confederation warriors took care not to light any fire that might announce their presence.

Blue Jacket assembled other chiefs. Warriors gathered to hear what was being said; among them was George Ash. As he remembered it, Blue Jacket addressed the council:

"Our fathers used to do as we now do—our tribes used to fight other tribes—they could trust their own strength and their number, but in this conflict we have no such reliance—our power and our number bear no comparison to those of our enemy, and we can do nothing, unless assisted by our Great Father above. I pray now that he will be with us tonight, and that tomorrow he will cause the sun to shine out clear upon us, and we will take it as a token of good; and we shall conquer."[1]

Eight-five years later at the Little Big Horn, before riding against Reno's troops, like Blue Jacket, Crazy Horse sought divine help.[2]

Through the night, scouts maintained a watch on the Americans. Some impetuous young warriors, too excited to sleep, prowled around the army's camp. Inside the camp that night, shots from sentries could be heard, but whether their targets were real or imagined was unknown. From the outposts, reports came back of Indians "skulking about in considerable numbers." "[U]nable to be up," St. Clair retired to his tent for the night.[3]

Lacking feed for the horses, the soldiers let them out of the encampment to graze, hobbled so that they could not go too far, with bells on to help locate them in the morning.

Captain Jacob Slough was setting up his tent when his uncle, Colonel George Gibson, appeared. Gibson was holding a raccoon he had killed. He invited Slough back to his tent to see how to dress the raccoon Indian style. Interested, Slough joined his uncle.

Slough, a Pennsylvanian, was about twenty-eight. He may well have known Richard Sparks for years before they became captains in Thomas Butler's battalion. To be appointed, Slough must have had frontier experience. Likely he was known to the Butlers or was recommended by someone they trusted.

Surgeon's Mate William McCrosky and Lieutenant Thomas Kelso were at Gibson's marquee when Slough and Gibson arrived. It was not long before Captain Edward Butler entered and said that a party might be sent out to catch some of the "rascals" who were trying to steal horses. Slough responded that he would like to command such a party. Then Captain Butler left to report Slough's willingness to lead a patrol. General Butler did decide to order a patrol. The stated purpose was to intercept horse-stealing Indians. Significantly, it was not described as a reconnaissance. Captain Butler returned to Gibson's tent. This time he was accompanied by "brigade major" John Morgan.[4]

Slough was asked to command the patrol and replied that he would if he was given good men.[5] Captain Butler assured Slough that he would have volunteers and told him he should get ready to see General Butler. Captain Butler obtained twenty-three or twenty-four volunteers, almost all of them sergeants from Colonel Gibson's levies.

When Slough walked over to General Butler's marquee, a number of men were congregated around a fire, warming themselves in front of the tent. Richard Butler asked Slough to come inside and told a servant to pour glasses of wine. Lieutenant Denny was also there. Butler warned Slough to be cautious and directed him to call on Colonel Oldham before continuing past the militia. After receiving the army's countersign for the night and presumably finishing his wine, Slough was ready.

With George Adams, Lieutenant John Cummings, Ensign McMickle and the sergeants following, Slough made his way to the militia camp. There he found Oldham lying down inside his tent, still fully dressed. Oldham advised Slough that he expected an attack in the morning. Certain that Slough's party would be cut off if they sortied out, he asked Slough not to proceed. Slough replied that he had his orders and must go. Accepting Slough's answer, Oldham directed him to the officer in charge of the sentries.

After fixing a watchword with the militia, Slough moved out, through the open ground and into the hostile forest environment. After about a mile they found a path. Slough dispersed his men, hoping to intercept skulking Indians. Half went to the right of the path under Cummings and McMickle. Slough took the rest to the left. When they were thirty to forty yards apart, with the path in the middle, Slough directed everyone to lie close to the ground and wait.

It was not long before they could see six or seven Indians approaching. When they were about fifteen yards to Slough's left, seven or eight guns fired at them. Surprised, the Indians ran. Slough's men thought they had killed one Indian, although they could not see a body.

Slough quietly ordered his men to reload and "lie down without budging." About fifteen minutes passed as they lay in the darkness. Then "a large group of Indians" approached as the first, smaller group had done, to the left of Slough's position. There were too many for Slough to want to engage them. The Indians passed by, then stopped. One of the Indians coughed. Slough suspected they were trying to provoke a reaction to find him. With the cough eliciting nothing but silence, the Indians proceeded on toward the militia camp. Slough "thought they meant to waylay" him. Then another large party of Indians passed, this time to the right of Cummings's position. After they passed, Cummings quietly moved over to Slough, asking if he had seen them. Cummings said that it was "a very large party" that he thought was out "to waylay" them. Cummings added "that it would be prudent to return to camp." George Adams also came over to Slough, echoing Cummings's opinion that "it would be prudent . . . to return."

Finding his men "uneasy," Slough decided to heed their advice. He ordered everyone "to fall into the path in Indian file and return to camp, and if they were attacked, to defend themselves with the bayonet altogether and not fire their pieces." The mood was tense. Every fifteen or twenty yards, they heard something moving in the woods on either side of the path, never seeing whatever it was. As quickly as possible, while still maintaining order and quiet, they returned to the militia camp. Slough had been both smart and lucky. By now it was about midnight. Stopping at Oldham's tent, Slough went in and woke Oldham to report what he had seen. Slough told Oldham that he agreed the Indians would attack in the morning. Oldham replied that he had been about to dress and inform St. Clair that he expected a morning attack. He asked Slough to tell St. Clair.

Proceeding back to the army's encampment, Slough dismissed his men and continued on to General Butler's marquee. Not seeing anyone awake except a sentry, he went to the tent that Colonel Gibson and Surgeon Mate's McCrosky were sharing. Waking them, he told them what he had discovered and asked Gibson to go with him to report to General Butler. Responding that he was stripped and would not go, Gibson directed Slough to see Butler and make his report.

As Slough returned to Butler's tent, the general came out to stand by the fire. Not wanting to be overheard by the sentry, Slough approached and asked Butler to come with him away from the fire. Then he described what he had seen and what Oldham had said. When Slough finished, he said he would go report to St. Clair if Butler thought that was proper. Butler "stood some time, and after a pause thanked [Slough] for [his] attention and vigilance, and said, as [Slough] must be fatigued [he] had better go and lie down." Slough did as Butler directed, almost certainly thinking Butler would convey his information to St. Clair. Still dressed, he lay down and fell asleep. Though expecting a morning attack, he was exhausted. Sleeping through the army's predawn muster, he woke to the sound of gunfire.

Slough's patrol had turned out to be important for its intelligence gathering, not for disrupting horse stealing. For the first time, significant numbers of Indians had been seen. When Richard Butler paused before answering Slough, he was thinking about the captain's information, not about the captain's fatigue. How significant was the information? Should anything be done in light of what Slough had observed? Should General St. Clair be told? Should anything else be ordered? Answering those questions for himself, Richard Butler went to bed.

Josiah Harmar by Raphael Peale, c. 1799–1803. (*US State Department*)

Arthur St. Clair by Jean Pierre Henri Elouis, c. 1795. (*National Portrait Gallery*)

Winthrop Sargent by John Trumbull, 1790. (*National Portrait Gallery*)

Ebenezer Denny, frontis piece of the *Military Journal of Major Ebenezer Denny*, 1860. (*Boston Public Library*)

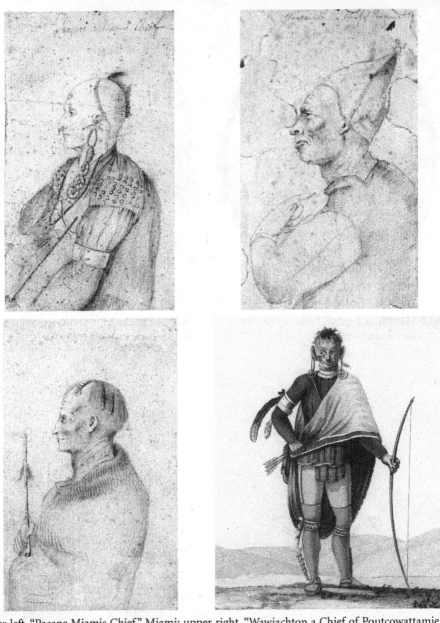

Upper left, "Pacane Miamis Chief," Miami; upper right, "Wawiachton a Chief of Poutcowattamie," Potawatomi; lower left, "Old Baby Ouooquandarong," Wyandot. These extraordinary illustrations were sketched by Henry Hamilton, c. 1778–1779, in the Illinois Country. (*Harvard University*) Pacanne was the chief of Kekionga. Hamilton described him as "dressed at the height of Indian fashion." He is holding a pipe-tomahawk, wearing a linen trade shirt and is adorned with silver brooches, ear wheels, arm bands, and a nose necklace made of glass trade beads. Wawiachton is wearing a European wool cap and coat. Hamilton described Ouooquandarong as "a very wise and moderate Sachem." Wrapped in a fringed trade blanket, he is holding "a decorated calumet-pipe, one of the most revered objects in Native America." See Martin J. West, *The Henry Hamilton Sketches: Visual Images of Woodland Indians*. Bottom right, "Indian of the Nation of the Shawanoes," Shawnee, engraving based on an original sketch by Georges H.V. Collot from his 1796 travels along the Ohio and Mississipi Rivers. (*Library of Congress*)

George Washington by Edward Savage, 1793. (*Chicago Art Institute*)

Henry Knox by Charles Peale Polk, after Charles Wilson Peale, after 1783. (*National Portrait Gallery*)

Thayendanegea (Joseph Brant), copy after Ezra Ames 1806 original. (*National Portrait Gallery*)

"Fort Washington erected in Cincinnati," mid-nineteenth century etching. Gen. Josiah Harmar described it as "one of the most solid substantial wooden fortresses . . . of any in the Western Territory." (*Huntington Library*)

Mihsihkinaahkwa (Little Turtle), chief of the Miami, etching based on a lost portrait by Gilbert Stuart, c. 1798.

Richard Butler by John Trumbull, 1790. (*Yale University Art Galler*)

"St. Clair's Defeat," lithograph, 1830. (*Anne S. K. Brown Military Collection, Brown University Library*)

"Death of Gen. Butler," mid-nineteenth century engraving. (*New York Public Library*)

Anthony Wayne by James Peale, c. 1795. (*National Portrait Gallery*)

"Wayne's defeat of the Indians," Lossing-Barritt, mid-nineteenth century engraving. (*Library of Congress*)

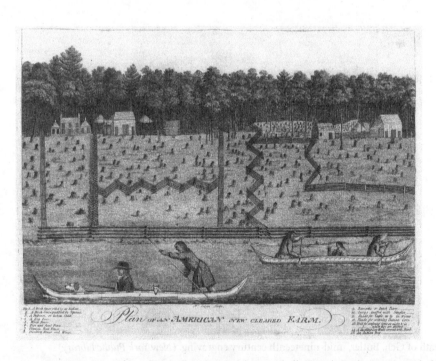

"Plan of an American New Cleared Farm," from Patrick Campbell, *Travels in the Interior Inhabited Parts of North America. In the years 1791 and 1792.* (*John Carter Brown Library*)

Chapter Twelve

The Sound of Bells

AT THE CONFEDERATION CAMP, "[a]bout an hour before day[break], orders were given for every man to be ready to march."[1] Word spread that fifty Potawatomi had left during the night. Warriors moved silently through the woods, wearing war paint, a breechclouts, and moccasins or mukluks. Some disregarded the cold, and some wore a hunting shirt or leggings. From trade, many of their loincloths, hunting shirts, and leggings were made of cloth, calico, or linen. The Three Fires' hunting shirts and leggings, though, were more likely to be buckskin. Most often their war paint was red or black or both. The colors symbolized war and death. For many, their only hair was a scalp lock. Others wore their hair full and long, sometimes braided. Some Wyandots had shaved the hair on one side of their head.[2]

In sight of the army's campfires, the warriors halted, probably on the high ridge. Among the Shawnee, Blue Jacket sang a "hymn" and a ceremony was performed.[3]

Chiefs formed the warriors into their half-moon attack formation. Then in good order, the warriors filed off the ridge. The Three Fires formed the left point of the crescent. The Wyandot, Seneca-Cayuga, and Du Quania's warriors formed the right point. Being small in number, and with their Haudenosaunee ties, the latter presumably attached themselves to the Seneca-Cayuga. With the largest contingent, the Wyandots were probably at the front of the right point. The Three Fires came off the ridge to the north, while the right point moved south. The crescent points moved to flank, envelop, and surround the army. Miami, Shawnee, and Delaware advanced through the woods toward the militia.[4]

As usual, fife and drums sounded reveille, and the army mustered before daylight. With the troops found present and accounted for, they were dismissed. The outposts remained on guard. The militia did not form to muster, but their camp was awake. Some were making coffee and breakfast. Sargent was on his way to see Oldham and to check on the militia patrols. Oldham must have seen Sargent approaching, for he met him before the adjutant general reached the militia's tents. Oldham admitted that no militia had gone out on patrol but assured Sargent that patrols would be dispatched without further delay. Perhaps flustered, perhaps assuming that Sargent already knew about it, Oldham did not mention Slough's patrol.

Why did Oldham fail to dispatch early patrols? Most likely it was a combination of thinking that too many of his men would refuse to go and a concern that those who did go would be easily picked off in the dark by the Indians. Oldham also did nothing to prepare for the attack he expected. Perhaps he thought that alerting his men to prepare for an attack would be ignored or, worse, trigger more desertions.

Thomas Irwin and the other wagon drivers were ordered to retrieve their horses early and prepare for the return trip to Fort Washington. They passed the camp's sentries as they went to find the horses. From the sentries, the drivers heard that Indians "had been round part of the camp nearly all night." Only some of the horses could be found. Others were gone, "stole by the Indians."[5]

While the army mustered, St. Clair was in his marquee, possibly still asleep. Butler still had not informed him of Slough's patrol or of Oldham's opinion about a morning attack. Butler's disdain for St. Clair certainly influenced and clouded his thinking. Did Butler think there was nothing else

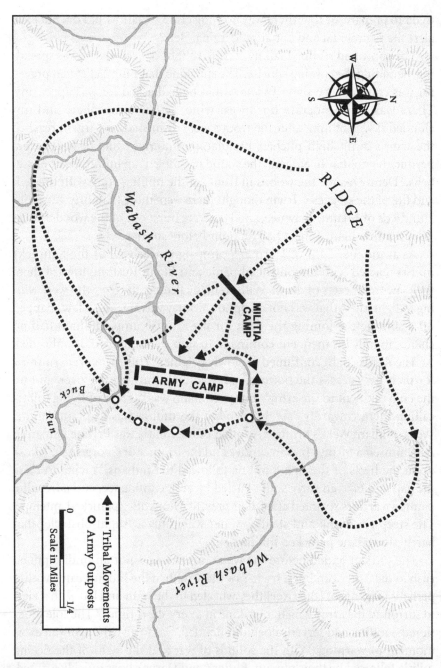

The US Army's encampment and the Native American line of attack, November 4, 1791.

to do to prepare, or that there was nothing else St. Clair would do, not even alert the regimental and battalion commanders?

The snow had stopped falling. The first light of early dawn was spreading, heralding the coming sunrise. The sunshine that Blue Jacket had prayed for was coming. The sign of victory that he had asked for was appearing. There was a "[m]oderate northwest wind, serene atmosphere and unclouded sky." Not long after the troops were dismissed, as Sargent reached the army's camp, high-pitched, undulating war cries could be heard from beyond the militia. To Sargent, the sound resembled "an infinitude of horsebells." Denny heard "the woods in front [of the militia] rung with the yells and fire of the savages."[6] Irwin thought there were more than fifty gunshots. Hundreds of Miami, Shawnee, and Delaware burst out of the woods. It was just after first light, almost half an hour before sunrise.[7]

As at the first fight of Harmar's campaign, nearly all of the Kentucky militia reacted with uncontrolled panic and flight. Rushing toward them they saw the specter of death. With so many fleeing, the few who were willing to fight knew that was not an option. To stay was suicide. A few snapped off a shot before joining the dash for the army's camp. Oldham had no chance to rally his men. His command to stop went unheard or unheeded.

The diffuse light continued to slowly brighten. Hundreds were running for their lives across the bottomland, splashing through the river, and up the embankment to the army's camp. Oldham was "at rear of flying militia calling them cowardly rascals." Among the militia was Captain Samuel Wells, William Wells's brother. Another of the militia was Private Benjamin Ash, himself a former Indian captive and the brother of George Ash. "Close upon the heels of the flying militia followed the Indians," racing to close the gap and take an early scalp. Fueled by zeal, confidence, and adrenalin, painted warriors sprinted after their prey, like lions after panicked antelope. The steep riverbank and shallow water were only a "slight obstacle" that barely slowed the panicked militia.[8]

The pursuit ended before the water, for this was not an undisciplined rush to the American lines. Irwin saw that "[w]hen the Indians came within perhaps 60 yards of [the river] they wheeled to the right and left with a view to surround the army which they done in a very short time."[9] The sole function the militia had served, albeit unintended, was to give the army an extra moment of warning. With the sounds of war and the sight of the fleeing militia followed by their pursuit, Butler's and Darke's lines quickly formed. The front line fired its first loud, though ineffectual volley. Consistent with the plan of attack, Miami, Shawnee, and Delaware found cover behind rocks and trees as they began to fire on Butler's front line. From their left to their right were the Delaware, the Shawnee, and the Miami. The latter faced Thomas Butler's battalion and the artillery. Where the river ran close to the knoll, the west bank was within effective musket range of the army's front line. Initially, most Delaware and Shawnee, and some Miami, found their cover on the west side of the river. Farther south, other Miami crossed the river, then quickly found cover as they closed to within effective musket range.

Most of the militia did not stop running when they reached the army's camp. Still panicked, they crashed through Butler's and Clark's battalions, briefly disrupting their line in the first moments of battle. Nevertheless, to Denny it seemed that "a smart fire from the front line met the enemy."[10]

The first sounds that registered with Benjamin Van Cleve were not bells or yells but gunfire from the direction of the militia's camp. He was behind the right side of the front line, with his horse half loaded in preparation for returning to Fort Washington for more supplies. Time compressed for the teenager as it seemed that "almost instantly" fleeing militia were rushing through the army's front line, though it took longer than that for the militia to run hundreds of yards. Van Cleve watched the militia crash through and disrupt the levies. Under the pressure of "tremendous fire from the enemy," the levies near Van Cleve fell back.[11] Suddenly, Van Cleve and his horse were in front of their line. Throwing his bridle over a tree stump, Van Cleve scrambled back toward the levies. They appeared to stabilize, and Van Cleve quickly turned to retrieve his horse. Despite the Indians' fire, Van Cleve started to lead the horse toward the troops when he saw the levies falling back again. Feeling too exposed, Van Cleve dropped the reins to run back to the levies. As he stepped away, his horse was hit by gunfire and fell.

Van Cleve's thoughts now turned to joining in the fight, the immediate problem being that he lacked a gun. The inexperienced teenager imagined that the army's strength must be "far superior to any the savages could assemble and that we should soon have the pleasure of pursuing them and I determined on being if possible, among the foremost in the pursuit."[12]

As they swung about a half a mile wide of the knoll, trees and the contour of the land largely shielded the Wyandots, Seneca-Cayuga, and Three Fires from the soldiers' line of sight.[13] While the Miami, Shawnee, and Delaware engaged General Butler's line, the points of the crescents swept toward both ends of the army's encampment.

The first outposts they reached were those of Ensigns McMickle and Purdy to the south and southeast, and of Ensign Cobb to the northeast. As if they stood in the way of a rushing flood, these three outposts were swept away. Purdy and Cobb were killed, as were many of their men.[14] McMickle was also probably killed when his outpost was overrun. The way back from the outposts to the shelter of the camp was hundreds of yards shorter than the paths of the oncoming Indians. That many of the outposts' guards failed to reach Darke's line suggests that the inexperienced ensigns lacked clear orders to return to camp in the event of an attack.

Having overrun the outposts on the army's flanks, the points of the crescent turned to complete their encirclement. The commanders of the eastern outposts had a small but critical amount of extra time before the Indian surge reached them. Captain Newman, Captain Hannah, and Ensign Turner all made it back inside of Darke's line. Presumably so did most of their men. It seemed to Darke that only a "few minutes" passed from the start of the attack to when the "[g]uards were drove in."[15]

Many, probably most, of the militia continued across the camp toward Darke's line. Some ran all the way through Gaither's battalion, knocking a few of his men forward. Indian gunfire from east of the camp abruptly stopped their flight. Finding cover close to the American position, Potawatomi, Ojibwe, Ottawa, Wyandot, and Seneca-Cayuga engaged Darke's line. There was no escape. The knoll was surrounded. Militia, who would have been happy to kill outnumbered Indians and loot their villages, were now ruled by fear. Unable to flee, they congregated by the women, children, baggage, and officers' tents, as if they could hide there. Some prowled the tents for food, as they would have done in an abandoned Indian village.

Within moments, St. Clair's effective force had been reduced by some four hundred men. Almost all of the militia and roughly half of the outposts' guards were dead, wounded, or too panicked to function. Confederation warriors had perfectly executed an eighteenth-century version of "shock and awe." To Denny, it seemed the battle was quickly "engaged in every quarter." To Darke, within "a few Minutes," the "whole Camp was Surrounded by Savages advancing" from "behind trees Logs etc.," creating "Grate Havok."[16]

The front line's artillery might have made a difference if it had been ready and able to fire over the fleeing militia and into the pursuing warriors while they raced across the hundreds of yards of bottomland. But there was no time for that.

As the sound of gunshots announced the attack, Arthur St. Clair's gout gave way to exigency. Not pausing to put on his uniform, he came out of his marquee dressed in a course, long coat, and a three-cornered beaver hat. In an instant, he saw how badly he had misjudged Indian intentions. Four of the remaining horses were his. They had been brought into camp before the attack began. The first was saddled and brought to him. Too scared by the gunfire, the horse refused to stand still. Despite the efforts of three or four men to help, St. Clair could not get astride. He moved to slightly higher ground, hoping it would make it easier to mount. Before he could try again, the horse fell, shot through the head, while "the boy that was leading him up [was shot] through the arm." While the saddle and bridle were removed from the dead horse, one of Sargent's servants brought the second of St. Clair's horses. As soon as that horse was saddled, shots killed both the servant and the horse. With surging adrenaline, impatience, and possibly alarm, St. Clair ordered a third horse to be brought to him, wherever he might be found and strode toward the left side of the front line. There, Major Butler's battalion and the artillery were "very warmly engaged." According to St. Clair, his "pains were forgotten, and for a considerable time, I could walk with a degree of ease and comfort that surprised everybody."[17] Near the artillery, a musket ball grazed St. Clair's face and clipped a lock of his long gray hair. It was the first of his close calls with death.

Within five minutes, Van Cleve found a nearby soldier, disabled with "his arm swinging with a wound."[18] The wounded soldier agreed to give his musket, gunpower, and ammunition to Van Cleve. Before turning to find a place to position himself, Van Cleve promised to return the levy's gun when the fight was over. With the benefit of growing up on the frontier, the eighteen-year-old knelt behind a tree. One knee on the ground, he waited to spot an Indian's head appear from behind a tree or an Indian moving to change position. Already a cloud of smoke from the gunpowder of the army's first volleys hung three feet above the ground.

John Hamilton was a packhorse master. Like Van Cleve he wanted to join in the fight to defend the camp but had neither a gun nor ammunition. Hamilton solved this by checking dead men's guns. When he found one that was loaded, he used it and then searched for another.

The regulars and the levies maintained or reestablished their lines. Though it soon seemed otherwise, numerically they still had the advantage. Standing, they fired volleys, reloaded, and fired again on the commands of their officers. On top of the rise, silhouetted against the sky, and mostly close together in a line, they were good targets. The exceptions were Clark's Pennsylvania battalion and Faulkner's Pennsylvania militia. The north half of the knoll was more wooded than the south, the south end being primarily open ground. Instead of having their men stand in a line to fire volleys, Clark and Faulkner made use of the trees, stumps, and logs in their sectors. Their men fired and reloaded from the available cover.

The artillery was soon in action. The cannons' roars were the loudest sounds of the day. The first artillery blast from Ferguson's battery appeared to startle and confuse some of the Indians. The quartermaster for Thomas Butler's battalion observed, "But they were soon rallied by their leader on horseback, dressed in a red coat."[19] Combining bravado and inspiration, the rider was obviously a leading chief. Wearing the scarlet coat of the British army and being near the center of the crescent marked him as Blue Jacket.

The artillery added greatly to the smoky haze as its gunpowder ignited. The "tremendous noise" of American artillery, muskets, and rifles cloaked the sound of Indian gunfire so that it could hardly be heard.[20] Heard or not, the smoke of ignited gunpowder came out of Indian gun barrels too. There were no war cries now, just what seemed like constant gunfire.

As American officers and soldiers stood, trying to maintain their lines, Indian muskets started to take a toll on them. For most of St. Clair's enlisted men and militia, this was their first real battle, and a determined enemy was trying to kill them.

Many Indians could recognize who the opposing officers were, whether by uniform, by acts of command, or by their being on horseback. As Americans had often done to the British, the officers were particularly targeted. Whether because of that or because they exposed themselves even more than their men, officers were falling in disproportionate numbers. In this first stage of the battle, General Butler was wounded in the arm and Major Butler was shot in the leg. Both needed to leave the front line to seek medical attention. Like his brothers, Captain Butler remained calm under fire. Unlike his brothers, whatever shots were aimed at him missed. Mounted, Colonel Darke suffered a flesh wound to his thigh. Able to control the bleeding, he never left the field.

The artillery was firing "a large quantity of cannister and some round shot."[21] Volleys from the infantry lines were fired on command. But their volleys and the artillery blasts were having virtually no effect. Unlike the army, the Confederation warriors gave the defenders little at which to aim. In contrast to the soldiers' static positioning, under cover of the smoke that spewed out every time a gun was fired, Confederation warriors moved from one tree, log, stump, and rock to another. This compounded the natural difficulty of aiming downhill through a smoky haze.

Army musket and rifle balls rattled against trees and clipped small branches. According to the Miami, "[m]ost of the Mihsi-maalhsa fire, both from muskets and cannon, was going into the treetops. In some cases, the fire was hitting tree limbs thirty feet over the heads of the Taawaawa Siiliipi men."[22]

As planned, the artillery crews received a disproportionate amount of Indian gunfire. Miami, led by Black Snake, focused on the artillery facing the river. A similar group, probably Wyandot, concentrated their shots at the artillery positioned in Darke's line. The breastworks of baggage that St. Clair and Ferguson had contemplated the night before were badly needed. Certainly, they would have blocked some of the shots that were striking the artillerymen.

Despite the peril, the artillery crews valiantly fired and reloaded. Their efforts were in vain. The canister and round shot only destroyed tree branches and leaves or struck the ground well behind the Indians. Through the smoke of the guns and the lingering haze, this may not have been apparent to either artillery battery. The gun crews and their officers stayed at their positions and kept trying.

The artillery barrages were sailing high over their targets because the artillery could not aim downhill. The cannon barrels could not be depressed to aim downward.[23] At their lowest degree of zero elevation, they were firing straight ahead into the trees over their attackers' heads. Despite years of artillery experience, before the battle, neither Major Ferguson nor his officers nor their commanding general visualized the artillery's field of fire. Inside of roughly one hundred yards, their cannons were reduced to being merely harmless annoyances. In the heat, desperation, and fog of battle, they never realized it.

For some time, Darke did not hear from St. Clair. On horseback, Darke directed the defense of his side of the camp, seeking to maintain the rear line. St. Clair was still on foot. His third horse never reached him, nor did he ever again see the man who had been sent for it.

As the engagement continued, musket and rifle balls smashed into bodies, shattering bone, shredding flesh, and piercing organs. Inexperienced soldiers were doing their best to follow orders as American casualties mounted, particularly among Heart's regulars, the artillery, Snowdon's cavalry, and Butler's, Bedinger's, and Gaither's battalions. Many of the officers in Bedinger's Virginia battalion were killed or wounded early in the action. For some, like Captain Van Sweringen, of Gaither's Maryland battalion, and Lieutenant James McMath, of Bedinger's Virginia battalion, conspicuous bravery crossed the line into foolhardy recklessness. Both died. To Sargent, they "seemed to have . . . thrown [their lives] away."[24]

Wounded were being brought back to the center of the beleaguered camp where surgeon's mates did what they could. Though not wounded, many militia and some soldiers congregated in the center, terrorized by the ongoing attack. Seeing this, twice General St. Clair, with other officers, attempted to rally these men and bring them back to the lines to fight. Once, Count Malartic saw St. Clair "draw his pistol and threaten" to kill one of the men who was refusing to fight.[25] At times, when officers were not there, some of the women, justifiably enraged and frightened, "drove ... skulking militia and fugitives of other corps from under wagons and hiding places with firebrands" and whatever else was available.[26]

Without giving it much thought, St. Clair and other senior officers had instinctively seen the steep, thirty-foot banks of the river as a natural impediment to potential attackers. Hard-driving legs of scared militia and determined Indians had quickly proven otherwise. Nor did the shallow depth of the river present a meaningful obstacle.

While not a significant obstruction, neither was the eastern riverbank inconsequential. The danger of an enemy trench or breastwork placed within fifty yards of the army's position would have been instantly understood. But American officers never visualized the riverbank as if it had been built to shield attackers. Confederation warriors, however, recognized opportune cover. For them "the steep bank ... served as a breastwork."[27] Aided by concealing clouds of smokey haze, Miami, Shawnee, and Delaware advanced across the river and up the slope of the bank. There, they lay prone while they aimed uphill, fired, and reloaded. From that part of the riverbank, they were within close range of Ferguson's artillery battery, Clark's battalion, and to a lesser extent, Patterson's battalion.

Using the available cover rather than standing up in a line, Clark's battalion and Faulkner's riflemen were only taking a few casualties. Winthrop Sargent deemed Clark to be "cool and brave" and praised Faulkner for his "coolness, spirit and judgment."[28] While their hilltop position did not afford cover for everyone, using the available cover was outside of the army's conventional, European concept of standing infantry lines firing volleys. Positioned between Clark and Faulkner but formed in the standard line, Patterson's men were taking moderate casualties.

The crews of both artillery batteries were models of tenacious bravery. What they lacked was an officer with the perspective to realize that the cannon were functioning only to bait a lethal trap—a trap in which, grouped together, they were an easy target for the concentrated gunfire being directed at them.

Through the carnage, Sargent assessed Major Ferguson as "cool, determined indefatigable and gallant," while "Captain Ford, Captain Bradford, and Lieutenant Spears fought bravely ... and evinced ... coolness and determination."[29] Captain Doyle of the 1st US Regiment attached himself to the artillery. Soon, he was wounded.

With the soldiers unable to target the Indians, their gunfire continued undiminished. The fight had been going on for an hour or more. It was around now that young Van Cleve settled down and realized his early thinking had been very wrong. Besieged and fraying, the army was not far superior to the Indians. Van Cleve was not alone in his realization. To the Americans' surprise, they were clearly losing the continuing exchange of gunfire. What St. Clair and other officers had seen as an excellent defensive position was proving to be a death trap.

Chapter Thirteen

Charging to Defeat

S EEING THAT THE ARMY'S FIRE WAS HAVING "no great effect," St. Clair concluded that with "confusion beginning to spread from the great number of
men who were falling in all quarters, it became necessary to try what could
be done by the bayonet."[1] To Darke, it seemed that "the enemy [was] Growing More bold and Coming to the very Mouths of our Cannon."[2] Like St.
Clair, he thought a bayonet charge was needed. St. Clair sent an order to
Darke to launch a bayonet charge and turn the Indians' flank.[3]

Darke ordered Heart's regulars, reinforced with levies from Gaither, to
fix bayonets. They were further reinforced by Captain Truman and some
of his dragoons. The plan was to charge forward, push back the Indians facing them, then wheel to the right and charge south to dislodge the remain-

ing Indians along the rear line. Assistant Surveyor Jacob Fowler welcomed the chance to be part of this first counterattack.

Mounted, with sword in hand, Darke led the bayonet charge. Initially it appeared successful, as they met little resistance. First, the Three Fires scattered. Then as the troops pushed south, outflanked Wyandot and Seneca-Cayuga ran to stay ahead of the bayonets. St. Clair observed that the charge "was executed with great spirit. The Indians instantly gave way, and were driven back three or four hundred yards."[4]

Pursuing those whose gunfire had been tormenting them since before sunrise, Darke's men must have felt a combination of blood lust and relief flooding through them. Instead of them standing and firing ineffectual volleys while men around them fell to Indian gunfire, now Indians were running from their bayonets "in all directions."[5] As the bayonet charge stretched out over hundreds of yards, it became less cohesive and more individual. Soldiers rushed for an opportune shot or bayonet thrust. With a single-minded focus on killing Indians, Darke led more by example than by command. There was no thought of maintaining an organized formation.

Rather than confront the bayonets, Confederation warriors gave way. But they had not run from the fight. Instead, they looked for an opportunity to outmaneuver their pursuers. As Darke's charge extended south of the army's camp to Buck Run, concealed by the woods, Wyandot and Seneca-Cayuga flanked the soldiers. Indian muskets and bows shot from close range. Charge metamorphosed into ambush. The risk of being outflanked and shredded materialized in dead and wounded soldiers. Truman was wounded several times. Still, he managed to stay astride his horse.

Worse, more Wyandot and Seneca-Cayuga circled back to the army's perimeter. With the rear line down to perhaps half strength, they took advantage of the depleted defenders and invaded the southeast sector of the army's perimeter. St. Clair observed how the Indians "soon returned, and the troops were obliged to give back in their turn."[6]

Even with what was happening south of the knoll obscured by the woods, Miami and Shawnee would have heard the sound of gunfire well south of the army's camp. That would have told war leaders like Little Turtle and Blue Jacket that some of the soldiers had left their positions to charge after Wyandot and Seneca-Cayuga warriors. Seeing the damage they had done to the soldiers facing them, the time was ripe to move forward. Thus, at about the same time that Wyandot and Seneca-Cayuga attacked from the southeast, Shawnee and Miami punched through Butler's weakened battalion on the southwest. Under pressure, Snowdon's dragoons pulled back from the south end of the knoll.

As Wyandot, Seneca-Cayuga, Miami, and Shawnee overran the southern part of the camp, including the artillery positions, havoc and slaughter reigned. Tomahawks and war clubs inflicted wounds and death on those unable to get away. Many who had been killed or who were incapacitated by wounds were scalped.

Years later, the Shawnee described the scene:

The fury of the Warriors increased, they mounted the bank, there was only between them and their enemies the tents and the baggage. The ground was covered with the [American] dead and dying whose groans mixed with the shouts of the combatants, all was stained with blood, a terrible slaughter ensued around the cannon which were resolutely defended by the Americans, who fell in heaps around their noisy implements of destruction.[7]

Near Buck Run, their charge ended, Darke and Heart must have been jolted to see the southern end of the camp penetrated through both lines. The need to return—both because their position was untenable and to save the camp—was clear. Major Heart hurriedly reorganized his regulars and began a quick march back.

Within the camp, St. Clair was organizing elements of Butler's and Clark's battalions to counterattack. Having received medical care for his leg wound, Thomas Butler, again on horseback, had resumed command of his battalion. In Sargent's view, despite "a wound . . . that might have excused a modest soldier from duty," Butler "returned to the charge with spirit."[8] Richard Butler was most likely still receiving medical attention for his arm wound.

The 2nd US Regiment's path back from Buck Run exposed them to more musket balls and arrows. Nevertheless, reentering the camp, they charged with bayonets, intent on driving the Indians out.

At about the same time Heart's regulars reentered the camp from the south, St. Clair began his counterattack from the north. With his adrenaline still dominating his gout pain, St. Clair led the bayonet charge with Butler's and Clark's troops.

The Confederation warriors made no effort to hold the ground. They had reason to be satisfied with their incursion, and for them, avoiding unnecessary casualties was axiomatic. Before the oncoming charges could close and crush the Indians between them, the warriors scattered back to the safety of the woods.

The lost ground and the artillery positions were retaken, but only a few Indians were killed or wounded. Jacob Fowler saw one of the wounded trying to crawl away, when Colonel Darke dismounted, raised his sword, and beheaded the unlucky Indian.

That the 2nd Regiment managed to accomplish what it did, Sargent credited to Major Heart and his officers, not to Colonel Darke. In Sargent's judgment, Darke was "brave," but so "passionately intent upon Indian-killing" that commanding a platoon was beyond his capacity.[9] Reflecting Sargent's assessment, Darke praised Lieutenant Bissell, not for leadership but because Bissell "made the freest use of the bayonet of any Man I noticed in the Carcases of the Savages."[10]

"[H]eavy and galling fire" had taken a serious toll on the 2nd Regiment.[11] It may well have been in this part of the battle that Captain Kirkwood, renowned for the number of engagements he survived in the Revolutionary War, was killed. This may also have been when Captain Newman suffered a serious arm wound and Lieutenant Richard Greaton was shot through his body. Greaton was still alive, but badly wounded.

Numerous scalped heads littering the ground appeared to emit smoke. Fowler described "freshly-scalped heads . . . reeking with smoke . . . in the heavy morning frost look[ing] like so many pumpkins in a cornfield."[12]

Surveying the carnage, Darke estimated that the Indians had scalped "a hundred men or more."[13] Many of those fell to Indian gunfire before the incursion into the camp. The contrasting lack of Indian bodies evidenced that the scalping had proceeded without pressure from army gunfire.

Failing to comprehend Native American tactics, Darke thought that if only the remaining troops could be formed for another "push," the Indians could be beaten back.[14]

With catastrophic artillery casualties, Lieutenant Cornelius Sedam and Ensign Bartholomew Schaumburg of the 1st US Regiment went to keep the cannons firing. Colonel Darke glowingly described Schaumburg as being "as brave Good and determined [a] Herow as any in the world."[15]

The exchange of gunfire resumed, much as it had before. Demoralized and confused, more troops congregated together on the north half of the hill, ignoring their officers, as if they could wish themselves away from the bloodstained ground, the trauma, the death, and the scalped heads. It was around this time that Richard Butler probably returned to the front line. Like St. Clair, General Butler was now on foot. Along the northwest and north edge of the knoll, where Clark, Patterson, and Faulkner faced Delaware and Three Fires, the battle was close to a standoff. But around the southern half of the camp, the continuing exchange of gunfire appeared unsustainable for the army. Confederation warriors advanced closer again.

From the length of the front line's artillery, around the south end of the army's line, through the length of the rear line's artillery battery, "the amazing effect" of the Indians' concentrated gunfire could be seen. It was not just from the bodies and the blood. "Every twig and bush seem[ed] to be cut down, as the sapling and larger trees [were] marked with the utmost perfusion of their shot." There were no such signs of concentrated army fire. Sargent concluded that the army's fire had been "very loose, and, even the artillery, to have been directed with very little judgment."[16]

St. Clair and his officers failed to comprehend that the Indians had effectively countered Darke's charge. Darke's initial success and the counterattacks that had driven the Indians back down the rise reinforced their preconception that bayonet charges would defeat the Indians. Thus, to relieve the increasing pressure, one or two more bayonet charges were ordered from the rear line. Sargent thought the Indians gave "ground to the powerful effect of their bayonets—but not till they had felt its force."[17] In reality, few Indians felt any force. The success of the bayonet charges was illusory. When the soldiers attacked again, though their charge was shorter and more controlled than Darke's had been, Confederation warriors countered as they had before. More officers and enlisted men were lost without gaining any tactical advantage.

As Denny saw it, the charges "forced the savages from their shelter, but they always turned with the battalions and fired upon them back; indeed they seemed to fear nothing that we could do. They would skip out of reach of the bayonet and return, as they pleased. They were visible only when raised by a charge." Mentally locked into relying on bayonet charges, St. Clair watched the charges "repeated several times, and always with success; but in all of them, many men were lost . . . particularly the officers."[18]

Benjamin Van Cleve had been fighting on the front line. From his musket being fired so much, the bands had flown off it. He was also out of ammunition. Hearing an unusually heavy amount of shooting behind him, Van Cleve moved across the hill to the rear line to see what was happening. Levy officers were ordering a charge. It was the rear line's last charge of the day.

Van Cleve saw a musket lying on the ground. Picking it up, he spotted a cartridge box that was almost full. Rearmed, he ran to position himself behind a large tree where he quickly loaded the newly acquired musket and fixed the bayonet to its barrel.

Leading his men's charge, Captain Benjamin Price of Gaither's Maryland battalion was among the officers cut down by Indian gunfire.

Van Cleve joined about thirty levies charging toward a group of Indians down below the bluff. They gave way and ran into a small valley filled with logs. Van Cleve and seven or eight levies ran into the valley. Losing sight of the Indians, they halted. The levies who had charged with them had gone straight ahead. They had also stopped. From the hollow, fifty to seventy yards away, Indians opened fire. With Van Cleve "being so near to where the savages lay concealed," their second volley left him "standing alone [behind] a small sugar tree scarcely large enough" to provide cover. Focusing on Van Cleve, Indian musket balls "struck the [sugar] tree & many ploughed into the ground at its root."[19] Firing back, Van Cleve noticed an Indian waiving a blanket up and down at the side of a tree. Aiming just past the edge of the tree, Van Cleve fired when the Indian appeared again. The Indian did not reappear. Nevertheless, Van Cleve was uncertain whether he had hit his target or any other Indian in the hollow. Out of ammunition, Van Cleve looked around. The levies who had been with him were halfway back to the rear line. Van Cleve quickly ran to follow them.

As before, taking advantage of the charge, Wyandot and Seneca-Cayuga closed on the weakened defensive line. Bedinger's battalion was driven back and became dispersed. Adjutant Grayson Burgis, an ensign, and Lieutenant James Stephenson tried to rally the remaining men. As they did so, a shot hit Burgis, killing him. Stevenson managed to reform "detachments from the scattered soldiers of the battalion" and get them back to the line.[20]

For a second time, Miami, Shawnee, Wyandot, and Seneca-Cayuga breached the army's perimeter. In Sargent's words, more than once or twice, the Indians "pushed with a very daring spirit upon the artillery of the front line and on the left flank of the army [the south end of the camp], and *twice gained our camp, plundering the tents and scalping the dead and dying*—but at both times they were driven back." (Emphasis added.) St. Clair was more succinct. "[W]here the artillery was placed," troops "were [temporarily], repeatedly driven [back] with great slaughter."[21]

Once inside the army's camp, the warriors sought to create as much terror and chaos as they could, as quickly as they could. The scared, shocked, demoralized men who were congregated around the marquees presented easy prey. If there was no need to shoot, soldiers and civilians, men and women, were tomahawked or clubbed. Scalps were taken from those being killed, those already dead, and those too wounded to escape. With the battle raging, taking prisoners was not practical, even if a warrior had any interest in doing so.

Not everyone was a passive victim. John Hamilton, the packhorse master who had been using dead men's guns, grabbed an axe to fight tomahawk-wielding Indians. Catherine Miller, known as Red-Haired Nance or Red-Headed Nance, reputedly fended off an Indian with a frying pan while holding her infant in her other arm. She had accompanied the army to be with her husband, an enlisted man.[22]

As Van Cleve made it back to camp, images of the ongoing battle flashed through his mind. Indians had taken the artillery again, and the army had retaken it again. "[A]bout 30 . . . men & officers laying scalped around the pieces of Artillery; it appeared the Indians had not been in a hurry for their hair was all skinned off."[23] In contrast, few Indian bodies lay inside the camp. Looking west, Van Cleve saw another charge beginning, this time from the front line toward the river.

Most of what was left of the 2nd US Regiment and of Major Butler's battalion were ordered to charge and drive the Indians back. It was desperately hoped that bayonets could still stem the army's bleeding and turn the tide. Despite his leg wound, Major Butler organized his levies.

The charge began, driving Miami, Shawnee, and Delaware who had closed on the front line back toward the river. Leading his infantry on horseback, Thomas Butler was a conspicuous target. He was quickly shot off his horse, seriously wounded in his other leg. One leg was broken. Unable to move, he lay on the slope of the knoll. Lieutenant Winslow Warren was also shot, dead or mortally wounded. Nevertheless, the charge continued, and ahead of its bayonets Confederation warriors ran through the water and disappeared into the woods. The charge's momentum dissipated at the river. But for the first time, the army had driven its attackers back across the water.

Some of the Indians who were pushed back found cover not far inside the woods, as they had at the start of the battle. Whether Little Turtle or Blue Jacket were in this area is unknown. Other Shawnee continued to withdraw, moving back and probably laterally, though there was no pursuit.

At the riverbank, there was uncertainty as to what to do next. Some soldiers forded the river; most did not. A withering volley of gunfire from the woods decided the issue.[24] The surviving regulars and levies retreated, knowing that those who had fallen would soon be scalped. The last bayonet charge of the day was over.

Badly wounded, Thomas Butler was at least fortunate that he had fallen early and that Edward saw him. Moving quickly, Edward Butler was soon carrying his brother back up the rise and inside the army's lines.

The retreating Shawnee were stopped by Black Fish, one of the Shawnee chiefs. George Ash described how, with a "voice of thunder," Black Fish asked, "what they were doing, where they were going, and who had given them orders to retreat?"[25] With "impassioned eloquence" he "exhort[ed] them to courage and deeds of daring." Black Fish declared that for him there would be victory or death. His challenge—"you who are like minded, follow me"—reaped an enthusiastic "war whoop" [meaning] 'We conquer or die.'"[26] Led by Black Fish, they rejoined the rest of the Shawnee.

Briefly, perhaps for fifteen minutes, perhaps for less, Indian gunfire slackened. Officers and soldiers wondered what this respite meant. Was it a harbinger of an unexpected, favorable development? St. Clair asked Denny if he knew how long they had been fighting. St. Clair "seemed pleased in the idea of repelling the savages and keeping the ground." Darke described "the enemys fire being almost over for Many Munites."[27] Then the Confederation attack resumed with full force.

Chapter Fourteen

Escape and Flight

THE BRIEF SLACKENING OF INDIAN GUNFIRE was most likely due to several factors. First, the Confederation was starting to run low on ammunition, so what was left needed to be conserved. Second, the Shawnee being rallied by Black Fish were temporarily out of the fight. Third, Blue Jacket and Little Turtle were likely organizing an assault to overrun St. Clair's camp.[1]

Then intense Indian gunfire resumed. The artillery was silent. Of the original four artillery officers, Captain Mahlon Ford was the only one still alive, and he was badly wounded. Captain Doyle, who had come to help, was wounded. Most of the men of the artillery battalion were also dead or wounded. The dead lay strewn around the artillery batteries. For the third and final time, Confederation warriors were penetrating the southern part of the knoll. Again, tomahawk blades and scalp knives sliced through flesh.

Wounds hemorrhaged. To Ash, this time, "[t]he attack was most impetuous and the carnage for a few moments was shocking. . . . Indians leaped in among the Americans and did the butchery with tomahawks."[2]

It was clear that the batteries could not be held. That meant the cannons needed to be spiked to render them useless. Spiking was accomplished by hammering or jamming a metal spike, or some other metal object, into the vent. An open vent was essential to pour in priming powder and to insert first a fuse, and then a slow match. That ignited the powder and fired the cannon. Often, artillery equipment included metal spikes to prevent them from being captured while still operable.[3]

Bedinger's battalion was mostly dead, wounded, or scattered. Without an effective command, Captain Hannah scanned the camp and went to help with the artillery. He joined Sedam, Schaumburg, and some enlisted men, who were still at the batteries. Disregarding the intense danger, they succeeded in spiking the cannons at both batteries. Colonel Darke described Hannah using a bayonet to spike what must have been the last of the cannons, as Indians closed to "within a few yards" before Hannah escaped to the new, constricted American line.[4] Of the officers who had been with the artillery, only Hannah, Schaumburg, and Sedam remained alive and unwounded.

Soldiers were falling back from their lines to the interior of the camp, as if they could somehow be safer there. In response, the Indians closed in, contracting around the Americans' false refuge. With diminished army gunfire, warriors could take more time to aim. The Confederation now controlled the southern part of the knoll.

One of the Americans still fighting aimed at George Ash. The musket ball went through the back of his neck. His next memory was of being carried off the field on an Indian's back.

General Butler had been walking up and down the front line since returning with his wounded arm in a sling. Someone offered him a horse. Butler probably welcomed the opportunity to lead again from horseback. Perhaps with more bravado than judgment, he mounted. It was around 9:00 AM when, like his brother Thomas, Richard Butler "was shot from his horse."[5] He had been hit twice. His leg wound was treatable. His chest wound was much worse. Unable to walk, Butler was placed on a blanket and four men carried him to the nearest medical tent.

Notwithstanding that he had few, if any, militia to command, Colonel Oldham fought to defend the camp throughout the bloody morning, "exhibiting more than personal coolness and bravery."[6] Like Richard Butler, it was about nine o'clock when Oldham was shot and fatally wounded. Winthrop Sargent was sure they were both mortally wounded, Butler with little time left to live and Oldham "not quite dead."[7]

With their lines compressed, soldiers were now "[e]xposed to a cross fire, men and officers were falling" everywhere. For Denny, "the distress . . . of the wounded made the scene such as can scarely be conceived."[8]

According to the Miami, running low on ammunition, "some of the men from the Taawaawa Siiliipi began to fire arrows into the center of the Mihsi-maalhsa camp, where most of their enemy was massed."[9]

Increasingly, Denny saw that men "became fearful, despaired of success, gave up the fight, and to save themselves for the moment, abandoned" their positions "and crowded in toward the center of the field." Their senses overwhelmed, unable or unwilling to continue to fight, these men were "perfectly ungovernable."[10] After hours of hard fighting, Sargent realized that "disorder and confusion" had consumed many of the men. Dispirited, they crowded together in various parts of the camp, unthinkingly making themselves even easier targets for the continuing hail of Indian musket balls and arrows. Confederation warriors sighted their targets "from behind trees and the most secure covers," while the remaining troops "could scarcely be led to discharge a single gun with effect."[11]

Jacob Fowler found his fellow surveyor, John Gano. They could see that the battle was lost and that, somehow, they needed to escape. They saw a group of soldiers or militia "gathered together, doing nothing." The group "appeared stupefied and bewildered with the danger." Fowler and Gano saw others in the large marquee tents of senior officers, guzzling down the breakfasts that had left uneaten, even though "some were shot down in the very act of eating."[12]

Evaluating their deteriorating defense, Denny concluded that retreat was the only option. To "[d]elay was death." Sargent assessed the situation as, "desperate . . . even Hope, that last consolation of the wretched, had failed the Army. . . . There was a mere possibility that some of the Troops might be brought off, though it could not be counted on among the probabilities. But there was no alternative."[13]

By now, eight musket balls had passed through St. Clair's clothes and hat. Almost miraculously, none had wounded him. Accurately judging that his men had suffered more than 50 percent casualties, St. Clair reached the same conclusion as Sargent and Denny. The only way out was to regain access to St. Clair's trace. Though St. Clair and his staff thought in terms of retreat, what they sought and what occurred was an escape.

Of St. Clair's staff, both Sargent and Count Malartic were wounded. The count had been trying to deliver an order from St. Clair when the general's last horse was shot out from under him, and he was wounded.

St. Clair had managed to function on foot throughout the battle, moving up and down the lines. Now he was "nearly exhausted."[14] Still functioning despite his wounds, Captain Truman brought one of the remaining horses to St. Clair. Had he stayed on foot, St. Clair's gout and fatigue would have doomed him to death or capture.

St. Clair and Sargent worked to gather as many of those who remained alive as they could, including the wounded who could "possibly hobble along."[15] To the extent possible, what was left of the army was reorganized. Most likely it was around 9:15 when orders were repeatedly passed to follow a vanguard through the Indians, then veer to the road to Fort Jefferson. Men who had seemed almost paralyzed, waiting to die, now regained thought and energy at the prospect of escape.

Richard Butler was brought to the medical tent where Surgeon's Mate Victor Gresom served as a doctor for the 1st Levies. Gresom determined that nothing could be done, other than to stem the bleeding and try to make the general comfortable. Butler was brought outside and propped up against a tree between two meal sacks. He too seemed certain that his chest wound was fatal. A small group of officers and soldiers gathered around him. According to Edward Butler, he brought Thomas to where Richard lay. Richard insisted that he was mortally wounded and should be left behind, and that Edward needed to save Thomas. As they left, Richard was "so nearly dead that [Edward] hope[d] that he was not sensible to any cruelty [the Indians] might willingly wreak upon him."[16] After his brothers left, Butler gave his ring, sword, and watch to Major Gaither. In exchange, Butler was given a loaded, cocked pistol. Then the rest of the group around the general left.[17]

All around Van Cleve, he saw "[t]he ground . . . literally covered with dead & dying men."[18] Shot through the hips, Daniel Bonham was unable to walk. Van Cleve spotted Bonham and was able to get him onto a horse. Van Cleve also found that his uncle had been shot. A musket ball had entered near Robert Benham's wrist and lodged near his elbow. Benham informed Van Cleve that General St. Clair had ordered a retreat. Both Benham and Bonham told Van Cleve to take care of himself. Bonham added that on horseback, he had a better chance of getting away than Van Cleve did.

With the most intact battalion, Clark was ordered to provide a rear guard. Sargent thought Clark "seemed to receive [the order] with reluctance," a rather natural reaction under the circumstances.[19] However Clark felt, he and his battalion prepared to cover the army's flight.

Close to three hours had passed since the Confederation's attack began. At about 9:30 AM, where the left side of Darke's line had once stood, a detachment feinted as if charging to turn the Indians' flank.[20] The best evidence is that Major Heart was killed leading this diversion.[21]

Thomas Irwin, one of the wagoners, saw that Chief Scout George Adams was with General St. Clair. Irwin heard a drummer beat the call to retreat, but the troops seemed to not understand its meaning. Adams gave "three sharp yells and said-'Boys, let us make for the trace.'"[22] Irwin was close to Adams as they ran forward to gain the road.

Fowler and Gano heard the order to charge to the road. They ran to join the breakout.

Heeding the advice to take care of himself, Van Cleve managed to get to the front of a group of "troops pressing like a drove of bullocks" to get into position. To his left, he saw Lieutenant John Morgan, General Butler's aide, with six or eight men, start to run. Van Cleve quickly ran to join them. In a short distance, they were suddenly among the Indians who had created their hellish morning. Again, the Indians avoided confronting a charge. The way out opened. Van Cleve thought two hundred men got through before more than "a chance shot" was fired.[23] Then, Indian gunfire increased.

Except for Clark's rear guard, the rest followed the vanguard as quickly as they could. St. Clair acknowledged that the retreat "was, in fact, a flight."[24] Reaching St. Clair's trace, the flight continued back down the road that had brought them to the banks of the river they still could not name.

Denny had been mounted since the militia was attacked. Both he and his horse remained unscathed. The horse was little but earned Denny's compliment of his having been "well-mounted." The horse that Truman gave St. Clair would do no more than trot. Once they reached the road, St. Clair and Denny stayed back "to see the rear."[25]

Fortunately, there was no immediate attack for Clark and his men to fend off. Once everyone who could had reached the road, their responsibility was over. They were not expected to stay with the slowest and sacrifice themselves. Everyone else was fleeing as quickly as they could. With discipline having evaporated and most of what remained of the army dysfunctional, no serious thought was given to organizing a rear guard to defend the road or to ambush pursuing Indians.

Like the artillery, the guns and the equipment of much of the army remained on the battlefield. Left behind was baggage, 384 regular tents, 11 larger tents, including the marquees, forges, tools, medicine chests, wagons, and all of the food.[26] Also captured or abandoned were 16 oxen, more than 300 packhorses, and dozens of artillery horses, wagon horses, dragoons' and officers' horses, and the remaining cattle. Infinitely more important, also left behind were those too badly wounded to walk, unless they were fortunate enough to have been put on a horse.[27]

Richard Butler remained propped against a tree waiting for an Indian to approach. A Shawnee warrior advanced toward Butler to take him prisoner. He might have recognized that Butler was an officer and wanted him for information, for ransom, or for torture. When the Shawnee told John Norton the story of the battle, they said Butler "snapped" off a shot.[28] It missed, and the warrior immediately finished Butler with a blow from his tomahawk. Wyandots said Butler was tomahawked by the son he fathered while living as a trader among the Shawnee. They said the young man did not realize the wounded officer was his father and he became deeply depressed after learning Butler's identity.[29] Coming from Native Americans, these are the best sourced accounts.[30]

In the army's former camp, warriors went through the tents and the baggage. Some enjoyed rum, other alcohol, or food they found. Some put on coats or cocked hats. In their war paint "they looked like an American Army in masquerade."[31] Cattle were slaughtered for a victory feast.

Wounded Americans were killed and scalped. Some of the dead Mihsimaalhsa bodies were mutilated, and some had dirt stuffed into their mouths. The dirt symbolized the price of land.

Other warriors were neither satisfied with what they had accomplished nor distracted by finishing off the wounded, scalping the dead, or finding prizes inside the camp. Most likely, these were primarily Potawatomi, Ojibwe, and Ottawa. They set off in pursuit of the fleeing survivors. Those toward the rear of the flight soon became aware they were being chased. Their terror increased. After about half a mile, most of the warriors quit the chase and went back to the battlefield to celebrate. But small parties continued to pursue the survivors.

About two miles into the flight, Van Cleve came to "a boy [who] had been thrown or fallen off a horse & begged [for his] assistance." For about the next two miles, Van Cleve "ran pulling" the boy with him. By then, Van Cleve was "nearly exhausted." A few horses were passing by them. Van Cleve heaved the boy up on a horse behind the two men it was already carrying. They were soon out of his sight. Van Cleve's thighs began to "cramp violently," and his pace slowed until he was barely walking. Nearby, a man with a wounded knee was doing his best to keep moving. By now, Van Cleve had dropped back to within one hundred yards of where the pursuit had caught up to some "old & wounded" stragglers. They were dying under Indian tomahawks. Van Cleve paused just long enough to tie his pocket handkerchief around the wounded man's knee. In Van Cleve's words: "[F]or a moment my spirits sunk & I felt in despair for my safety. I hesitated whether to leave the road or whether I was capable of further exertions. If I left the road the Indians were in plain sight & could easily overtake me. I threw the shoes off my feet & the coolness of the ground seemed to revive me."

The cramping started to ease, and Van Cleve began to trot. At a bend in the road, his renewed pace allowed him to bypass half a dozen would-be escapees. Focused on survival, as he passed, he instinctively "thought that it would occupy some time of the enemy to massacre these before my turn would come."[32]

Newman's arm wound sapped his strength until he just gave up and laid down. Companions put him on a stray packhorse. Then they were on the move again. Not much later, a musket ball struck Newman in the back and killed him.[33]

Slowed by his wound, Samuel Turner knew he could no longer stay ahead of the Indians' pursuit. The ensign stopped and waited. Offering to surrender, to his relief, he was taken prisoner. Ultimately, Turner was brought to Detroit, where he was ransomed and released. He returned to the United States in early 1792.[34]

Holding her infant, Red-Haired Nance struggled to continue. Her husband was dead or presumably dead. Private James McDowell came up to Nance and her child. McDowell estimated the infant to be a year old. For a time, he carried the child. After the respite, McDowell handed the infant back to Nance and went on ahead.[35] As she continued, mentally exhausted, not having eaten since the night before, and fearful of oncoming Indians, physical exhaustion set in again. Nance stopped. If they were overtaken, both she and her child would probably die. Given the horrors of the day, Nance may have thought it was a certainty. What is known is that she laid her infant down on the ground along the trail and trudged on alone. The story is told in two ways. In one version, Nance thought that leaving the child behind was the infant's best chance for survival.[36] In the other version, she left the child to save herself, believing that otherwise they would both die.[37]

It was said that the infant was saved by "Indians [who] carried it to the Sandusky towns and reared it."[38] If so, the child was exceptionally lucky to have been found by someone unusually kindhearted, or by a warrior who knew a family who wanted to replace a child they had lost. If true, the child was never identified. Wyandots lived on the upper Sandusky.

Fortuitously, soon after Van Cleve thought about how much time it would take the Indians to kill those he had passed, the last of the pursuers decided they had done enough. Now satisfied, they turned back toward the battle site. Their pursuit had continued for at least four and possibly as far as six miles.

After the pursuit ended, St. Clair sent Denny ahead to try to call a halt and allow the remainder of the army to consolidate. Denny's orders were treated as no more than suggestions. To the extent of their varying capabilities, men set their own pace. In the rush to Fort Jefferson, half or more of the soldiers who were not wounded "threw away their arms and accoutrements." For St. Clair, that was "the most disgraceful part of the business."[39] Winthrop Sargent described how "[t]he road for miles was covered with firelocks, cartridge-boxes and regimentals."[40] Ebenezer Denny observed that "[a]rms, ammunition and accoutrements were almost all thrown away, and even the officers in some instances divested themselves of their fusees ... exemplifying by this conduct a kind of authority for the most precipitate and ignominious flight."[41]

After eleven more miles, Van Cleve was in the middle of the retreat. Like the others, he had slowed to a walk. Next to him Corporal Josiah Mott and Red-Headed Nance were crying, Mott for his wife who had been killed and Nance for her child. A "nearly exhausted" Bartholomew Schaumburg hung on to Mott's arm. Van Cleve took the officer's fusil and accoutrements and carried them for him. With his free hand, Van Cleve helped to guide Nance's steps. Ahead, Van Cleve saw the boy he had put on the horse. The boy had fallen off and was walking. No longer pursued, they continued on toward Fort Jefferson.[42]

That afternoon, the first remnants of the army were met by a detachment of the 1st US Regiment. Hearing the cannons' explosive roars from miles away, Major Hamtramck marched his regiment back toward St. Clair until they encountered fleeing militia. Perhaps to avoid being treated as deserters, perhaps because they believed it, they told Hamtramck "that the army was totally destroyed."[43] Accepting their story as true, Hamtramck sent a detachment to reconnoiter ahead. Concerned that victorious Indians would advance to attack Fort Jefferson, Hamtramck took the rest of the regiment back to secure the fort. Darke castigated Hamtramck's behavior as "cowardly."[44] Perhaps affected by his son being badly wounded and by his own wound, Darke claimed that many of the wounded would have been saved if Hamtramck had advanced with his full regiment. The timing and distance, however, suggest Hamtramck was too far away to have arrived before the battle ended or even to have arrived in time to save the stragglers in the retreat.

The flight continued for twenty-nine miles to Fort Jefferson. The first refugees reached the fort by seven o'clock that evening. Having not marched more than nine miles in a day during the campaign, fear and hunger pushed them to traverse more than three times that distance within nine hours. More arrived over the next hours.

Both Van Cleve and the unknown boy reached Fort Jefferson. Daniel Bonham did not. He had fallen off his horse and been left on the trail. Robert Benham's luck held. He too was among the survivors at Fort Jefferson, as were Fowler, Gano, Irwin, and Nance.

There was no meat and far too little flour for the influx of refugees at Fort Jefferson. Quickly discovering the food shortage and driven by hunger, levies and militia continued on toward Fort Hamilton. Despite the regulars' exhaustion, after hearing from Colonel Sargent, Colonel Darke, Major Hamtramck, Major Ziegler, and Major Gaither, at ten o'clock that night, St. Clair ordered the regulars to begin the march to Fort Hamilton and then on to Fort Washington.

Having completed their scout, Piominko and Sparks were on their way back to rejoin St. Clair when they encountered an Indian riding a dragoon's horse and wearing a dragoon jacket. He was armed with a sword and a rifle. Someone, perhaps Sparks speaking Shawnee, hailed the unsuspecting Indian. Thinking that the scouting party were Confederation warriors, he told them of the great victory over the Americans, boasting that his arm had tired from tomahawking and scalping so many. The talkative warrior soon became one of the dead and scalped. Now knowing that there was no army to rejoin, the scouts headed for Fort Jefferson. When they reached it, Sparks carefully appeared first and hailed the guard to avoid being shot by nervous sentries. It was soon known that they had brought back five scalps.

Overall, St. Clair's army suffered 632 killed or missing, of which 39 were officers. This included Colonel Gibson and Captain Darke who lingered into December and January. Most likely they succumbed to infections that developed from their wounds. An additional 281 were wounded, including 29 officers. Captain Slough was one of the wounded, as was Lieutenant Cummings, who was with Slough on the night patrol. Some of the wounded enlisted men may have eventually died, as Gibson and Darke did, but there is no record of it.[45]

The casualty rate for the regulars and the levies exceeded 50 percent. With 913 dead, wounded, or missing, the overall casualty rate was barely under 50 percent. The ultimate casualty rate was similar for officers and enlisted men. The Kentucky militia's casualty rate was only about half of the overall rate.[46]

The levies suffered the heaviest casualties. The 1st Levy Regiment had 11 officers and a surgeon's mate killed, 1 officer captured and 8 wounded, while the 2nd Levies had 11 officers killed and 7 wounded.[47] Presumably the casualties of the enlisted men were proportional.

The 2nd US Regiment suffered 7 officers killed and 1 wounded.[48] A regimental monthly return dated December 1, 1791, shows 101 enlisted men killed and 52 "present sick." From the overall casualty numbers, it is safe to infer that nearly all of the "sick" had been wounded.[49]

Notably, Major Clark, Captain Hannah, Lieutenant Stevenson, Captain Faulkner, Lieutenant Sedam, Ensign Schaumburg, and Major Gaither survived without a wound. So did militia Captain Samuel Wells, William's brother. George's Ash's brother was not so fortunate. Militia Private Benjamin Ash was among the dead.[50]

Of the civilians, at least 14 artificers, 10 packhorse men, 2 of the 6 artillery's wagon drivers and the artillery's cook were killed, and 13 artificers and packhorse men were wounded.[51] According to Winthrop Sargent, of approximately 33 women, all but 3 were killed or missing and presumed dead.[52] Sargent gave no numbers for children, and there are none. The absence of such numbers suggests that few children were with the army. Anecdotally, besides Red-Haired Nance's infant, the unknown boy helped by Van Cleve, and the questions concerning Heart's and Newman's sons, Margaret Pedrick's child was tomahawked.[53]

Although the image of wholesale slaughter was imprinted on the Americans who escaped, Ensign Turner was not the only prisoner taken. On December 2, Alexander McKee wrote to Sir John Johnson and referred to "the testimony of many Prisoners who have been delivered up to me."[54] McKee also reported that agents of the Indian Department had secured the release of several prisoners. Sergeant Reuben Reynolds, an American spy posing as a deserter, reported seeing several prisoners who had been taken in the Wabash battle in an Indian village. Reynolds referred to the prisoners as "slaves," some of whom "were treated well, others ill."[55] Reynolds probably observed the prisoners in June 1792. Oliver Spencer named Henry Ball and Polly Meadows as a soldier and his wife who were taken prisoner, though the difference in last names suggests they were not married. According to Spencer, Ball and Meadows were living at the Glaize and working to pay ransom, "he by boating to the rapids of the Maumee, and she by washing and sewing."[56] Mary McKnight and Margaret Pedrick were also captured. Months later, each escaped.[57] There are no accounts from these survivors of any prisoners being tortured.[58]

Sargent objectively assessed that the Indians had probably suffered few casualties, notwithstanding some that "pretend to have seen great numbers dead." Based on Du Quania's first-hand account, Alexander McKee reported, "The loss of the Indians is indeed very trifling and scarcely credible, the number of killed being only 20 or 21, and of wounded 40."[59]

In 1810, consistent numbers were given by the Shawnee to John Norton: six Shawnee, four Wyandot, two "Mingoes," five or six Delaware, and a smaller number of Ottawa killed. Apparently, either Norton or the Shawnee who told him the story conflated all of the Three Fires with the Ottawa. A more significant caveat to the history related to Norton was that it named the Shawnee and Delaware in the center, with "the Wyandots and Mingoes taking the right . . . and the Ottawas on the left," without mentioning the Miami.[60] While this might have just been a mistake, by 1810, a degree of mutual disdain had developed between the Shawnee and the Miami. This arose from Little Turtle's claim that he commanded the Confederation's force, from the Shawnee insistence on fighting at Fallen Timbers in 1794, and from their sharply divergent 1810 policies. Little Turtle and the Miami had accepted the futility of war and worked to adapt to white, agrarian living. This starkly contrasted with the rise of Tecumseh and his brother, the Prophet, and with Shawnee advocacy for Native American ways and Native American unity to preserve their remaining land. George Ash's recollection was that thirty-five Indians were killed or mortally wounded.

Alexander McKee advised John Johnson that:

The astonishing success of a few Indians, not more than 1040, who have opposed and destroyed, the whole American force will most probably cause a more numerous collection of Indians . . . than was ever before known in this part of the Country. This circumstance will naturally lead you to consider the necessity of sending forward at as early a period as possible, all the supplies for the year as well as the extraordinaries, which will become indispensably necessary for so numerous a Body of Indians. . . . It must now, more than ever, most evidently appear that whilst we keep the Western Indians our friends, this post may bid defiance to any enemy, from any land expedition, that may be contemplated against it; and I am persuaded myself that the Provisions & Supplies which Government have allowed, or may hereafter allow to them, either from benevolence, or a desire to cultivate their friendship, and good will, exclusive of the advantages derived from their trade, are most apparently useful and advantageous to Great Britain. The Country which the Americans are endeavoring to wrest from the Indians; is the only Part in which they could subsist, and it would seem the greatest injustice to deprive the natural and perpetual possessors thereof of their only means of existence. If the terms of peace proposed by the Indians, last summer had met with the success they merited we should not now have occasion to deplore the effusion of so much Blood, and I most sincerely wish, that the Americans, now convinced of the difficulty of subduing a Brave & warlike race of People, may listen to the Voice of Equity and Reason and establish a firm & lasting Peace on the Principles of natural Justice & Humanity.[61]

Chapter Fifteen

The Consequences
of Victory

I N 1792, GEORGE WASHINGTON EXERCISED the first presidential veto, and
won reelection. The US Mint was established. Kentucky became the fif-
teenth state. The Mississippi River was the country's western border. In the
south, Spain still ruled Florida and West Florida, which included southern
Alabama and southern Mississippi. The impact of Native Americans routing
St. Clair's army continued to reverberate as the war continued.

For the Maumee Confederation, with a victory of unprecedented proportion, hope, optimism, and confidence were never higher. Several generations later, Potawatomi Chief Simon Pokagon, a man both literate and
schooled in tribal oral history, wrote of this time:

We fought most heroically against overpowering numbers for home and native
land; sometimes victory was ours, as when, in the last decade of the eighteenth cen-

tury, after having had many warriors killed, and our villages burned to the ground, our fathers arose in their might, putting to flight the alien armies of Generals Harmar and St. Clair, hurling them in disorder from the wilderness across our borders into their own ill-gotten domain.[1]

Describing "alien armies" being hurled out of the "native land . . . wilderness" reflected Native American awareness that the natural forest ecosystem would not continue to stand in a white "domain."

Despite their unprecedented success in routing St. Clair's army, Kekionga and the surrounding towns were deemed to be too exposed to American attack. They were abandoned, and the Confederation moved about fifty miles upriver, in and around the Glaize, where the Auglaize flows into the Maumee. This brought the Shawnee, Miami, and Buckongahelas's Delaware closer to the Wyandot and Ottawa, and closer to McKee, shortening the British supply line. Raids and the threat of raids continued to stymie further large-scale American expansion. England continued to maintain its forts, its trade, and its support for the Maumee Confederation.

An unintended consequence of the Confederation's victory was the restructuring of the US Army. Recognizing that reliance on levies was undesirable, Washington and Knox quicky developed a plan to more than double the size of the army so it would total more than five thousand men, plus officers. The expanded army would have five regiments of infantry instead of two. The artillery would be expanded to a battalion of four companies, and the cavalry would be expanded to a squadron of four troops.[2] Even with the expanded army, militia would still be used to supplement the regulars. Linked to expanding the army was Washington's intention to continue the war with no change in the government's land goals or its Indian policy.

The administration's request for approximately $1.25 million to fund the war and expand the army sparked vehement congressional debate. On January 26, 1792, the House met as a committee of the whole. Both the wisdom of the president's plans and the war's justification were questioned. Representatives Anthony Wayne, Benjamin Goodue, Elias Boudinot, Samuel Livermore, Samuel Steele, Josiah Parker, and Benjamin Bourne, representing Georgia, Massachusetts, New Hampshire, New Jersey, North Carolina, Rhode Island, and Virginia, argued against the administration's policies:

[The Indian war was] as unjustly undertaken [as it has been] unwisely and unsuccessfully conducted . . . depredations had been committed by the whites as well as the Indians; and the whites were most probably the aggressors, as they frequently made encroachments on the Indian lands, whereas the Indians showed no inclination to possess our territory.... Peace ... may be obtained ... at much less expense than ... war.[3]

They contended that fighting a war to gain Indian territory was pointless

as we already possess land sufficient—more, in fact, than we will be able to cultivate for a century to come. Instead of being ambitious to expand our boundaries, it would answer a much better national purpose to check the roving disposition of the frontier settlers.... If kept closer ... they would be more useful ... and would not so frequently involve us in unnecessary and expensive wars with the Indians. ... If the citizens of the United States were recalled within their proper boundaries [for years to come they could] cultivate the soil in peace, neither invaded nor invading. As the country progresses in population, and our limits are found too narrow, it will then be soon enough to contemplate a gradual extension of our frontier.

They complained that after three years of war "no one, except those who are in the secrets of the Cabinet, knows for what reason the war has thus been carried on for three years."

Representatives Alexander White and Andrew Moore, both of Virginia, spoke in support of the administration's plan. They referred to the "savages," arguing that the war was one of self-defense, that the few white depredations had been provoked, and that relations on the frontier were so acrimonious that peace was impossible. The Indians were blamed for not making peace in the treaties the United States sought. They claimed that it no longer mattered whether the war was justly begun because to stop fighting would "abandon our fellow-citizens on the frontier to the rage of their savage enemies."

The debate reveals that perhaps neither the war's inception nor its continuation were inevitable. If Washington and Jefferson had different visions of the future, or less focus on immediate expansion, different decisions about war and peace might have been made.

The same day, at the president's direction, Secretary Knox sent Congress a report titled *The CAUSES of the existing HOSTILITIES between the UNITED STATES and certain Tribes of Indians north-west of the OHIO stated and explained from official and authentic Documents, and published in obedience to the orders of the PRESIDENT of the UNITED STATES,* January 26, 1792. This public report was in stark contrast to Knox's private reports to the president in late 1790 and early 1791, where he had identified multiple causes for the war. Those causes had included treaties taking Indian land for "pitiful" amounts and expanding settlements encroaching on Indian land.[4] Despite the title stating that it was based on "official and authentic Documents," this public report to Congress explained the causes of the war quite differently. After reviewing the treaties and asserting that Indian lands had been properly acquired by "purchase," the report stated that it did "not appear that the right of the Northern and Western Indians, who formed the several aforementioned treaties to the lands thereby relinquished to the United States, has been questioned by any other tribes; nor does it appear that the present war has been occasioned by any dispute relatively to the boundaries established by the said treaties."[5] That statement was blatantly false and was known to be false. Washington, Knox, and others knew that the Maumee Confederation rejected the validity of the treaties and claimed all of Ohio was still rightfully Indian land. They were well aware that peace could be obtained for Ohio land. The report reiterated the claim that had originally been made to justify the war. "[I]t appears that the unprovoked aggressions of the Miami and Wabash Indians upon Kentucky and other parts of the frontiers, together with their associates, a banditti, formed of Shawanese and outcast Cherokees, amounting in all to about one thousand two hundred men, *are solely the causes of the war*."[6] (Emphasis added.) Washington and his administration could have argued that this was a cause of the war. But to assert that it was the sole cause of the war was as false as claiming that the sole cause of the war was the attacks of Kentuckians and Virginians on the Indians. It appears that Washington and Knox tailored their messaging to play to the deeply rooted emotional belief of most of the frontier, and some in Congress, that blamed only the Indians, while implicitly absolving the administration of a scintilla of fault. In this, their communication was all too modern.

Senator Benjamin Hawkins, formerly a member of Washington's Continental army staff and of the Continental Congress, was one who did not accept the report. In a letter to President Washington, he wrote that after the Revolutionary War, "we seem to have forgotten altogether the rights of the Indians. They were treated as tenants at will, we seized on their lands and made a division of the same. . . . It is the source of their hostility." Unknown to Hawkins, his description was consistent with Knox's private description fourteen months earlier. Hawkins recounted how St. Clair was ordered to obtain a new treaty to resolve Indian complaints about the prior treaties ceding land. Hawkins commented that most Indians did not accept St. Clair's invitation, thinking that he only wanted them to relinquish their claims to the land. Hawkins recognized that "it was natural to expect that [refusal] as from our conduct they conceived themselves deprived of what they deemed most precious, that they would be in a state of hostility against us, and the more so, as the British in Canada were ready enough, to misrepresent, all our conduct, to furnish them with military stores, and . . . to encourage them." Hawkins charged that those responsible for western affairs "were for war, all who are dependent on the department, are for war, this is their harvest." Hawkins was likely thinking about the land investments of St. Clair, Sargent, and Duer, among others. Hawkins warned that war would continue "[a]s long as we attempt to go into their country, or to remain there."[7]

Neither Hawkins's letter nor congressional dissent had any effect on the administration's plans and objectives. A key House vote to advance the bill was 34 to 18 in favor.[8] The House and Senate approved a final version of the bill on March 4, 1792. The president's plans would proceed.

In April, General Anthony Wayne was appointed to replace St. Clair as the Army's major general. This time there was no rush to launch a major offensive. Unlike the hurried campaign of 1791, time was taken to recruit and train the soldiers of the newly expanded army. There was no major American offensive in 1792. In December, the army was designated the Legion of the United States and was reorganized into four sublegions. Each sublegion consisted of its staff, a troop of dragoons, a company of artillery, two battalions of infantry armed with muskets, and one battalion of riflemen.[9]

While the United States was recruiting and beginning to train new soldiers, conflict on the northwestern frontier continued. In spring and summer 1792, the impact of Native American raiding parties was felt even east of the Ohio River. In late June 1792, Absalom Baird, a militia officer and justice of the peace for Washington County, in southwest Pennsylvania, reported to President Washington, "The people in general were more intimidated this year. . . . [N]umbers have moved from the frontier into the interior settlements."[10]

In summer 1792, William Wells visited his white family in Kentucky. He briefly returned to the Miami but soon decided it would be better to live as a white man. Little Turtle accepted Wells's decision, and they remained on good terms.[11] His first wife was released and returned to her village. Sweet Breeze, Little Turtle's daughter, stayed with William Wells for the rest of her life. Wells soon became an army interpreter.

For the First Peoples, internal debate continued on what peace terms were acceptable. This was the subject of a large and argumentative intertribal conference that began September 30, 1792, and lasted ten days at the Glaize. After a calumet was passed and smoked by all the chiefs of the confederacy, the speeches began. Throughout, as was customary, belts and strings of wampum signified past and current messages. Depending on the historical power, status, and relationship of the tribes, it was customary to address others as brothers, elder brothers, uncles, or nephews. Father was still reserved for the king and the British.

Initially, Egushawa favored the compromise for peace advocated by the Six Nations' leaders, which focused on the Muskingum rather than the Ohio as their eastern boundary. The Miami, Shawnee, and Delaware, however, insisted that the Ohio River was the only rightful boundary. Their lead speaker was Red Pole (Messquakinoe), Blue Jacket's half-brother.[12]

On the third day, Red Pole reminded the "Elder Brothers of the Six Nations" that four years before, they had advised the tribes "to all be strong and united as if one nation. . . . You know when we last met at the foot of the Rapids four years ago it was unanimously agreed on by all Nations, to be strong, and to defend our Country; But we have never seen you since that time."[13] Buckongahelas followed. "Uncles Six Nations. Don't think, because the Shawanoes only have spoke to you, that it is their sentiments alone, they have spoke the sentiments of all the Nations." At their next meeting, Cow Killer, a Seneca chief, urged everyone to "unite, and consider what will be the best for us, our women and children, to lengthen our days and be in peace." His message was to not be too "proud spirited" to make peace and "to go on in the best manner we can to make peace" with the Americans.

Words and emotions reached a crescendo on the sixth day when Red Pole spoke of how everyone knew that the Six Nations had been talking to the Americans and that they had come with "a bundle of American Speeches under their Arm." Then he challenged them to "lay that bundle down here and explain what you have been talking with [the Americans] these last two years. . . . All the different nations here, now desire you to speak from your Heart, and not from your mouth, and tell them what that Bundle was which you had under arm when you came here,—We know what you are about. We see you plainly." With that, Red Pole threw the Six Nations' wampum at Cow Killer's feet. Disconcerted, the Senecas had no immediate answer, complaining that they had been talked to "a little too roughly" and had been "thrown on their backs." Then they separated to consider what to do.

When they returned, they acknowledged having met in Philadelphia with "the 13 States and Washington. . . . Brothers, Washington asked us what was the cause of the uneasiness of the Western Nations. We told him it was in regard to their lands." Cow Killer said that Washington wanted peace;

that Washington promised that if the real owners had not sold the land, then satisfaction would be given to the Indians; that there should be a council to determine this. But Washington never said that any land would be relinquished. Then Cow Killer offered the bundle of papers and speeches they had received.

On the eighth day of the council, Red Pole spoke of how while the Six Nations talked to Washington about peace, the Confederation had defeated two invading American armies. "[H]ad the Great Spirit been favorable to them instead of us, you would have found them here, their strong forts, and only a small remnant, or perhaps none of your Western Brethren to deliver their sweet speeches to." Red Pole explained that after defeating St. Clair, they had his captured papers translated. So they knew that if they had been defeated, the Americans would have built forts and driven all the Indians away. They knew that if they had not fought, the American plan was to subjugate them and turn them into farmers who labored "like beasts." Then Red Pole announced the consensus agreement that the true boundary line, as set at Fort Stanwix, was the Ohio River; that what the Confederation wanted was the restitution of their lands, not compensation for lands held "under false pretenses."

In December, Seneca chiefs Cornplanter and New Arrow informed General Wayne of the Shawnee demands:

The Shawanese say, that if they make peace, it will be on these terms: The Americans to allow them all the lands they held in Sir William [Johnson's] time; or, at least, that the river Ohio shall be the line, and they will be paid for the lands improved on the south side of said river Ohio. These, they say, are the terms, and the only ones, on which they will make peace.[14]

The reference to Sir William Johnson's time vividly sent the message that no treaty the United States had entered into, whether it be with the king of England or with any Indians, had validly affected the Shawnees' right to Ohio. The additional demand for compensation for Kentucky land south of the Ohio was more than the Confederation had agreed it needed. So either this was not accurate or it may have been a negotiating ploy, a bargaining chip to be conceded.

Benjamin Lincoln, Timothy Pickering, and Beverly Randolph were selected as the American commissioners who would meet with a large tribal council to negotiate a peace agreement. They knew that leaders of the Six Nations, including Joseph Brant, would advise the Confederation to compromise on land, at least to the Muskingum River.

The commissioners arranged with Captain Hendrick Aupaumut, chief of the Stockbridge band of the Mohicans, to try to influence the Confederation. Their written instructions asked him "to suggest some things for their consideration . . . in order to discover how far they may be persuaded to depart from their rigid demands." These suggestions included that in reliance on treaties, "the great council of the United States" had sold "large tracts of land along the Ohio," and that people had settled there, from Pennsylvania to the Great Miami, so that "it may be very difficult, if not impossible, now to give them up." It was also suggested that the commissioners might agree to relinquish land west of the Great Miami, pay for the land east of the Great Miami, and perhaps even give up some of the land south of the line established in the treaties of Fort Harmar and Fort McIntosh. The Great Miami flows approximately two hundred miles west of the Muskingum, so these suggestions would still concede most of Ohio to white settlement. An additional suggestion concerned the forest:

Consider, further, what are the advantages you derive from the lands which the United States wish to retain. They are furs, skins, and meat, which you would every year obtain by hunting. But suppose the commissioners should offer to pay a large annual rent for those lands; in money, in goods, or provisions; would not such terms be better than war? But, probably, besides this rent, you may hunt on these same lands as long as you can find any game.[15]

Hendrick reportedly had the written message translated and then destroyed it.

John Graves Simcoe was the lieutenant governor of Upper Canada (Ontario) and the commander of British forces there. In early June, the American commissioners wrote to Simcoe seeking to discover what the British were telling the Indians. It was suspected that the British were advising the Confederation not to make any land concessions. While the British had been, and were prepared to continue, providing logistical support to the Confederation, peace was in Britain's interest. They were not opposed to the Confederation conceding some land.

The commissioners disclosed that "altho' it is now impossible to retrace all the steps then taken, the United States are disposed to recede as far as may be indispensable . . . and for the lands retained make ample compensation." They concluded the governor "must be aware that the sales and settlements of the lands over the Ohio founded on the Treaties of Fort McIntosh, and Fort Harmar, render it impossible now to make that River the boundary. The expression of [the governor's] opinion on this point in particular will give [the commissioners] great satisfaction."[16]

In response, Governor Simcoe denied he had advised the Indians not to give up any land, explaining that the Indians had not asked for his advice on the subject and were not likely to do so. Simcoe wrote that while the British government's principle was that the tribes should be united so all treaties have "universal concurrence," it appeared the Confederation was convinced the United States wanted tribal disunity.[17]

Two weeks later, Simcoe's message to the Confederation affirmed that the British would deliver provisions and provide observers to the council, that the king had never ceded Indian land ownership to the United States, and that the king's boundary under the Fort Stanwix Treaty was the Ohio. The message wished for peace but refrained from suggesting what terms should be accepted to achieve it.

After various preliminary efforts, talks between the Confederation and the government were finally held in summer 1793 at the Canadian farm of Matthew Elliott of the British Indian Department. But the Confederation did not gather there. Hundreds of the Six Nations, the Wyandot, the Shawnee, the Delaware, the Munsee, the Miami, the Ottawa, the Chippewa, the Potawatomi, the Seneca-Cayuga, the Cherokee, and the Nanticoke gathered some ninety miles away at the Maumee River Rapids. The Confederation sent deputations to Elliott's farm while they met at the rapids to decide how to respond to developments in the negotiations.

The council between the American commissioners and the Confederation deputation began July 7. After three weeks, Joseph Brant expressed his concern to Governor Simcoe that his plan to negotiate a boundary at the Muskingum was not being followed, contrary to the wishes of the Three Fires and others. A Creek delegation had arrived at the rapids, and Brant thought the shift toward demanding all of Ohio might be because of the Creeks' news of whites encroaching on their lands.

Doubts about American credibility probably deepened further because of letters Creek leaders had received six months earlier. Those letters came from James Seagrave, the government's Indian agent in the south. Seagrave warned the Creeks not to listen to the "bad talks" of war from the Shawnee or "Northern" Indians who had come to visit them. Seagrave claimed these bad Indians were now begging for peace. In one letter, he even claimed that out of leniency, President Washington had not sent "a large army against them, and, by this means, they have had an opportunity to kill a number of his people, and do a great deal of mischief."[18] The visiting Indians were eight

Shawnee. They were led by Red Pole and included George Ash.[19] In addition
to the Creek, they also visited the Chickamauga Cherokee.

Seagrave's claims that the Shawnee and others were begging for peace
and that no large army had been sent against them were foolish, easily exposed lies. The Creeks could hear for themselves that the Shawnee were not
begging for peace. News of the victories over Harmar and St. Clair was
widely known.

On July 30, Captain Johnny, by now the Shawnee civil chief, Sawaghdawunk (Carry-On-About or Carry-All-About) of the Wyandot, and Buckongahelas led the Confederation's deputation.[20] Among others present were
McKee and Elliott. Consistent with the decision of the Confederation's
council the prior October, their message was that the rightful boundary was
the Ohio River.

With Simon Girty translating, Sawaghdawunk spoke. "We have thought
it best, that what we have to say should be put in to writing, and here is the
meaning of our hearts." The paper stated that it was from the whole Confederation and listed the Wyandot, Delaware, Miami, Shawnee, Ottawa,
Chippewa, Potawatomi, Mingo, Conoy, and Munsee. Absent from the list
of tribes was the Six Nations of the Haudenosaunee. The key provisions of
the paper presented to the commissioners stated:

Brothers: You know very well that the boundary line, which was run between the
white people and us, at the treaty of Fort Stanwix, was the river Ohio. Brothers: If
you seriously design to make a firm and lasting peace, you will immediately remove
all your people from our side of that river.

Brothers: We therefore ask you, are you fully authorized by the United States to
continue, and firmly fix on the Ohio river, as the boundary line, between your people and ours?[21]

Late in the afternoon of the next day, the American negotiators responded. They reiterated prior statements that peace would require mutual
concessions. They said it would be best to discuss those concessions face-
to-face and asked to meet with the confederacy "in full council without
more delay."[22]

Then the commissioners outlined their position. They conceded that the
Treaty of Paris could only have ceded Britain's land claims, not Indian land
rights. They said the United States had sought peace and had made treaties
with the Iroquois, the Wyandot, the Delaware, the Ottawa, the Chippewa,
and the Shawnee. The United States had disposed of "large tracts of land
[that were] ceded" and "a great number of people" had moved and settled

on those lands. Hearing of dissatisfaction, St. Clair held a new council at
Fort Harmar in 1789, with over six hundred Indians from many nations.
There the old treaties were reconfirmed by the Six Nations of the Iroquois,
and the Wyandot, Delaware, Ottawa, Chippewa, Potawatomi, and Sac joined
in the new treaty. With this rationale, the commissioners reached their key
points.

Accordingly, large tracts have been sold and settled. . . . And now, brothers, we answer explicitly, that for the reasons here stated to you, it is impossible to make the
river Ohio the boundary, between your people and the people of the United States.

Brothers: You are men of understanding, and if you consider the customs of
white people, the great expenses which attend their settling in a new country, the
nature of their improvements, in building houses, and barns, in clearing and fenc-
ing their lands, how valuable the lands are thus rendered . . . you will see that it is
now impracticable to remove our people from the northern side of the Ohio. . . .
[T]he United States cannot make the Ohio between you and us.

The commissioners wanted the Confederation to "finally relinquish . . .
some of the land on your side of the river Ohio." They wanted everything
ceded in the Fort Harmar treaty, plus land claimed at the Falls of the Ohio
for George Rogers Clark and his men. For this, the United States would give,
in money or goods, the largest sum ever given for Indian lands. "And because those lands did every year furnish you with skins and furs, with which
you bought clothing and other necessaries," every year the United States
would furnish "a large quantity of such goods as are best suited for the wants
of yourselves, your women and children." But if there could not be an agreement for all of that land, then there should be an agreement on a new
boundary line and the United States would provide "generous compensation" with an initial payment and "yearly rent . . . forever."

What unsettled land the United States might concede was not delineated.
Nor was it specified whether this would be limited to unsettled and unsold
land or would include unsettled land, even if it had been sold.

The commissioners sought one further concession: that any future sales
of Indian land be made to the United States only. With that, a copy of the
speech and a belt of white wampum containing thirteen black stripes were
handed to the Confederation representatives.

The next day, August 1, with Simon Girty translating, Sa-wagh-da-wunk
spoke briefly. He told the commissioners that the past treaties were incomplete and had not been made by all of the chiefs; that their lands had not
been bought and still belonged to them. Sa-wagh-da-wunk reiterated that

they all knew "the Ohio was made the boundary." He said that they knew, and George Washington knew, "you have your houses and people on our land; you say you cannot move them off; and we cannot give up our land." As translated by Girty, Sa-wagh-da-wunk concluded: "Brothers: We don't say much; there has been much mischief on both sides. We came here upon peace, and thought you did the same. We shall talk to our head warriors. You may return whence you came, and tell Washington."[23]

It appeared that the council had come to an abrupt end. But Elliott went to Captain Johnny and told him that the last part of the translation was wrong. They went to Girty, who maintained that he had translated correctly. After some additional discussion, Girty addressed the commissioners: "Brothers: Instead of going home, we wish you to remain here for an answer from us. We have your speech in our breasts, and shall consult our head warriors."[24]

With that request, the commissioners agreed to wait to hear from the Confederation's council at the rapids.

With the risk of an impasse hovering, tensions mounted. A week elapsed with no word from the Confederation. Then, over the next days, the commissioners heard from a number of Indians that the Six Nations, the Seven Nations of Canada,[25] the Ottawa, the Chippewa, and the Mississauga were particularly strong for peace and that the weight of opinion favored terms that the Americans could accept. However, the Wyandot, Shawnee, Miami, and Delaware remained opposed to any land concessions, though even among those tribes a substantial minority was said to disagree. Thus, the tribes on the front line of the struggle were willing to fight for all of Ohio while the tribes who lived farther west, like the large majority of the Three Fires, or farther north in Canada, such as Brant and some of the Six Nations, or farther east under American control, like the rest of the Six Nations, were willing to make concessions for peace.

The critical voice was that of the Three Fires. Because of Egushawa's influence and because of those tribes who were open to conceding some land, only the Three Fires could be relied on to provide the substantial number of additional warriors the Confederation would need for a reasonable chance of victory in the next campaign. While unanimity was politically useful, a unanimity for war, with too few tribes willing to actually fight, would be self-defeating.

For perspective, the number and locations of settlements should be considered.

In 1793, John Heckewelder, a Moravian missionary, estimated there were approximately 3,220 settlers north and west of the Ohio River. He was apparently referring to residents of lawful settlements, not to however many squatters remained scattered around Ohio.[26] Nearly all of the settlers Heckewelder listed lived within ten miles of the Ohio River. Eleven hundred were at Columbia at the mouth of the Little Miami. Nine hundred lived in Cincinnati. Three hundred fifty were at Marietta at the mouth of the Muskingum. Three hundred were at Gallipolis near the mouth of the Kanawha (Great Kenhawa) River. Two hundred eighty lived at North Bend and South Bend, named for bends in the Ohio. The amount of land occupied by these settlers was still relatively small.

Why then, for the Shawnee, Wyandot, Miami, and Delaware, was it worth continuing the war to insist that these settlers leave? Beyond a matter of principle, it recalls the suspicion that Blue Jacket expressed to Antoine Gamelin, that American peace offers would lead to the loss of land "by degrees" and that "a certain proof that they intend to encroach on our lands, is their new settlement on the Ohio."[27] And that suspicion had been reinforced by the Creeks' news. Furthermore, was it realistic to expect that artificial boundary lines around existing settlements would be respected? Or would such boundaries be the starting points for additional settlers to gradually encroach farther north and west of the Ohio?

Another week passed before two Wyandot runners delivered a written answer on August 16. Dated August 13, it listed the Wyandot, the Seven Nations of Canada, the Delaware, the Shawnee, the Miami, the Ottawa, the Chippewa, the "Senecas of the Glaize" (the Seneca-Cayuga), the Potawatomi, the Conoy, the Munsee, the Nanticoke, the Mohican, the "Messasagoes" (Mississauga), the Creek, and the Cherokee Nations. Conspicuously absent were the Six Nations.

To the Americans' point that the treaties ceding land to the United States were peace treaties, the council responded:

Brothers: This is telling us plainly, what we always understood . . . and it agrees with the declarations of those few who attended those treaties, viz: That they went to meet your commissioners to make peace, but, through fear, were obliged to sign any paper that was laid before them . . . deeds of cession were signed by them, instead of treaties of peace.[28]

The answer reminded the commissioners that before St. Clair's Fort Harmar treaty, the Confederation had clearly announced that "no bargain or sale" of any Indian land "would be considered as valid or binding, unless agreed to by a general council," and that no such council agreed to St. Clair's treaty. Then the response rhetorically asked, "How then was it possible for you to expect to enjoy peace, and quietly to hold these lands, when your commissioner was informed, long before he held the treaty of Fort Harmar, that the consent of a general council was absolutely necessary to convey any part of these lands to the United States?"

Next, the critical American rationale that the sale and settlement of land could not be undone was addressed. "[N]o consideration whatever can induce us to sell the land on which we get sustenance for our women and children." Turning the commissioners' offer of payment against them, a "mode" was suggested

by which your settlers may be easily removed, and peace thereby obtained. . . . Divide . . . this large sum of money, which you have offered to us, among these people: give to each also, a proportion of what you say you would give to us, annually, over and above this very large sum of money. . . . If you add, also, the great sums of money in raising and paying armies, with a view to force us to yield you our country, you will certainly have more than sufficient for the purposes of re-paying these settlers for all their labor and their improvements.

The justification for mutual concessions was rejected since why should nations being invaded be obligated to make mutual concessions? "Restore to us our country, and we shall be enemies no longer."

Even the proposal that if land was sold in the future it could only be sold to the United States was rejected.

The Confederation explained that it had not met in council directly with the commissioners because the commissioners had never met their precondition for direct talks, an acknowledgment that the boundary line was the Ohio River. The Confederation's answer continued:

We desire you to consider, brothers, that our only demand is the peaceable possession of a small part of our once great country. Look back, and review from whence we have been driven to this spot. We can retreat no further, because the country behind hardly affords food for its present inhabitants, and we have therefore resolved to leave our bones in this small space to which we are now confined.

With maintaining settlements north and west of the Ohio River an essential, uncompromisable goal for the United States, and respecting the river as the rightful boundary line an essential, uncompromisable goal for the Confederation, no terms could satisfy both. Negotiations were at an end. The war would continue.

The rationales for the opposing positions reflected their views of the forest and conflicting visions of the future. For the Americans, land could not be given back because sweat and money had improved it by clearing the forest for homes, barns, and fenced fields and pastures. For white settlement, less forest was unequivocally better. Explicitly recognizing that this diminished the tribes' ability to carry on the fur trade, and implicitly recognizing that it also limited their ability to hunt sufficiently, the commissioners offered money and goods to compensate for the loss of forest and its consequences.

Less forest meant less wildlife. It also meant less biodiversity, something the First Peoples, but few whites, were likely to recognize. For Native Americans, controlling the land and living in the natural woodland ecosystem meant economic independence with the resources needed to obtain enough food, clothing, and shelter. While the Confederation's written answer did not use the word "forest," given that more than 90 percent of the land was still dense woodlands, land meant forest. Moreover, if the settlers vacated Ohio, over time, what they had cleared would return to being forest, reclaimed by nature. The inability to agree on peace terms was intertwined with these fundamental differences.

But suppose the Confederation council had been persuaded, not by those who would have agreed to peace on virtually any terms but by the moderate peace advocates. Would a peace agreement have been reached? In October, still hopeful he could broker the peace agreement he had long envisioned, Joseph Brant was in council with Israel Chapin, deputy agent to the Iroquois and a former general in the Continental army. As he had been proposing for years, Brant asserted that the Muskingum should be the boundary. But that for peace, the Indians would "give up such part of those lands [along the Ohio west of the Muskingum] as are actually settled and improved; which settlements are to be circumscribed by a line drawn around them, and no further claims are to be admitted beyond such line."[29] So the boundary line was to be the Ohio to the Muskingum, then north along the Muskingum to its portage to the Cuyahoga and eventually to Lake Ontario, with exceptions for established settlements inside that line.

The response to Brant's proposal was not even a conditional yes. President Washington responded through Secretary of War Knox, who wrote:

The same principles of moderation and humanity which before dictated the offers to the Indians, and sincere friendship for the Six Nations, have induced your Father, the President, to consider attentively your proposition for a new boundary. Although the lines you mentioned are considered as liable to considerable objections, yet, it is hoped, when all difficulties are discussed at a treaty or a conference by moderate men, with upright view, that some agreement may be made which will lead to a general peace. On this ground, the President consents that a conference should be held at Venago, on the 15th, or middle of May, next.[30]

It appears that Washington considered the most moderate Indian proposal that might be obtainable to be a starting point for negotiations. So even if the Confederation had agreed to Brant's plan, whether a peace agreement would have been reached remains uncertain. For both sides, at some point, land was more important than peace, and bargaining for land was a zero-sum game.

With no agreement, Anthony Wayne began a new American offensive. It was October 1793, twenty-three months after the Battle of the Wabash.

Chapter Sixteen •

The Irony of
Fallen Timbers

WAYNE'S AIDE-DE-CAMP IN THE NEW CAMPAIGN against the Maumee Confederation was William Henry Harrison, the future ninth president of the United States.[1] Operating without time pressure, Wayne's plan was to build a string of forts and gradually solidify control over more and more of the contested land before ultimately seeking a major battle. Fort St. Clair was built between Forts Hamilton and Jefferson. Fort Greenville was erected less than ten miles north of Fort Jefferson. When constructed, it was the largest wooden fort on the continent.[2]

In response to Wayne's advance, Little Otter (Nekeik) led an Ottawa war party south. After ambushing a patrol, they successfully attacked a supply train and then a small settlement.

In December, despite the winter weather, Wayne and three hundred men advanced twenty-four miles north to the site of St. Clair's debacle. There they constructed Fort Recovery.

In the spring, Wayne's slow advance and fort building resumed. Knowing that Wayne would advance north, the British constructed Fort Miamis along the Maumee. About fifteen miles from the mouth of the river, it was an earthworks fortification, surrounded by a deep trench lined with stakes. Most importantly, the British garrison was equipped with fourteen cannons.[3]

Seeking to disrupt Wayne's supply line, Blue Jacket, Egushawa, and Little Otter led some 1,200 Shawnee, Three Fires, Seneca-Cayuga, Wyandot, and Miami warriors south in June 1794. Blue Jacket wanted to bypass Fort Recovery and cut off Wayne's supplies and communications south of Fort Greenville. The Three Fires, though, strongly favored attacking around Fort Recovery. With an agreement on the course of action a necessity, Blue Jacket acceded.

On June 30, a large packhorse train left the fort heading south for more supplies. Warriors with red and black war paint, clad only in breechclouts and moccasins, waited in the woods. Their ambush began with volleys of gunfire. Then they quickly rushed to close on the soldiers with tomahawks and war clubs. The troops that could ran for the fort.

Hearing gunfire, Major William Mahon led infantry and dragoons out of the fort to aid the packhorse escort. There was a brief exchange of gunfire before the rescuers joined the flight of those they had come to rescue. Most made it back inside the fort. Major Mahon and some twenty others did not.

Feeling the thrill of success and bloodlust, Ojibwe and Ottawa warriors wildly charged the fort. It was the mistake the defenders needed. Muskets fired through loopholes in the walls. Cannon fired canister and six-pound balls toward the reckless Indians. Feeling obligated to support the attack and uncontrolled by their chiefs, more warriors joined the assault. Nearly their only targets were the fort's loopholes, on the off chance that they could hit the men behind them. Although the siege lasted into the next day, the fort was never at risk. A clear victory had disintegrated into a costly draw. All, or virtually all, of the army's losses came before the fort was assaulted. The army's losses were twenty-two dead, including Mahon, twenty-nine wounded, and three pack-horsemen missing and captured. More than two hundred packhorses were captured, fifty-nine were killed, and twenty-two were wounded.[4] Ambushing the convoy had cost the Confederation three dead and a few wounded. Attacking the fort had cost fourteen dead, with eleven falling so close to the walls that their bodies could not be recovered.

About the same number were wounded as were killed. In the aftermath of the failed attack, recriminations erupted between the Three Fires and the other tribes. Three Fires complained that the others had not really tried to take the fort. Shawnee, Miami, Seneca-Cayuga, and Wyandot complained that the Three Fires' attack was foolish and not part of the agreed plan. With the chiefs unable to restore harmony, the Three Fires headed home. Blue Jacket reluctantly returned to the Glaize, his plan to disrupt Wayne's campaign shattered.

William Wells was now the captain of one of Wayne's scout companies. He was in an army that included veterans of the battle at the Wabash: Captains Jacob Slough, Edward Butler, Mahlon Ford, Richard Greaton, Benjamin Price, and Joseph Brock, and Lieutenants Bartholomew Schaumburg, John Reed, and Piercy Pope. Captain Sparks was also in Wayne's Legion. Whether any of them talked to Wells, or talked among themselves, about Wells's role in their defeat, or whether Wells and Sparks talked of their lives as adopted Indians are intriguing but unanswerable questions.

Wayne's advance continued. Marching toward the Glaize, he had close to 2,000 federal troops, plus 1,500 mounted Kentuckians.[5]

Facing this threat, the Confederation's council revealed a fundamental divide. The basic issue was not where or how to fight but whether to fight or seek peace terms. Perhaps influenced by Wells, Little Turtle concluded that the war was futile and advocated for peace talks. Either Blue Jacket, Egushawa, or both, forcefully responded that they must continue to fight for their lands. That was the consensus. Reluctantly, Little Turtle accepted it.

Finding Wayne more difficult to attack than St. Clair, and unable to launch a surprise attack, the Confederation chiefs decided to meet the army's advance in an area of tall grasses and woods on the floodplain of the Maumee. The area was known for the number of trees that lay on the ground, uprooted by a past tornado. The terrain would provide cover and concealment for the Confederation warriors as they waited to fire their first volley at Wayne's approaching army. The Confederation leaders resolved to defend Ohio, the Maumee, and the forest ecosystem at Fallen Timbers. The appellation came from the downed trees.

Fallen Timbers was downriver from the Glaize. Once again, Indian homes and cornfields would be abandoned and burned.

Overcoming the disharmony that arose after being repulsed at Fort Recovery, some 1,500 Confederation warriors assembled, substantially more than had defeated St. Clair. They were joined by fifty to seventy Canadian militia under Blue Jacket's brother-in-law, the veteran Captain William Caldwell.[6] To create deniability for the British, Caldwell and his Canadians did not wear uniforms. Also joining the Confederation force were several French-Canadian traders, including Antoine Lasselles.

Alerted by a deserter more than a week before, Indian scouts monitored Wayne's movement.[7] Confederation chiefs knew where the army camped on August 18 and knew that when Wayne marched the next day, the soldiers would reach Fallen Timbers before noon. They knew they would be out-numbered more than two to one, but they had expected similar odds thirty-three months before when they marched to intercept St. Clair.

Thus, the next morning, Blue Jacket, Egushawa, Little Otter, Tarhe, and an unenthusiastic Little Turtle led their men into position in Fallen Timbers. They were just four miles from Fort Miamis. Hidden in the tall grass and behind trees and logs, the Confederation warriors waited expectantly for the first soldiers to appear. They waited, but Wayne chose not to move that day. There was a widespread emotional letdown among the warriors at the soldiers' nonappearance.

A patrol Wayne dispatched reported that Indians were ahead. The next day, in the early morning hours of August 20, there was heavy rain. When it stopped around 7:15, Wayne assembled his men and resumed their march north. Having left about two hundred men behind to secure new camps and forts, Wayne had approximately 1,800 regulars, plus the 1,500 mounted Kentucky militia.

As they had the day before, Blue Jacket, Egushawa, Little Otter, Tarhe, and Little Turtle waited in Fallen Timbers. Among the Shawnee were Tecumseh, an increasingly well-known young war leader, and his close friend Stephen Ruddell. Also there and ready to fight were Caldwell with his Canadians and Lasselles and the other French-Canadian traders.

But the Indian discipline, focus, and spirit that was evident when they marched from Kekionga to intercept St. Clair was missing. Disappointed that the Americans had not appeared the prior day, and with the heavy early morning rain, many were still in their camps. Many others were at Fort Miamis to obtain supplies. After years of a national war, hundreds of the Confederation force failed to follow their chiefs to Fallen Timbers. Instead of 1,500 warriors, estimates range from 1,100 to barely more than 500. Now those ready for battle were outnumbered at least three to one, and possibly by more than six to one.[8] Nevertheless, Blue Jacket, Egushawa, Buckonga-helas, Little Otter, and Tarhe were determined to fight Wayne's Legion.

The legion advanced in columns with the river to their right and brigades of mounted Kentuckians to their left and rear. At a distance ahead of the legion, a battalion of mounted Kentuckians commanded by Major William Price slowly rode through the tall grass. Wayne was uncertain whether the Indians would fight or seek peace. If there was to be a fight, Price's advance guard would engage first, alerting Wayne and the rest of the army.

With the Indians having insufficient numbers to utilize the half-moon and with Wayne on the march, Fallen Timbers was an entirely different type of battle than had been fought along the Wabash.

After about five miles, as Price's horsemen moved forward, the first blast of gunfire erupted from the woods and high grass. Six of the militia were killed and others were wounded. The Kentuckians quickly turned their horses back.

With the woods and the many fallen trees preventing a direct cavalry charge, Wayne ordered the legion to form two lines. To Wayne's eye, "The savages were formed in three lines, within supporting distance of each other, and extending for near two miles, at right angles with the river."[9] Confederation chiefs tried to follow up on their initial advantage, but Wayne's main force held. Wayne ordered the mounted Kentuckians to circle around to the left to outflank the Indians and the legion cavalry to move right to outflank the Indians at the river. At the same time, Wayne ordered the first line of infantry, probably about seven hundred men, "to charge with trailed arms, and rouse the Indians from their coverts at the point of the bayonet, and when up, to deliver a close and directed fire to their backs, followed by a brisk charge, so as not to give them time to load again."[10] Badly outnumbered and with Wayne's troop movements threatening to outflank them, Confederation warriors were soon on the defensive. Under pressure, Tecumseh on the left, and Tarhe and Caldwell on the right, led a fighting, controlled withdrawal. Unable to either directly stop Wayne's advance or to outflank him, Blue Jacket could not maintain the fight. The battle was over in barely more than an hour.

Many of the retreating warriors sought refuge in Fort Miamis. But the fort's commander, Major William Campbell, refused to open the gates to his supposed Indian allies. Campbell's overriding priorities were to avoid giving Wayne a reason to attack the fort and to avoid accidently sparking a war between Britain and the United States. Blue Jacket later described the scene: "They have often promised to help us and at last, when we could not withstand the army that came against us, and we went to the English fort for refuge, the English told us, 'I cannot let you in. You are painted too much, my children.' It was then we saw the British dealt treacherously with us."[11]

With the Indians forced to retreat farther north, Wayne's men set more vegetable fields ablaze for miles along the Maumee. Again the Indians would face a severe food shortage.

The number of Native Americans killed was in the thirties or forties. Egushawa, Little Otter, and Tarhe were among the wounded. Antoine Lasselles was captured. Wayne's casualties have been reported as 44 to 47 killed and 89 to 103 wounded. Wayne reported 2 officers and 42 men killed, including 11 who died of their wounds, plus 7 officers and 82 men wounded.[12] The psychological damage to the Confederation was strategically worse than the military defeat. Native American confidence in the British shattered on the closed gates of Fort Miamis. Confederation leaders had understood for years that their success required substantial logistical support from the British. With the British no longer seen as trustworthy friends, self-confidence in their capacity to prevail in the struggle for Ohio was undercut.

In October, the abandoned site where Kekionga and Miamitown had long flourished saw new construction. It was Fort Wayne.

Nevertheless, it was not until six months later, on February 22, 1795, that the Shawnee, Delaware, Three Fires, Wyandot, and Miami agreed to cease hostilities, exchange prisoners, and meet Wayne for a peace conference in June. Exercising the authority given to him by President Washington, Wayne made this agreement without consulting, or even informing, Governor St. Clair. Like the public, St. Clair had to read a proclamation that began, "By his Excellency Anthony Wayne, Esquire, Major-General and Commander-in-chief of the Legion, and Commissioner Plenipotentiary of the United States of America for establishing a permanent peace with all of the Indian tribes and the nations north-west of the Ohio."[13]

Gradually, more than 1,100 Shawnee, plus the tribes of the Miami nation, the Ottawa, Ojibwe, Potawatomi, Wyandot, Delaware, Kickapoo, and Kaskaskia (an Illinois tribe) gathered for the peace conference. The leaders of the Maumee Confederation attending included Little Turtle, Blue Jacket, Buckongahelas, Egushawa, and Tarhe.

When Tarhe rose to speak on July 22, though he addressed General Wayne as "Elder Brother," his first words might have sounded ominous:

Elder Brother: Now listen to us! The Great Spirit above has appointed this day for us to meet together. I shall now deliver my sentiments to you, the Fifteen Fires. I view you lying in a gore of blood; it is to me, an Indian, who has caused it. Our tomahawk yet remains in your head; the English gave it to me to place there.

But Tarhe's next words revealed his real "sentiments":

Elder Brother: I now take the tomahawk out of your head; but, with so much care, that you shall not feel pain or injury. I will now tear a big tree up by the roots, and throw the tomahawk into the cavity, which they occupied, where the waters will wash it away where it can never be found. Now I have buried the hatchet, and I expect that none of my color will ever again find it out. I now tell you, that no one in particular can justly claim this ground, it belongs, in common, to us all; no earthly being has an exclusive right to it; the Great Spirit above is the true and only owner of this soil, and he has given us all an equal right to it.

Brothers: The Fifteen Fires, listen! You now see that we have buried the hatchet; we still see blood around you, which, together with the dirt that comes away with it, we bury with the hatchet, in the hole we have made for them, and replace the great tree as it stood before, so that our children, nor our children's children, can ever again discover it.[14]

During the days of the council, there was much talk of burying the hatchet forever. Though he made some efforts to argue for better terms, Little Turtle told the council that Wayne's "words" were what he had expected.[15] A day later, addressing the Wyandot, Delaware, and Shawnee as the Miami's "uncles," "grandfathers," and "younger brothers," respectively, Little Turtle asked them to consent to the "Fifteen Fires" terms and smoking "the calumet of peace."[16]

With pressure exerted by Wayne to obtain the terms he wanted, and with war no longer considered a viable option by the Confederation leaders, the council was less a negotiation than an acceptance of American terms. The result was the Treaty of Greenville. It was signed on August 3, 1795, nearly four years after a jubilant Maumee Confederation celebrated its victory at the Wabash. All the tribes agreed to the treaty.

Wayne's terms reconfirmed prior treaty concessions and extended Indian land concessions into western Ohio and eastern Indiana. The treaty line ran from the mouth of the Cuyahoga, south to the portage at the Tuscarawas headwaters, west-southwest to the headwaters of the Great Miami near the portage to the St. Marys, west to Fort Recovery, then southwest to the Ohio at the mouth of the Kentucky River.

Sixteen additional strategic sites were forced to be ceded. These included six square miles around Fort Wayne; six square miles around Fort Defiance at the Glaize; twelve square miles at the Maumee Rapids where Fort Miamis stood; six square miles at the mouth of the Maumee; Fort Detroit and the land north, south, and west of it; the island where Fort Michilimackinac stood and the adjacent mainland; six square miles at the mouth of the Chicago River; and twelve square miles at the mouth of the Illinois River. Apparently to emphasize American dominance, the treaty recited that these sites were given as "evidence of the [Indians'] returning friendship" and "confidence in the United States," and for "mutual benefit."[17] Although the treaty then recognized all other land north of the Ohio, east of the Mississippi, and west and south of the Great Lakes as Indian land, it exempted four sites. These included one hundred fifty thousand acres in southern Indiana for George Rogers Clark and his soldiers. The treaty's land acquisitions exceeded American expectations.[18]

The Cherokee did not attend the Greenville conference but soon afterward agreed to leave Ohio and return to their traditional homeland in the south.

The Maumee Confederation's victory at the Wabash succeeded in maintaining Native American control over northwestern Ohio and northeastern Indiana for forty-five months, continuing a free tribal life, albeit in a time of war, and preserving the forest that dominated the landscape. Measured by geography, not by population, further American settlement in Ohio was largely stymied during those years. The ripple effect of the floodgates of settlement remaining closed in northwestern Ohio and northeastern Indiana meant expansion farther west, in the rest of the Northwest and ultimately into the Great Plains, was also impeded. Thousands of lives were impacted, both Native American as well as those of would be white settlers who otherwise would have immigrated west years earlier.

In 1790, whites in the Northwest Territory were estimated to number three thousand. Most were in Ohio. In 1796, there were still only about five thousand whites in Ohio. All lived within fifty miles of the Ohio River.[19] Four years later, the first Ohio census showed a population 45,365.[20] Native Americans were not counted. The land mass for farms and towns increased exponentially with the population. Like a law of physics, what was left for the old forest and its wildlife decreased proportionately.

Had the decisive Native American victory at the Wabash instead been a defeat, the population would have burgeoned years earlier. The Maumee Confederation's resistance bought those extra years for their way of life and for the woodland environment that was home to that life. The eighteenth-century English satirist and Tory politician John Shebbearne advised that "[g]aining time is gaining everything in love, trade and war." Meeting Shebbeare's definition of victory, the Maumee Confederation had gained time. Colonial-Native American conflict began in the early 1600s on the East Coast. Almost three hundred years later, Geronimo and his band, including Lozen, surrendered in the Southwest. Through those centuries, no other battle in the Indian wars impacted as many people as the army's defeat at the Wabash did.

In addition to slowing the timeline of American expansion, the Battle of the Wabash demonstrated the potential for the military and political success of a pan-tribal confederation. In the coming decade, this would aid Tecumseh as he built a new, even broader confederation to oppose the continuing efforts to obtain more Indian land and to further alter the landscape in the Old Northwest. The fundamental issue of whether Native Americans would concede or would resist the expansion of white settlement continued as did the intertwined issue of woodland versus farmland. Tecumseh spoke to these issues as he sought to build a confederation even larger and more powerful than the Maumee Confederation. Twenty years after the Battle of the Wabash, Tecumseh exhorted the Choctaw and the Chickasaw to join this new alliance, arguing that unless every tribe combined together to "check . . . the ambition and avarice of the whites, they will soon conquer us apart and disunited." In part, he spoke of history and evoked the image of the forest:

Where today is the Pequot? Where the Narragansetts, the Mohawks, Pocanokets, and many other once powerful tribes of our race? They have vanished before the avarice and oppression of the white men, as snow before a summer sun. In vain hope of alone defending their ancient possessions, they have fallen in the wars with the white men. Look abroad over their once beautiful country, and what see you now? Naught but the ravages of the pale-face destroyers, meet your eyes. So it will be with you Choctaws and Chickasaws! Soon your mighty forest trees, under the shade of whose wide spreading branches you have played in infancy, sported in boyhood, and now rest your wearied limbs after the fatigue of the chase, will be cut down to fence in the land which the white intruders dare to call their own.[21]

That white expansion must be stopped to preserve their forest home was undoubtedly repeated by Tecumseh as he exhorted tribes to commit to a new confederation. As remembered in Potawatomi oral history, Tecumseh warned that the expanding white population

will destroy these forests whose branches wave in the winds above the graves of your fathers, chanting their praises. If you doubt it, come, go with me eastward or southward a few days' journey along your ancient mi-kan-og [trails] and I will show you a land you once occupied made desolate. There the forests of untold years have been hewn down and cast into the fire! There be-sheck-kee and waw-mawsh-ka-she [the buffalo and the deer], pe-nay-shen and ke-gon [the fowl and fish], are all gone. There the woodland birds, whose sweet songs once pleased your ears, have forsaken the land, never to return. And the wild flowers which your maidens once loved to wear, have all withered and died.[22]

Almost certainly, Tecumseh's warnings about the dire threat to the forest echoed the words he had heard in Shawnee, and in intertribal councils, years earlier from Blue Jacket, Captain Johnny, and others.

Chapter Seventeen

The Investigation
of Defeat

IN HIS BRILLIANT HISTORICAL SATIRE *Flashman*, George MacDonald Fraser writes, "This myth called bravery, which is half-panic, half-lunacy ... pays for all; in England you *can't* be a hero and bad. There's practically a law against it."[1] (Emphasis in original.) Fraser's observation, though made in the context of nineteenth-century England, applies equally to the eighteenth century and England's former American colonies. The influence from English culture, the frontier psyche, and national politics all sought examples of courage more than dissections of failure. Courage as redemption for foolish, arrogant leadership was a theme in one of John Ford's classic westerns, *Fort Apache*. Against the advice of his more experienced subordinate Captain York (John Wayne), Colonel Thursday (Henry Fonda), a Custer-like commander, splits his outnumbered troops and engages the

Apaches. In the battle, Thursday becomes separated from his doomed main force. He chooses to ride to his men and die with them. The Apaches wipe them out but opt not to attack York's remaining unit. Later, speaking to reporters, York has only praise for Thursday, though he knows it was the colonel's refusal to listen and his fatally underestimating the Apaches that led to the deaths of most of the regiment.

His unquestioned bravery would aid St. Clair as he sought to weather the storm of criticism that engulfed him in the aftermath of his disastrous defeat at the Wabash. At stake were both his reputation and his political career.

Five days after the flight from the battlefield, St. Clair wrote to Secretary Knox. He began, "Yesterday afternoon, the remains of the army under my command got back to this place, and I have now the painful task to give you an account of as warm and as unfortunate an action as almost any that has been fought, in which every corps was engaged and worsted, except the first regiment," which had been dispatched to meet the supply train. Despite all the problems that delayed his campaign, despite the militia's abysmal performance, despite the tactical failures, St. Clair's explanation for the catastrophic defeat was simply, "We were overpowered by numbers." With the memory of the hellish morning likely still feeling to St. Clair as if it were an open wound, his conclusion reflected neither analysis nor self-critical introspection. What it did reflect was that a thousand attacking Indians seemed like two thousand or three thousand to the beleaguered general. To his credit, St. Clair acknowledged that the sole basis of his conclusion was "the weight of the fire, which was always a most deadly one, and generally delivered from the ground—few of the enemy shewing themselves afoot, except when they were charged; and that, in a few minutes, our whole camp, which was extended above three hundred and fifty yards in length, was entirely surrounded, and attacked on all quarters."[2]

While mentioning that the Indians shot "from the ground" and generally showed themselves only when they were charged, St. Clair's assessment failed to affirmatively recognize the effectiveness of the Indians' tactics and the concomitant ineffectiveness of his own tactics.

As to detaching the 1st US Regiment days before the battle, St. Clair wrote, "I incline to think it was fortunate: for I very much doubt whether had it been in the action, the fortune of the day had been turned; and if it had not, the triumph of the enemy would have been more complete." Ultimately, he would concede that a contributing factor to the defeat "was the absence of the first regiment."[3]

Not until a "PS" did St. Clair note that the night before the attack, his orders to Oldham to send out patrols "which were of much consequence, were not executed" and that General Butler had not informed him of some "very material intelligence" obtained by Captain Slough's patrol.[4] What, if anything, St. Clair would have done with information from militia patrols or Slough's "material intelligence" was left unsaid.

Later, in response to a congressional investigation, St. Clair asserted that in addition to the Indians' superior numbers, the principal causes of the defeat were the delays resulting from the contractor's failures, the quarter-master's failures, and the conditions on the Ohio River. St. Clair maintained that those delays prevented him from reaching the Maumee before frost destroyed the horses' grazing. He also contended that the delays diminished the effects of Wilkinson's and Scott's raids.[5]

Additionally, St. Clair suggested that the delays resulted in hundreds of Wyandot, Potawatomi, Ottawa, and Ojibwe arriving in time for the battle, "many" just "a few days before the action."[6] The evidence is to the contrary. Warriors were gathering in the summer, hence the need for more British supplies and provisions. There is no credible evidence that a large influx of warriors arrived in late October. Moreover, had the army marched in August instead of September, warriors from outside the Maumee could simply have responded to the earlier threat. St. Clair admittedly planned on potentially being opposed by a force of 1,200 to 1,400 Indians.[7] Not only was he not outnumbered, he was opposed by fewer than what he anticipated he might have to face.

St. Clair listed desertion among the contributing factors. Paradoxically, he did not include the expiration of levy enlistments.[8]

As to their conduct in battle, St. Clair praised his troops:

[They were] beaten after [an] obstinate struggle by a greatly superior force . . . [having] continued the combat until two thirds of their number were stretched upon the ground. . . . All this happened to our little beaten, but not disgraced army, and would have shed a lustre upon the best disciplined troops in the world. They were not disciplined, but their native valour supplied the want of it.

[N]o troops ever behaved with more firmness, or charged the enemy with the bayonet with more intrepidity; neither did the officers of any army display, on any occasion, more gallantry or make greater exertions, of which the great number who fell or were wounded, is a melancholy proof.[9]

Although the president may have heard rumors that St. Clair's army had been defeated, he probably received St. Clair's dispatch to Knox on December 9, while he and Martha Washington were entertaining guests.[10] Staying in control, he concealed his emotions until their guests departed. Once they were gone, Washington exploded with fury. He immediately assumed that the disaster was due to St. Clair's failing to heed his warning not to fall victim to a surprise attack. As a colonial officer serving under British General Edward Braddock in 1755, Washington had survived the disastrous Battle of the Monongahela. That engrained in Washington the need to avoid being surprised by an Indian attack. Although the militia was surprised, the main body of the army was in formation when the attack came. Washington's reaction suggests that he too failed to consider the possibility of the American army being outmaneuvered and outfought. St. Clair's defeat had more in common with Washington's own ignominious defeat as a young, inexperienced commander at Fort Necessity in 1754, where he chose to defend a position that turned into a trap.

Like his commander, Colonel Darke did not understand why the army had been decimated. He wrote to Washington, declaring that if given command of the army he would march on the Miami towns and retake the lost cannons. Darke assured Washington that the Indians had "Lost Many of their bravest Warriors" and had been greatly "weakened."[11] In writing of his bayonet charge, Darke had no idea that he had fallen into the trap of the Indians' run-and-hit tactic. With no evidence other than the course of the battle, Darke expressed the belief that several white officers were with the Indians, as if they could not have maintained their attack without such assistance. This was not merely factually incorrect. It revealed a racist underestimation of Indian military prowess.

Though not in the army, wagoner Thomas Irwin showed more insight:

The troops on that campaign ought to have been drilled 8 or 10 months and learned them how to handle a gun. I think a number never had handled a gun or shot one. There was two excellent companies of artilary men commanded by Capt'ns Bradford and Ford. If they would have had a good breast-work to shelter thmselves all the Indians that was there could not have fazed them. That battle always reminded me of one of those thunderstorms that comes up quick and rapidly.[12]

Irwin's critique about untrained troops was correct. But even trained troops would not have had much success shooting at a well-concealed enemy. Irwin's second critique was partially correct. A breastwork would have reduced the rate of artillery casualties. It would not, however, have fully protected the artillery battalion, nor would it have changed the futility of their cannon blasts.

Unlike his general, Colonel Sargent realized that the army was not overwhelmed by a vast number of Indians. He estimated that there were more than one thousand but did not suggest that there were many more than that. Totally discounting the 80 military servants, the 220 outpost guards, all of the militia, and the civilians, Sargent considered the army's "efficient numbers" to be only 1,080.[13] While somewhat overstated, his point that the army's effective strength was substantially reduced at the very beginning of the attack was valid.

Sargent accurately described all but the 2nd US Regiment as "raw and undisciplined troops, *ignorant totally of the Indian and indeed all other mode of fighting* . . . new raised troops . . . without the time for instruction and never having fired even a blank cartridge."[14] (Emphasis added.) Though almost certainly unintended, this assessment implicitly faulted the political and military command structure from the top through at least the regimental commanders. It was Washington, Knox, and Congress who decided that six-month levies would constitute much of the army and that they would rely on militia to bring the expedition up to an acceptable number. As for the senior officers in the field, with days and weeks of waiting at Forts Pitt, Washington, Hamilton, and Jefferson, was there really no time for drills or for musket training?

Three months later, Sargent was with the army detachment that returned to the site of the battle to try to recover the lost cannons. They still mistakenly thought they were at the St. Marys. Sargent could not accept that the choice of ground on which to camp was a tactical error, writing:

The immediate spot of the encampment appears very strong, and is *certainly so defensible against regular troops* that I believe any military man who has not had the fatal experience of the late misfortune would unhesitatingly have pitched upon it. It is, however, (I must confess) *surrounded by close woods, thick bushes and old logs, which afford the best cover for an Indian attack*; but these appear now to be very much increased since I observed them before the action.[15] (Emphasis added.)

Regardless of how they appeared to Sargent, the woods and bushes did not increase during the intervening three months of late fall and winter.

Unlike St. Clair and Darke, Sargent credited Native American tactics. He was among the few to recognize "the superiority of the Indian mode of fighting."[16]

Just before Christmas, John Armstrong, a general in the Continental army, wrote to President Washington. Armstrong first received acclaim as the "Hero of Kittanning" for leading a raid against a Delaware village on the Pennsylvania frontier during the French and Indian War. Armstrong criticized the use of standard army tactics and the reliance on artillery, which resulted in troops being a static, "large and visible object, perhaps in close order too, to an enemy near enough to destroy" them. Armstrong noted that Indians were known to be able to fight while "comparatively invisible." While St. Clair and others talked of how the Americans had been badly outnumbered, Armstrong concluded "that five hundred Indians were fully sufficient" to have destroyed the army.[17]

The day after Christmas, Secretary Knox issued his own assessment of the campaign. He concluded that the "principal causes" of St. Clair's defeat were: "1st. A deficient number of good troops, according to the expectation, in the early part of the year. 2d. Their want of *sufficient discipline, according to the nature of the service.* 3d. *The lateness of season.*"[18] (Emphasis in original.)

Knox added that "another cause" was that instead of the originally estimated 1,200 Indians, there were actually "somewhere about three thousand," with the increase coming from Wyandot, Delaware, Potawatomi, Ottawa and Chippewa (Ojibwe).[19] In this, Knox and his sources of information were wrong.

Controversy continued to swirl around St. Clair and the army's disaster. On March 26, 1792, St. Clair wrote to inform Washington that he wished to resign his military commission for health reasons, but not before a court of inquiry was held. St. Clair expected that such a court would exonerate him, as Harmar had been exonerated seven months earlier. Nevertheless, in his letter to the president, St. Clair acknowledged that if "the result of the inquiry be that" he had neglected any duty, or failed to take advantage of every opportunity, or that the army was "delayed one moment" by his illness, he would "patiently submit to the merited censure."[20] Washington responded two days later, explaining that it was impossible to grant St. Clair's request because the army lacked enough officers of sufficient rank to form a court for a major general.[21]

By the end of March, the House of Representatives provided the inquiry St. Clair wanted when it directed a committee to determine why the campaign failed. This was the nation's first congressional investigation. It would soon lead to the first invocation of what we now call executive privilege.

St. Clair wrote to Washington again on March 31, explaining that he preferred to maintain his commission until the congressional inquiry concluded, to avoid public perception that he was resigning because of the "volume of calumny and defamation, invented by malice, which is daily pouring from the press into the public ear."[22] Nevertheless, he offered to resign if necessary. On April 4, the president responded. While expressing sympathy for his position, Washington told St. Clair that his resignation was necessary, as the law allowed for only one major general and "the essential interests of the public require that your successor should be immediately appointed, in order to repair to the frontiers."[23] Three days later, St. Clair formally resigned his commission.

Before holding hearings, the House first sought all relevant documents from Secretary Knox. To consider this request, Washington met with Knox and the rest of his cabinet, Jefferson, Hamilton, and Attorney General Edmund Randolph. All agreed that the House was entitled to make an inquiry and could make a general request for papers. There was also unanimous agreement that the executive had discretion to determine what papers should be produced and that documents should be withheld if producing them would harm "the public good." It was also decided that the congressional request should have been directed to the president, not to the secretary of war. Following conversations between Cabinet members and congressmen, a new request was issued, directed to the president. This time the request sought "such papers of a public nature, in the Executive Department, as may be necessary to the investigation of the causes of the failure of the late expedition under Major General St. Clair." The addition of the word "public" to the request signaled an acceptance that the executive might have relevant papers that were private and could remain confidential. After determining that the public good did not require withholding anything, there was full compliance with this request, and all papers deemed relevant were produced. Without any real controversy, the principle of executive privilege was established.[24]

Having received the documents, the House committee heard from witnesses, including survivors of the campaign. Issues concerning the quality of the army's gunpowder, its weapons, and its tents were put into perspective. Some gunpowder got wet from the rain, but no one claimed the army lacked enough gunpowder during the battle. The inspector of the army, Colonel Francis Mentges testified that neither the quantity nor quality of the army's guns caused any delay. He correctly concluded that although only two battalions had tents that kept the rain out, bad tents were simply not a cause of the defeat.[25]

At the conclusion of the hearings, the committee made findings and reached conclusions concerning what had occurred, what caused the defeat, and St. Clair's performance. Among the committee's factual findings were, "[t]he army was delayed five or six days in their march from Fort Jefferson,

for the want of provisions, and the season was so far advanced, that sufficient green forage for the horses could not be procured," which led to the
loss of many of the horses. St. Clair's orders were "express and unequivocal,
to proceed with the expedition, so much as . . . to preclude the commander-
in-chief from exercising any discretion" about whether to continue. The
committee concluded that "the principal causes . . . of the failure" of the expedition were:

The delay in furnishing the materials and estimates for, and in passing the act for
the protection of the frontiers; the time after the passing of which was hardly sufficient to complete and discipline an army for such an expedition, during the summer months of the same year.

The delays consequent upon the various gross mismanagements and neglects
in the quarter master's and contractor's departments: the lateness of the season at
which the expedition was undertaken, the green forage having previously been destroyed by the frost, so that a sufficiency of subsistence for the horses, necessary
for the army, could not be procured.

The want of discipline and experience in the troops.

Exonerating St. Clair, the report concluded:

The committee conceive it but justice to the commander in chief, to say, that in their
opinion, the failure of the late expedition can in no respect be imputed to his conduct,
either at any time before or during the action; but that, as his conduct, in all the
preparatory arrangements, was marked with peculiar ability and zeal, so his conduct,
during the action, furnished strong testimonies of his coolness and intrepidity.[26]

On February 15, 1793, the House committee submitted a supplemental
report. Various factual details were revised. But the conclusions regarding
the principal causes of the defeat and the exoneration of St. Clair remained
unchanged.[27]

The subjects the committee omitted were as significant as its findings
and conclusions. None of the following was deemed to be a cause of the defeat:

Failing to obtain a guide.

Failing to obtain scouts capable of effective long-range reconnaissance.

Reducing the effective fighting force by three hundred men, plus officers,
when Hamtramck's regiment was ordered south to meet the supply train.

Choosing a campsite surrounded by cover that attacking Indians could
and did use.

Not considering the artillery's line of fire.

Standing to fire volleys against unseen Indians.

The bayonet charges from the rear line and the final bayonet charge from the front line, charges that cost heavy casualties without gaining more than a momentary advantage.

The Indians' successful tactics.

Omitting all of these matters from its list of the "principal causes" of the defeat implied that every battlefield decision, by the army and by the Indians, was ultimately inconsequential. That implication was clearly erroneous.

This was the extent to which the committee's report said anything related to these subjects:

[T]he first regiment was detached with a view to cover a convoy of provisions which was expected, and which it was supposed was in danger from the deserted militia, and to prevent further desertions. . . . [S]everal charges were made by part of the army, which caused the enemy to give way, but produced no good effect; the attack was unexpected . . . the fire of the army was constant, but not well directed . . . the commander in chief appears to have been cool and deliberate in the whole of the action, and the officers in general active and intrepid; the whole order of march, as far as the committee are capable of expressing on opinion, appears to have been judicious, and the ground for action well chosen.[28]

In trying to understand the committee's thinking, it is plausible that the committee did not understand the causal effect of some of the mistakes that were made and that St. Clair benefitted from goodwill he accrued while serving in the Confederation Congress. It seems unlikely, though, that these two factors are sufficient to explain all of the committee's omissions. What does seem likely is that the personal bravery St. Clair exhibited overshadowed the hard truths of his questionable and failed decisions. Likewise, the committee made no mention of Oldham's failure to have early patrols out the morning of the attack. Nor was there a word about Butler's failure to inform St. Clair of Slough's patrol. Criticizing officers who demonstrated courage under withering fire, two of them among the dead, apparently felt unseemly, ill mannered, or inappropriate. Those feelings may also help explain the generally positive image of Red-Haired Nance, a woman who proved her courage armed with a frying pan yet broke under immeasurable stress and abandoned her infant. It was almost as if bravery created a protective bubble against disapproval.

What causes victory and defeat is often a complex tapestry of the skill of the victors and the mistakes of the vanquished—not infrequently interwoven with luck. For the Battle of the Wabash, the outcome was no accident. The causal factors broadly fall into five categories. Two are the effective planning and skillfully executed tactics of the Maumee Confederation. The other three are the army's organizational, informational, and battlefield failures.

The Confederation chiefs utilized the intelligence reports they obtained and their knowledge of how the army and the militia fought and reacted. Thus, they rushed the militia but began a battle of attrition against the regulars and the levies, taking care not to expose their warriors. Then, the run-and-hit tactic countered the bayonet charges. Armstrong alluded to the effectiveness of the Indian tactics in his letter to the president. Sargent privately recognized the "superiority" of Indian tactics in his diary.

The House committee did address the American organizational failures. The first was the fundamentally flawed plan from President Washington and Secretary Knox that was approved by Congress. The timetable for recruiting and marching from Fort Washington was simply too short. Intertwined with this was the reliance on six-month levy enlistments for half of the army's strength. That the 1791 timetable and the use of six-month levies were serious mistakes was tacitly admitted by the unhurried timetable and disuse of levies for Wayne's campaign.

Exacerbating these problems were the abysmal logistics due to the misfeasance and malfeasance of Hodgdon, the quartermaster general, and Duer, the War Department's general contractor. The committee was correct that St. Clair was not responsible for these organizational failures. He was responsible for the last organizational mistake, sending the entire 1st US Regiment back down the trace after the militia desertion on October 31.

The organizational failures cost time and morale, which in turn resulted in the loss of levies whose enlistments expired, more desertions, and dispatching the 1st US. Thus, ultimately, they left St. Clair with substantially fewer fighting men, as well as with troops with little to no training. This may have doomed the campaign to failure. It did not, however, control the course of the battle or doom the army to the devastation it suffered.

The informational failures of not obtaining a guide and of inadequate scouting were St. Clair's. Had there been a capable guide, the army most likely would have followed a better route and never been near the ill-fated site at the Wabash. Of course, whether that would have resulted in a campsite with terrain less favorable to the Indians' attack cannot be known. A more direct route would have increased the possibility of Sparks and Piominko intersecting the Confederation force moving toward the army. When the Chickasaws arrived, St. Clair failed to use any of them to scout defensively. More than one thousand approaching Indians went undiscovered. This was the one deficiency Denny acknowledged in his journal.

General St. Clair, General Butler, Colonel Sargent, and the regimental commanders, Colonel Darke, Colonel Gibson, and Major Heart, shared varying degrees of responsibility for camping in terrain that favored an Indian attack, for having their troops exchange musket fire from exposed positions, and from undisciplined bayonet charges. Darke's bayonet charge, in particular, was problematic. He futilely chased after Indians for hundreds of yards while others who had essentially sidestepped his charge pierced Darke's depleted rear line. Other battle-site failures were Butler's choosing not to inform St. Clair of Slough's intelligence, Oldham not getting patrols out as ordered, and placing the cannons without calculating their field of fire.

Ultimately, what happened at the Wabash resulted from superior Native American planning and tactics. The magnitude of the Maumee Confederation's victory and the army's defeat speaks to the degree to which better planning and tactics controlled the course of the battle.

EPILOGUE: ENDURING LESSONS

It is easier not to engage in the often-difficult and sometimes-stressful work of planning. But planning generally increases the chances for success, be it in war, politics, negotiations, business, or games. The starting point for planning is to gather information. This should be an ongoing process because even after a plan is put into effect, new information may show that the plan needs to be modified. Information is an asset. Closely related to gathering information is recognizing informational gaps.[1] This is also an ongoing process.

Just as planning increases the chances for success, information and understanding what is uncertain or unknown increases the ability to plan effectively. To borrow a phrase from Eric Rodwell, winner of seven world bridge championships, life "is a game of incomplete information."[2] Frequently, decisions must be made in the harsh context of uncertainty, without the benefit of complete information. It is crucial to be aware of the degree to which decisions are based on assumptions, on inferences, on opinions, on faith, on possible or probable facts, or on definite facts. Recognizing that a decision is based entirely, or in part, on an assumption, an inference, an opinion, a belief, or on possible or probable facts enables us to judge the level of confidence the decision merits. Comprehensive planning requires alternatives to address what may happen when events do not go as expected.

THE MAUMEE CONFEDERATION PLANNING AND TACTICS

Before the war council met, the strength and movement of the oncoming American army was gathered from scouts, from prisoners, and from deserters. To this the chiefs added their knowledge of how the army fought and of how the militia fought. Taking another step in the planning process, the chiefs assessed the strengths and weaknesses of their warriors and of their opponents.[3] In doing so, they recognized important differences between the militia and the army. This enabled them the to visualize how to attack, as well as how the battle could and should proceed. Thus, they chose their strategy and tactics.[4] The last key piece of information came when they observed where the army and the militia were camped and saw the gift of abundant cover in the surrounding terrain.

Critical to their plan was what not to do. Their warriors must have been told in the strongest terms not to charge the army's line in the initial attack. Instead, they were to find cover and begin the process of attrition, until the army's lines were so weakened that they could be penetrated with few casualties. At the Wabash, Native American warriors followed that plan to near perfection. Had they immediately rushed the knoll in a bloodthirsty frenzy, they would have run into volleys of musket fire. The entire course of the battle might have been altered. Ironically, by not immediately charging up the rise, the Indians exhibited more discipline than the army displayed in Darke's bayonet charge.

THE ARMY'S ORGANIZATIONAL DECISIONS

There was planning for the army's campaign. President Washington and Secretary Knox planned the expansion of the army, the reliance on levies and militia, building forts, and the goals of the campaign. St. Clair's plans were reflected in his orders of march, of encampment, and of battle. Both the process and the product of their plans, however, were deeply flawed.

How could men as intelligent as Washington and Knox, former generals with years of wartime experience, plan the army's expansion and the ensuing campaign with such an unreasonably tight schedule? Most likely, feeling pressure to act decisively, they imagined the best-case scenario without considering either the probability that all would not go as rapidly as they hoped or the consequences if it did not. Blinded by optimism, they confused what they wanted to be true with the realities of circumstances beyond their control. Unconsciously, decision making was dominated by emotion rather than by objective reasoning. It is an aspect of the human condition that clouds decision-making as much today as it did centuries ago. Millions of people believe false claims because they want to believe them, disregarding the utter lack of any actual evidence for the claims. How to avoid this decision-making pitfall could fill volumes by experts in various fields. Here, suffice it to say that consciously attempting the hard work of objective analysis is a useful first step.

When Washington and Knox knew the campaign was significantly behind schedule, they might have given St. Clair discretion to stop if he deemed it unwise to continue, despite the embarrassment and the money spent on the levies. Alternatively, they might have directed St. Clair to stop building forts, or given him discretion to do so, or directed him to leave a small force behind to construct the forts while moving ahead with the rest of the army.

It appears that Washington and Knox were what poker players call pot committed. Instead of being flexible and adjusting to a changing, frustrating situation, their thinking was rigid. Having invested money, resources, and prestige, when the odds worsened, they demanded that fate deliver the victory they needed. Even men like Washington and Knox can fall victim to such unconsciously emotional decision-making.

Thorough planning helps to avoid this pitfall. Whether recruitment and moving the army across the country might suffer delays were certainly foreseeable possibilities. Their plans should have included contingencies for what to do if delays occurred, with decisions made before frustrations reached a boiling point.

Why were hiring a guide and obtaining capable, long-range scouts not priorities? Knox had first suggested a regiment of five hundred rangers and then suggested recruiting fifty to one hundred Iroquois and Chickasaw scouts. In raising and organizing the expedition's forces, a unit of rangers could have been formed to provide ongoing scouting. St. Clair must have known of Rogers' Rangers exploits with the British army during the French and Indian War. And in 1774, St. Clair led an effort to raise a company of rangers to patrol the Pennsylvania frontier to counter the threat of Indian war parties.

Nevertheless, in organizing his expedition, not even a small unit of rangers was formed. A guide and good scouts could have kept St. Clair informed as to where the army was, how they could best reach the Maumee, and what was ahead of them. Literally and metaphorically, St. Clair proceeded without knowing the path to his goal.

The implicit judgment was that the army, with its Revolutionary War officers, artillery, and bayonets, was too powerful, even with largely untrained, inexperienced troops, to be defeated by any force of supposedly undisciplined Indians. Confident that the Indians would not attack and that his men would defeat them if they did, it seems St. Clair thought a guide and long-range scouts might be helpful but were by no means necessary. In this, he undervalued acquiring basic information.

Symptomatic of misplaced conventional thinking and overconfidence were the officers' servants and the women and children. Taking eighty soldiers out of their combat roles and assigning them as officers' servants, if not inappropriate from the beginning, became so as the number of troops shrank.

Following the custom of allowing women and children, unnecessary noncombatants, to accompany the expedition badly underestimated the danger involved. Dozens died who never should have been near the battlefield.

DETACHING THE 1ST US REGIMENT

Why did St. Clair dispatch Major Hamtramck and the 1st US Regiment, lowering his troop strength by more than three hundred, in response to sixty to seventy militia deserting? St. Clair's threefold explanation was that he did so to protect the oncoming large supply train, to deter additional militia desertions, and to possibly apprehend the deserters. But that raises the question of why he chose his most experienced regiment and sent the entire unit.

While protecting the supply train was critical, dispatching Hamtramck's entire regiment was out of proportion to the threat posed by the militia. St. Clair could hardly have thought that man for man the militia were more dangerous than the Indians. One hundred to one hundred fifty troops could have been sent. His order must have stemmed from his conviction that the Indians would not attack. St. Clair's conviction that an attack was unlikely, however, was really no more than conjecture.

Even if St. Clair's opinion had been based on better evidence, risk should be evaluated both quantitatively, by the likelihood it will occur, and qualitatively, by its degree of danger. Weakening his force by unnecessarily detaching the 1st US Regiment failed to account for the lethal risk if an attack came.

Despite changing circumstances, St. Clair never seriously considered modifying the campaign plan. One moment to do so was the arrival of the Kentucky militia at Fort Washington. As Winthrop Sargent and Ensign Piercy Pope each observed, most of the militiamen were clearly unfit for Indian fighting. Add to that the dismal performance of the militia infantry in Harmar's campaign. It would have taken political courage to send most of the militia back to Kentucky. Whether St. Clair ever regretted not doing so is speculative. If he had sent them back, the mass desertion would have been avoided and the 1st US Regiment would have been in the fight.

THE ARMY'S BATTLE SITE DECISIONS

It appears that St. Clair and his senior officers acted on a number of assumptions as if they were immutable facts. That conventional tactics would work as well against Indians as they did against European troops. That Indians could not withstand bayonet charges. That Indians could never overrun the army's camp or win a pitched battle against the valor and discipline of an American army.

In choosing where to encamp and in fighting with standing lines of infantry firing volleys, St. Clair and his senior officers commanded as if they were fighting the British or the French. Certainly, had the Maumee Confederation warriors marched out of the woods, across the clearing, and through the bottomland, then charged up the knoll as if it were Bunker Hill, they would have taken heavy casualties. The outcome, if not an American victory, might have been a costly draw. Even the artillery would have been useful against an opposing army marching hundreds of yards across open land. Of course, that type of attack was never going to happen. St. Clair, Butler, and their regimental commanders followed their methods and routines from the Revolutionary War. None had commanded troops in a battle against Native Americans.

Clearly, it is essential to know one's craft. If not already known, learning it must be an essential part of information gathering. St. Clair, Butler, Sargent, Darke, Gibson, and Heart failed to learn the best methods for Indian fighting. Nor did they take the next step and imagine, visualize, or mentally script out how the Indians might attack; what would happen to infantry standing in the open; what might be more effective than maintaining static, exposed positions; what the Indians might do next after running from bayonet charges; whether extended bayonet charges would undermine defending the camp's perimeter; or other battlefield scenarios.

Meticulous planning requires contemplating how the battle, the negotiation, or the interaction may proceed, what scenarios may transpire, and what contingencies may be needed. While military war games did not start to become an accepted practice for over a century, the best leaders have always understood how to think through alternate scenarios that may ensue.[5]

The placement of the artillery was the nadir of the army's planning. Certainly, not just St. Clair but also Major Ferguson and the artillery officers bore responsibility. So did Butler and Darke as the commanders of the front and rear lines. There could not have been any thought given to where attacking Indians would be or to where cannon balls and cannister would strike from the battery positions.

Suppose that General St. Clair, or General Butler, or Colonels Sargent, Darke, and Gibson, or Major Heart, anticipated a battle in which the Indians would "seldom expose their persons to danger, and depend entirely upon their dexterity in concealing themselves during an engagement, never appearing openly, unless they have struck their enemies with terror, and have thereby rendered them incapable of defense." Suppose any of them had visualized that when he was "attacked by the savages":

"He cannot discover them, tho' from every tree, log or bush, he receives an incessant fire, and observes that few of their shots are lost. He will not hesitate to charge those invisible enemies, but he will charge in vain. For they are as cautious to avoid a close engagement, as indefatigable in harassing his troops; and notwithstanding all his endeavors, he will still find himself surrounded by a circle of fire, which, like an artificial horizon, follows him everywhere.

"Unable to rid himself of an enemy who never stands his attacks, and flies when pressed, only to return upon him again with equal agility and vigour; he will see the courage of his heavy troops droop, and their strength at last fail them by repeated and ineffectual efforts."

What if they had learned that the Indians fought guided by three principles:

"The first, that their general maxim is to surround their enemy.

The second, that they fight scattered, and never in a compact body.

The third, that they never stand their ground when attacked, but immediately give way, to return to the charge."[6]

All of these descriptions come from William Smith's *An Historical Account of the Expedition against the Ohio Indians, in the MDCCLXIV. Under the Command of Henry Bouquet Esq., Colonel of Foot, and Now Brigadier General in America*. Smith explained that his depiction of a futile effort to defend against an Indian attack was "not an imaginary supposition, but the true state of an engagement with the Indians, experienced by the troops who have fought against them."[7]

Smith was the provost of the College of Philadelphia. His account of Bouquet's expedition was published in Philadelphia in 1765. Over the next thirteen years, later editions and printings were published in London, Amsterdam, Dublin, and Paris. It has been described as "the most widely circulated and read work on warfare and diplomacy in the Ohio country to emerge following the Seven Years' War [whose] literary reputation and impact . . . surpassed all similar contemporary works published on either side of the Atlantic."[8]

It is very likely that St. Clair would have heard of it and that the book would have been of interest to him. In 1765, St. Clair and his wife were prospering in the Ligonier Valley. Bouquet marched from Fort Ligonier the day before Bushy Run. Whether St. Clair or any of his officers read Smith's *Historical Account* is unknown, though St. Clair claimed he had "joined theory to practice, by an attentive perusal of the best military books, in most languages."[9] If St. Clair did attentively peruse Smith, twenty-five years later either he had forgotten it or he decided he knew more than Smith did.

Beyond describing the Indians' methods, Smith also warned of a mistake to avoid and explained a countermeasure to employ. Troops "are not to be drawn up in close order, which would only expose them without necessity to a greater loss."[10] "When the firing begins, the troops will have orders to fall on their knees, to be less exposed till it is thought proper to attack."[11] Smith's admonitions were consistent with Rogers' "Rules of Ranging." Unknown, forgotten, or disregarded were the instructions written in 1757 by the continent's most renowned Indian fighter. Rogers' seventh rule of ranging began: "If you are obliged to receive the enemy's fire, fall, or squat down, till it is all over; then rise and discharge at them." It continued:

"If the enemy push upon you, let your front fire and fall down, and then let your rear advance thro' them and do the like, by which time those who before were in front will be ready to discharge again, and repeat the same alternatively, as occasion shall require, by this means you will keep up such a constant fire, that the enemy will not be able to easily break your order, or gain your ground."[12]

Smith and Rogers would have scoffed at the notion that American valor and discipline alone would prevail over the Indians. Or that bayonet charges would rout them. Rogers and Smith knew better.

Nor, despite the talk of discipline, were the army's bayonet charges planned so they would maintain the control and cohesion explicated in Bland's *Treatise*. While following Bland's teachings still would not have routed the Maumee Confederation warriors, it might, at least, have minimized the army's casualties.

From the conception to the destruction of St. Clair's expedition, too many decisions were rooted in misunderstanding Native American tactics, confusing hope and opinion with fact, and in arrogant overconfidence tinged with an attitude of racial superiority. Closed-mindedness naturally followed. Add to this the fatigue, carelessness, and interpersonal conflict that burdened the army when it camped on November 3, and the recipe for disaster was complete.

Confidence is often helpful and sometimes necessary. Arrogant overconfidence is often fatal. Too much uncertainty can create paralyzing fear. Too little can create a false sense of security. The right amount is a gift, unmasking what we do not know. It is an aspect of what Zen Buddhism calls "beginner's mind" (*shoshin*). In part, it motivates realistic appraisals of alternative possibilities.

Today, centuries after the 1791 campaign that culminated along the Wabash, too often the effort required for thorough, effective planning is still not made. Gathering objective, reliable information is too often undervalued, assumptions and beliefs are treated as hard facts, and fallacious certitude overlooks uncertainties and ignores contingencies. This complicates our so-called culture wars and generates false issues. By working to escape this self-defeating mental maze, we can ease our conflicts and illuminate the real issues.

In the blood-soaked conflict over the Old Northwest, there was wisdom, folly, courage, determination, and savagery on both sides. Focused on its frontier and beyond was the agrarian-minded, ambitiously expansive, young American republic. Inhabiting the frontier and beyond were the woodland Native American tribes, living on the bounty of nature and their vegetable gardens, their boys raised to be warriors. Inextricably linked to this clash of disparate cultures was the fate of the vast forest.

While Ohio and Indiana were once 95 percent and 90 percent woodlands, respectively, 120 years after the Battle of the Wabash, only 10 percent of Ohio and less than 7 percent of Indiana were forested.[13] While that has tripled through the twentieth century and into the twenty-first, only 4 percent of Ohio woodlands, barely more than 1 percent of Ohio land, and only about 3 percent of Indiana woodlands, less than 1 percent of Indiana land, is publicly owned, protected forest.[14] Even with reforestation and the return of some wildlife, it is not the same old-growth forest that once existed.

Carbon storage is the lifetime accumulation of carbon, sometimes referred to in terms of carbon dioxide or CO_2e. The latter encompasses all carbon gases, not just CO_2. Carbon accumulates not only in the trees but also in the other plants, the forest floor, and the soil.

To explore the magnitude of the deforestation, suppose that the Maumee Confederation had succeeded and had maintained 14 million acres of the Ohio forest, a little less than 50 percent of the original acreage, as the equivalent of national forest. As of 2020, 8.1 million acres of Ohio forest were storing approximately 610 million metric tons of carbon.[15] Fourteen million acres of forest, hundreds of years old, would far exceed that amount through a combination of acreage and because of the greater carbon storage capacity of older forests. If our hypothetical forest existed, the amount of carbon sequestration, the current or annual intake of carbon, would also be dramatically higher, and greater biodiversity would have been preserved. The imbalance of nature that concerned Humboldt and Madison, and the effects of viewing the forest as an obstacle to be cleared, continue to impact us today.

The struggle of indigenous people to control their lands and block the powerful forces of deforestation continues. A five-year study in the Brazilian Amazon found that indigenously controlled land lost seventeen times less vegetation than was lost in uncontrolled areas.[16] It also found that the indigenous controlled areas contributed two to three times more regrowth of native vegetation than in uncontrolled land. Naturally, this also preserves the rich biodiversity in these areas. A long-term study of Wisconsin forests also found that indigenously controlled forests overall have more mature trees, higher tree volumes, higher rates of tree regeneration, more plant diversity, and fewer invasive species, and are more accommodating to wolves and other predators, than comparable nontribal, public-managed forests.[17]

Control requires legal title. In the Peruvian Amazon, helped by the Centro para el Desarrollo del Indígena Amazónico (Center for the Development of the Amazonian Indigenous) and the Rainforest Trust, more than 150 indigenous communities have gained title to millions of acres, allowing them to sustainably manage their lands.[18] Titling these traditional communities recognizes their long history of occupancy and land management.

This work is continuing. In Peru, efforts are underway to help 160 indigenous communities secure control and legal title to more than 3.825 million acres of their traditional rainforest lands. This will preserve the natural ecosystem and prevent land grabs for megafarms and commercial logging.[19] In the Brazilian Amazon, the Rainforest Trust and the Instituto Internacional de Educação do Brasil (The International Institute of Education of Brazil) have begun a project to protect 2,262,878 acres in five reserves where fewer than eight thousand people dwell. As in Peru, this project will seek to place title with the indigenous communities and to jointly develop long-term plans to preserve the natural ecosystems.[20]

Now, the fate of the earth's remaining forests, from Alaska's Tongass to the Amazon to Borneo's Danum Valley, is inextricably tied to our conflict with climate change. It is a conflict that people have been losing, in large part because of short-term greed, relentless carbon emissions, and continued deforestation. Like the Maumee Confederation, we are in a battle to preserve our homes, our way of life, and our environment. As the nation once envisioned and committed itself to expansion, as essential for future generations, we have to envision and commit to a carbon-neutral, biodiverse world, creating it for our own sake and the sake of future generations. Repairing the environment is a sine qua non for prosperity and national security.[21] Unlike the St. Clair expedition, we have to understand where we are, appreciate the existential danger we face, plan effectively, think flexibly, and choose efficacious strategies and tactics. Now as then, "the work is play for mortal stakes."[22]

NOTES

INTRODUCTION

1. St. Marys is the spelling used by the US Geological Survey. US Geological Survey, St. Marys River at Rockford, OH-04180988,https://waterdata.usgs.gov/monitoring-location/04180988/#parameterCode=00065&period=P7D&showMedian=false. The name is sometimes written as St. Mary's.

2. Mingo is the tribal name commonly used by whites in the 1700s and in histories for over two hundred years. It was not used by the tribe itself, except in dealing with whites. The people to whom it applied were mostly Seneca who migrated west and settled in Ohio. Other tribal members came from the Cayuga. A small number also came from other tribes. The tribe's name for itself now is Seneca-Cayuga. Muriel H. Wright, "A Guide to the Indian Tribes of OK: Seneca," May 23, 2016, Seneca Cayuga Nation. https://sctribe.com/history/05-03-2016/guide-indian-tribes-ok-seneca; Muriel H. Wright "A Guide to the Indian Tribes of OK: Cayuga," July 2, 2015, Seneca Cayuga Nation, https://sctribe.com/history/07-02-2015/guide-indian-tribes-ok-cayuga.

3. Mihsihkinaahkwa is the Miami spelling. Sources have spelled it Mishikinakwa, Michikinqua, Michikinikwa, and Meshikinquah.

4. Custer is often referred to as General Custer. He was breveted to general during the Civil War, a temporary promotion that ended when the war did.

5. For tribal members, Lakota, not Sioux, was and is the proper name. Edward Clown Family, as told to William B. Matson, *Crazy Horse: The Lakota Warrior's Life & Legacy* (Layton, UT: Gibbs Smith, 2016), 10.

6. Kingsley M. Bray, *Crazy Horse: A Lakota Life* (Norman: University of Oklahoma Press, 2006), 245.

7. Wade Davis, *Photographs* (Madeira Park, BC: McIntyre & Douglas, 2016), 46.

8. Eleanor Jones Harvey, "Who Was Alexander Von Humboldt?," *Smithsonian Magazine*, March 24, 2020, https://www.smithsonianmag.com/smithsonian-institution/who-was-alexander-von-humboldt-180974473/.

9. Andrea Wulf, "Founding Gardeners: The Revolutionary Generation, Nature, and the Shaping of the American Nation," 2013, 22-23, Yale University, https://agrarianstudies.macmillan.yale.edu/sites/default/files/files/colloqpapers/04wulf.pdf.

10. Ibid., 27.

11. Climate change can be significantly diminished through the natural capture and storage of carbon. Rainforest Trust, "Climate," https://www.rainforesttrust.org/fighting-climate-change/. Preserving and replanting forests would also stem the increasingly dangerous loss of biodiversity. While not the complete answer, the fate of the forests remains a critical issue in the twenty-first century.

12. The account of William Kennan is fundamentally contrary to the known facts. Kennan falsely refers to himself as a ranger, rather than as Kentucky militia. Moreover, some descriptions of personal exploits challenge credibility. These include the descriptions of Kennan, Robert Branshaw, also Kentucky militia, and Assistant Surveyor Jacob Fowler. Various sources have repeated and continue to repeat these accounts. See Fort Wayne and Allen County Public Library Staff, eds., *St. Clair's Defeat* (Fort Wayne, IN: Boards of the Public Library of Fort Wayne and Allen County, Indiana, 1954), 9-14, 16-22, 27-31; Alan C. Gaff, *Field of Corpses: Arthur St. Clair and the Death of an American Army* (Nashville, TN: Knox Press, 2023), 303-309, 320, 335-36, 357.

13. Chayefsky wrote the script for *The Americanization of Emily*. Heller, of course, authored *Catch-22*.

14. Colin G. Calloway, *The Victory with No Name: The Native American Defeat of the First American Army* (New York: Oxford University Press, 2015).

CHAPTER ONE: THE FATE OF THE FOREST

1. Helen Hornbeck Tanner, ed., *Atlas of Great Lakes Indian History* (Norman: University of Oklahoma Press, 1987), 14-15.

2. Deborah Fleming, "Resurrection of the Wild: Ohio Ecology as Regeneration," *Organization & Environment* 13, no. 4 (December 2000): 487, JSTOR, https://www.jstor.org/stable/26161500.

3. Writing in 1765, William Smith suggested that a European who had not lived "in the vast forest of America . . . will hardly be able to conceive a continuity of woods without end." William Smith, *An Historical Account of the Expedition against the Ohio Indians, in the Year MDCCLXIV. Under the Command of Henry Bouquet Esq., Colonel of Foot, and Now Brigadier General In America,* (1765), 44, Hathi Trust, https://archive.org/details/cihm_41689/page/n5/mode/2up.

4. Tanner, *Atlas*, 14-15.

5. Ohio Department of Natural Resources, *History of Ohio State Forests*, ohiodnr.gov; Fleming, "Resurrection," 488.

6. Sam F. Carman, *Indiana Forest Management History and Practices*, 2013, US Department of Agriculture, Forest Service, https://www.fs.usda.gov/research/treeresearch/42897.

7. Treeplantation.com. "Tree Spacing Calculator." https://treeplantation.com/tree-spacing-calculator.html.

8. John F. Ross, *War on the Run: The Epic Story of Robert Rogers and the Conquest of America's First Frontier* (New York: Bantam, 2011), 27-28.

9. J. Donald Hughes, "Forest Indians: The Holy Occupation," *Environmental Review* 1, no. 2 (1976): 3, 7-8, JSTOR, https://www.jstor.org/stable/3984362?seq=7.

10. Ebenezer Denny, *Military Journal of Major Ebenezer Denny: An Officer in the Revolutionary and Indian Wars*, 145 . https://exploreuk.uky.edu/catalog/xt76dj58d796# page/1/mode/1up.

11. US Department of Agriculture, Forest Service, *Timeline of Activity on the Lands of the Hoosier National Forest,* https://www.fs.usda.gov/detail/hoosier/learning/history-culture/?cid =fseprd576369.

12. Hughes, *Forest Indians,* 11.

13. Ibid., 9, 10.

14. Ibid., 3-4.

15. John Sugden, *Tecumseh: A Life* (New York: Henry Holt, 1997), 118-19.

16. Wayne E. Stevens, "The Organization of the Fur Trade 1760–1800," *Mississippi Valley Historical Review* 3, no. 2 (Sept. 1916): 172-202, JSTOR, https://archive.org/details/jstor-1886434/page/n1/mode/2up.

17. US Department of Agriculture, Forest Service, Wayne National Forest, "Early Settlement," https://www.fs.usda.gov/detail/wayne/about-forest/?cid=fsm9_006138; US Department of Agriculture, Forest Service, *A History of the Daniel Boone National Forest 1770–1990,* ch. 24, "Early Forests & Forest Industry in Eastern Kentucky," http://npshistory.com/publications/ usfs/region/8/daniel-boone/history/chap24.htm.

18. Calloway, *Victory with No Name,* citing Papers of Sir Frederick Haldimand (Additional MSS., 24, 322:112-13), 42n24, British Museum.

19. Andrew Roberts, *Churchill: Walking with Destiny* (New York: Viking, 2018), 415.

20. George Washington to George Mercer, 7 November 1771, National Archives, founders. archives.gov. https://founders.archives.gov/documents/Washington/02-08-02-0359.

21. Library of Congress, "Thomas Jefferson: The West," https://www.loc.gov/exhibits/jefferson/jeffwest.html.

22. Gov. St. Clair's Address at Marietta, July 15, 1788, St. Clair Papers (hereafter cited as SCP), 2:55, 2:56, Hathi Trust, https://babel.hathitrust.org/cgi/pt?id=nyp.33433081765376&seq=14.

23. Gov. St. Clair to the President, Sept. 14, 1789, SCP, 2:124; Major Hamtramck to Governor St. Clair, December 2, 1790, SCP, 2:198; John Sugden, *Blue Jacket: Warrior of the Shawnees* (Lincoln: University of Nebraska Press, 2000), 75, citing Northwest Territory Collection, Indiana Historical Society, Indianapolis.

24. John Norton, *The Journal of Major John Norton, 1816,* Carl F. Klinck and James J. Talman, eds. (Toronto: Champlain Society, 1970), 170.

25. Ibid.

CHAPTER TWO: QUAGMIRES OF HATE, OASES OF HUMANITY

1. The Royal Proclamation—October 7, 1763: By The King. A Proclamation. George R., Avalon Project, https://avalon.law.yale.edu/18th_century/proc1763.asp.

2. Silver friendship medals had been sent to various chiefs of England's Native American allies during the French and Indian War. In a favorable biography of George III, Andrew Roberts suggests that an additional reason for the proclamation was the king's unwillingness to "betray" those allies. Andrew Roberts, *The Last King of America: The Misunderstood Reign of George III* (New York: Viking, 2021), 125. Observing that not alienating many American colonists and unleashing them to flow west would have best served England's imperial interests, Roberts wrote, "Britain behaved with an honorable punctiliousness towards her treaties with the Indigenous Nations that verged upon the pedantic." Ibid. 126. That disdain for honoring commitments even to friendly tribes is minor compared to the attitude of most colonial Americans of the time.

3. Edward Redmond, *Washington as Land Speculator,* Library of Congress, quoting George Washington's correspondence to William Crawford, September 20, 1767, https://www.loc.

gov/collections/george-washington-papers/articles-and-essays/george-washington-survey-and-mapmaker/washington-as-land-speculator/.

4. Fintan O'Toole, *White Savage: William Johnson and the Invention of America* (New York: Farrar, Straus and Giroux, 2005), 158, 165, 271, 274-76.

5. Frederick Wulff, *Alexander McKee—The Great White Elk: British Indian Agent on the Colonial Frontier* (Parker, CO: Outskirts Press, 2013), 108, 115n71-72; Smith, *Historical Account*, 20.

6. The charge of inciting domestic insurrections among the colonies refers both to Britain's Native American allies and to Lord Dunmore's November 1775 offer of freedom to slaves who enlisted in the British army. Roberts, *Last King*, 307. Within three years, a number of states matched the offer of freedom for slaves willing to enlist in the Continental army. Thousands of slaves gained freedom through military service, while thousands of others took advantage of the chaos of war and escaped. Digital History, Explorations: The Revolution, "Slavery, the American Revolution, and the Constitution," https://www.digitalhistory. uh.edu/active_learning/explorations/revolution/revolution_slavery.cfm#:~:text=Several%20 thousand%20slaves%20won%20their,the%20colony%27s%20prewar%20total%2C%20es-caped.

7. Ross, *War on the Run*, 93, 174.

8. Calloway, *Victory with No Name*, 66, 75; Glenn F. Williams, *Dunmore's War: The Last Conflict of America's Colonial Era* (Yardley, PA: Westholme, 2017), 66-67, 72, 193.

9. Governor St. Clair to the Secretary of War, Sept. 14, 1788, SCP, 2:90.

10. Phillip W. Hoffman, *Simon Girty, Turncoat Hero: The Most Hated Man on the Early American Frontier*, illustrated ed. (Staunton, VA: American History Press, 2009), 296-97, citing Draper Manuscripts, microfilm, 2-W-385-387. Lyman Draper, Draper Manuscript Collection: Harmar Papers, Wisconsin Historical Society, Madison.

11. Brigadier General William North, Muskingum to ___, Northwest Territory Collection, 1721–1825, M0367, box 1, folder 26 1786 08 07 005, Indiana Historical Society, images.indianahistory.org; quoted in Sugden, *Blue Jacket*, 75.

12. Kentucky was part of Virginia until it became a separate state in 1792, so the reference to Virginia backwoodsmen may have included Kentuckians.

13. Gov. St. Clair to the President, Sept. 14, 1789, SCP, 2:124.

14. Major Hamtramck to Governor St. Clair, December 2, 1790, SCP, 2:198.

15. General View, Communicated to Congress, December 30, 1794, American State Papers, Indian Affairs (hereafter cited as ASPI), Library of Congress, 1:543-44, https://memory.loc. gov/cgi-bin/ampage?collId=llsp&fileName=007/llsp007.db&recNum=; Governor St. Clair to the Secretary of War, Philadelphia, Jan. 27, 1788, Territorial Papers of the United States, 2:89, Hathi Trust, https://babel.hathitrust.org/cgi/pt?id=mdp.39015071159 142&seq=9.

16. Major Hamtramck to Governor St. Clair, December 2, 1790, SCP, 2:198; Governor St. Clair to the Secretary of War, Pittsburgh, July 5, 1788, Territorial Papers of the United States, 2:119.

17. George E. Lankford, "Losing the Past: Draper and the Ruddell Indian Captivity," *Arkansas Historical Quarterly* 49, no. 3 (Autumn 1990): 214, quoting Draper Manuscripts, 2-YY-120-133, 225. Lyman Draper, Draper Manuscript Collection, Tecumseh MSS, Wisconsin Historical Society, Madison, JSTOR, https://www.jstor.org/stable/40030798. However, in an extensive biography, after research to identify a documented attack that fit the circumstances Ruddell described, John Sugden concluded that Tecumseh was twenty at the time and that decades later, Ruddell's memory was mistaken on this detail. Sugden, *Tecumseh*, 49-51. For

Shawnee pronunciations, see Native Languages of the Americas, "Shawnee Pronunciation and Spelling Guide," http://www.native-languages.org/shawnee_guide.htm.

18. Sugden, *Blue Jacket*, 54, 63, 80.

19. Ibid., 76.

20. Henry Hay, *Narrative of Life on the Old Frontier: Henry Hay's Journal from Detroit to the Mississippi (i.e. Miami) River*, ed. Milo M. Quaife. Madison: Historical Society of Wisconsin, 1915, 248-49, Hathi Trust, https://babel.hathitrust.org/cgi/pt?id=osu.32435015062847&seq=3.

21. O. M. Spencer, *Indian Captivity: A True Narrative of the Capture of Rev. O. M. Spencer by the Indians in the Neighborhood of Cincinnati*, ed. Milo M. Quaife (Chicago: R. R. Donnelly & Sons, 1917), 98, 100, 101, Internet Archive, https://archive.org/details/omspencercapti00spenrich/page/n9/mode/2up.

22. Hoffman, *Simon Girty*, 147-54.

23. Sugden, *Blue Jacket*, 81-83.

24. Ibid., 81, 283n7.

25. Ibid., 86-87.

26. Benjamin Franklin to Peter Collinson, 9 May 1753, National Archives, https://founders.archives.gov/?q=%20Author%3A%22Franklin%2C%20Benjamin%22%20Period%3A%22Colonial%22%20Recipient%3A%22Collinson%2C%20Peter%22&s=2111311111&r=17.

27. James Axtell, "The White Indians of Colonial America," *William and Mary Quarterly* 32, no. 1 (Jan. 1975): 62-63, JSTOR, https://www.jstor.org/stable/1922594.

28. Denny, *Military Journal*, 84.

29. Franklin to Collinson, 9 May 1753, National Archives.

30. Ross, *War on the Run*, 54, citing Robert Rogers, *A Concise Account of North America* (London: Robert Rogers, 1765), 157.

31. Cari Nierenberg, "What Is Stockholm Syndrome?" June 27, 2019, Live Science, https://www.livescience.com/65817-stockholm-syndrome.html.

32. Lisa Louise Broberg, "Sexual Mores among the Eastern Woodland Indians" (master's thesis, William and Mary, 1984), ScholarWorks, Dissertations, Theses, and Masters Projects, paper 1539625275, https://dx.doi.org/doi:10.21220/s2-hd8b-0y78.

33. Axtell, *White Indians*. 62, 65, 67, 77-79.

34. Ibid., 88.

CHAPTER THREE: THE DRIVE FOR LAND, THE DESCENT INTO WAR

1. Tanner, *Atlas*, 70.

2. *Report of the Secretary of War Relative to Intruders on Public Lands*, April 19, 1787, Territorial Papers of the United States, 2:26-27.

3. R. Douglas Hurt, *The Ohio Frontier: Crucible of the Old Northwest 1720–1830* (Bloomington: Indiana University Press, 1996), 158-161.

4. O'Toole, *White Savage*, 173, 175.

5. The Maumee was sometimes referred to as "the Omee," "the Miami of the Lakes," "the other Miami," or just "the Miami." The Great Miami River was sometimes referred to as just "the Miami" or the "Big Miami." To avoid confusion, references to these rivers will be to the Maumee and the Great Miami.

6. George Washington to James Duane, 7 September 1783, National Archives, https://founders.archives.gov/?q=%20Author%3A%22Washington%2C%20George%22%20Recipient%3A%22Duane%2C%20James%22&s=2111311111&r=20.

7. George Washington to Thomas Jefferson, 3 May 1790, National Archives, https://founders.archives.gov/documents/Washington/05-05-02-0241.

8. Brigadier General William North, Muskingum to ___, Northwest Territory Collection, quoted in Sugden, *Blue Jacket*, 75.

9. Nonhelema was known to whites as the Grenadier Squaw because she was over six feet tall. Whites may have called other tall Shawnee women Grenadier as well, and it has been suggested that Butler's relationship might have been with a Grenadier other than Nonhelema. At the time of Tamanatha's birth, Nonhelema would have been about forty-five, or unrealistically older according to some accounts, while Butler was twenty. That Butler's relationship and son were with Nonhelema is accepted by the Piqua Shawnee. Nonhelema had several marriages and also had a child with British Indian agent Alexander McKee. Piqua Shawnee Tribe, "Nonhelema Hokolesqua (Cornstalk's Sister) c.1718–1786," *Piqua Shawnee Tribe: History, Culture* (blog), Piqua Shawnee Tribe, August 31, 2018, https://piquashawnee.blogspot.com/2018/08/.

10. Breveting is a temporary promotion. Typically, it was given in recognition of an officer's outstanding service during wartime and lasted for the duration of the officer's assignment or possibly the duration of the war.

11. Treaty of Fort McIntosh (1785), *Treaty With the Wyandot etc.: 1785*, Avalon Project, https://avalon.law.yale.edu/18th_century/wya1785.asp.

12. Harry M. Ward, *When Fate Summons: A Biography of General Richard Butler, 1743–1791* (Washington, DC: Academica Press, 2014), 70.

13. Colonel Harmar to the Secretary of War, Nov. 15, 1786, SCP, 2:19.

14. Sugden, *Tecumseh*, 73-74.

15. Sugden, *Blue Jacket*, 76, 80; George Blue Jacket, "A Story of the Shawanoes," 3, Eastern Shawnee Tribe of Oklahoma Digital Collection. https://ohiomemory.org/digital/collection/p16007coll27/id/364#:~:text= George %20Bluejacket%20was%20the%20son,signed%20the%20Treaty%20of%20Greeneville.

16. Sugden, *Blue Jacket*, 77.

17. Speech of the United Indian Nations at Their Confederate Council, Held Near the Mouth of the Detroit River, the 28th November and 18th December 1786, ASPI, 1:8.

18. Ibid., 1:9.

19. Williams, *Dunmore's War*, 165-66, 213-15.

20. Northwest Ordinance (1787), National Archives, https://www.archives.gov/milestones-documents/northwest-ordinance.

21. Ibid.

22. Instructions to the Governor of the Territory of the United States Northwest of the River Ohio, Relative to an Indian Treaty in the Northern Department, Oct. 26, 1787, ASPI, 1:9; SCP, 2:37.

23. Colonel Harmar to the Secretary of War, May 14, 1787, SCP, 2:20; Brigadier-General Harmar to Secretary of War, Jan. 10, 1788, SCP, 2:38.

24. Governor St. Clair to Secretary of War, Jan. 27, 1788, SCP, 2:42.

25. Governor St. Clair to Secretary of War, July 5, 1788, SCP, 2:48-49.

26. Treaty of Fort Harmar (1789), *Treaty With the Wyandot etc.: 1789*, Avalon Project, https://avalon.law.yale.edu/18th_century/wya1789.asp.

27. To George Washington from Henry Knox, 23 May 1789, National Archives, https://founders.archives.gov/documents/Washington/05-02-02-0267.

28. From George Washington to Arthur St. Clair, 6 October 1789, National Archives, https://founders.archives.gov/documents/Washington/05-04-02-0097.

29. Sugden, *Blue Jacket*, 84.

30. Mark K. Schoenfield and Rick M. Schoenfield, *Legal Negotiations: Getting Maximum Results* (New York: Shepards/McGraw-Hill, 1988), 247-53.

31. Governor St. Clair to the President, Sept. 14, 1789, SCP, 2:123.

32. C. A. Buser, "Tarhe," Wyandot Nation of Kansas, http://www.wyandot.org/sachem.htm.

33. Blue Jacket, "Story of the Shawanoes."

34. Secretary of War to the President of the United States, Jan. 4, 1790, ASPI, 1:60.

35. Extract of a Letter from the Lieutenants of the Counties of Fayette, Woodward, and Mercer, to the Secretary of War, 14 April 1790, ASPI, 1:86.

36. Hay, *Narrative of Life*, 259.

CHAPTER FOUR: FALSE VICTORY

1. This first undeclared war has been compared by some to the so-called war on terror. Doing so denigrates the legal status of Native American tribes as sovereign nations. Instead, this first undeclared war is more properly compared to undeclared wars fought against sovereign nations, such as North Korea, China in the Korean War, North Vietnam, Grenada, Panama, and Afghanistan (where the Taliban was the ruling government). See *McGirt v. Oklahoma*, 140 S.Ct. 2452 (2020); *United States v. Sioux Nation of Indians*, 448 U.S. 371 (1980); Edward Lazarus, *Black Hills White Justice: The Sioux Nation Versus the United States, 1775 to the Present* (New York: HarperCollins, 1991). The comparison also implicitly suggests that the Indians were terrorists, a fallacious suggestion notwithstanding that the Indians' mode of warfare often involved acts of terror. The suggestion reflects the attitude of the average Kentuckian in the late eighteenth century more accurately than it does the complex historical facts.

2. Statement Relative to the Frontiers Northwest of the Ohio, Dec. 26, 1791, ASPI, 1:97.

3. Ibid., 1:98.

4. There is a surprising discrepancy among secondary sources on whether Kekionga or Le Gris's village, was on the east bank of the St. Joseph, though there is no question they were across the river from each other. John Reed Swanton, "The Indian Tribes of North America," *Bureau of American Ethnology Bulletin* 145, 238, places Kekionga on the east bank, as do Sword, Calloway, Warner, and Dillon. Wiley Sword, *President Washington's Indian War: The Struggle for the Old Northwest 1790–1795* (Norman: University of Oklahoma Press, 1993); Calloway, *Victory with No Name*; Michael S. Warner, "General Josiah Harmar's Campaign Reconsidered: How the Americans Lost the Battle of Kekionga," *Indiana Magazine of History* 83, no. 1 (March 1987): 43-64, JSTOR, https://www.jstor.org/stable/27791042; John Dillon, *History of Indiana, from the Earliest Exploration by Europeans* (Indianapolis, IN: Bingham Doughty, 1859), https://digital.library.pitt.edu/islandora/object/pitt:31735054853399. But Tanner's *Atlas* and Bert Anson's *The Miami Indians* place Kekionga on the west bank. Bert Anson, *The Miami Indians* (Norman: University of Oklahoma Press, 2000). Sugden and Ironstrack cite Tanner. Sugden, *Blue Jacket*; George Ironstrack, "The Mihsi-maalhsa Wars, Part 2, The Battle of Kiihkayonki," Aacimotaatiiyankwi, https://aacimotaatiiyankwi.org/2014/03/31/the-mihsi-maalhsa-wars-part-ii/. Ironstrack also cites Anson. Two contemporary descriptions appear to place Le Gris's village on the west bank and Kekionga on the east bank. Lieutenant Denny drew a map of Maumee villages when Harmar occupied Kekionga in 1790. See "View of the Maumee Towns Destroyed By General Harmar, October 1790," ch. 4, 57. He placed the largest village on the east bank of the St. Joseph, and everyone agrees that the largest village was Kekionga. Arriving from Detroit in December 1789, Henry Hay de-

scribed Le Gris's village as "a very pretty place . . . the River St. Joseph . . . falls in the Miami River very near the town at the S.W. end of it." Hay, *Narrative of Life*, 216-17, 221. The southwest end of the St. Joseph puts Le Gris's village on the west bank. Moreover, as Kekionga was sited to control the portage at the Maumee, logically it would have been located between the St. Joseph and the Maumee, rather than across the St. Joseph from the portage. For the Miami pronunciation, see Miami Tribe of Oklahoma, Indigenous Languages Digital Archive: Miami-Illinois, https://mc.miamioh.edu/ilda-myaamia/dictionary/entries/7263.

5. Some later writers have done the same.

6. Hay, *Narrative of Life*, 217-23.

7. Calloway, *Victory with No Name*, 100.

8. Otho Winger, "The Indians Who Opposed Harmar," *Journal of Ohio History* (Jan.-March 1941): 55-59, Ohio History Connection, https://resources.ohiohistory.org/ohj/browse/displaypages.php?display[]=0050&display[]=55&display[]=59.

9. Hay, *Narrative of Life*, 255; Sugden, *Blue Jacket*, 54; Spencer, *Indian Captivity*, 88.

10. Sugden, *Blue Jacket*, 25–27, 43.

11. Ibid., 31–32.

12. Norton, *Journal*, 189. In April 1809, Norton embarked on a fourteen-month, thousand-mile trip from Canada through Ohio and Kentucky to Tennessee. His goal was to meet and learn about the Cherokee and the other indigenous nations he met along the way. Norton's interest came naturally. His father was Cherokee by birth but British by upbringing. Norton's father was taken as a boy when his village was attacked and brought back to Britain. Norton's mother was Scottish. Coming to America as a soldier in the 1780s, Norton became an interpreter. Eventually he met Joseph Brant and was adopted by the Mohawk. In the War of 1812, Norton led a force of Haudenosaunee, fighting with the British army and Tecumseh's warriors.

13. Spencer, *Indian Captivity*, 87-88.

14. Ibid., 88.

15. *Joseph Moore's Journal*, Territorial Papers of the United States, 2:649.

16. Spencer, *Indian Captivity*, 88.

17. Ibid., 88. Oliver was not aware of it, but the fairer complexion of Blue Jacket's daughter was presumably due to their maternal grandfather being French-Canadian.

18. Ibid., 88.

19. Ibid., 89.

20. Tanner, *Atlas*, 82; Hoffman, *Simon Girty*, 42-45, 174, 201-203, 221, 233, 269-71; Sugden, *Blue Jacket*, 131; Robert S. Allen, *The British Indian Department and the Frontier in North America, 1755–1830*, app. D: "Indian Leaders and Notables of the British Indian" (Oct. 24, 2006), Parks Canada, http://parkscanadahistory.com/series/chs/14/chs14-1n.htm.

21. Wulff, *Alexander McKee*, 1-8.

22. Reginald Horsman, "McKee, Alexander," *Dictionary of Canadian Biography*, 1979, http://www.biographi.ca/en/bio/mckee_alexander_4E.html.

23. Reginald Horsman, "Elliott, Matthew," *Dictionary of Canadian Biography*, 1983, http://www.biographi.ca/en/bio/elliott_matthew_5E.html.

24. Christopher B. Coleman, "Letters from Eighteenth Century Indiana Merchants," *Indiana Quarterly Magazine of History* 5, no. 4 (December 1909): 149, IUScholarWorks Journals, https://scholarworks.iu.edu/journals/index.php/imh/article/view/5703/5127.

25. David R. Farrell, "Adhemar, Saint-Martin, Toussaint-Antoine," *Dictionary of Canadian Biography*, 1983, http://www.biographi.ca/en/bio/adhemar_toussaint_antoine_5E.html.

26. Court of Inquiry on General Harmar, American State Papers, Military Affairs (hereafter cited as ASPM) 1:31, Library of Congress, https://memory.loc.gov/cgi-bin/ampage?collId= llsp&fileName=016/llsp016.db&recNum=4.

27. Secretary of War to Governor St. Clair, August 23, 1790, and Sept. 12, 1790, ASPI, 1:98, 100.

28. General Knox to Governor St. Clair, Sept. 14, 1790, SCP, 2:181.

29. Ibid., 2:181-82; Governor St. Clair to the Secretary of War, Sept. 19, 1790, SCP, 2:184.

30. Governor St. Clair to Major Murray, or Officer Commanding the British Troops at Detroit, Sept. 19, 1790, ASPI, 1:96; SCP, 2:186-87.

31. Blue Jacket, "Story of the Shawanoes"; Ironstrack, "Mihsi-maalhsa Wars, Part 2."

32. Native Languages of the Americas, "Shawnee Pronunciation and Spelling Guide."

33. Major John Smith to Capt. LeMaistre, Oct. 20, 1790, Colonial Office Records, Michigan Historical Collections (hereafter cited as COR), vol. 24, 107-108. https://quod.lib.umich.edu/ cgi/t/text/text-idx?c=moa;idno=0534625.0024.001.

34. Colonel A. McKee to Sir John Johnson, Oct. 18, 1790, COR, 24:106.

35. It was later suggested by a Detroit merchant and fur trader, William Macomb, that once Harmar reached Kekionga, instead of looting and burning the villages, Harmar could have easily negotiated a peace treaty. *Conversation upon the State of Affairs in the western Country*, Philadelphia, January 31, 1791, COR, 24:170.

36. *Additional News from Detroit*, Dec. 11, 1790, COR, 24:159-160; Court of Inquiry on General Harmar, ASPM, 1:23 27.

37. General Orders, Oct. 29, 1790, ASPI, 1:105; Court of Inquiry on General Harmar, ASPM, 1:23, 27.

38. Capt. Mathew Elliott to Col. A. McKee, Oct. 23, 1790, COR, 24:108-109; Major John Smith, Information Respecting Action of Indians Obtained from Mr. Godfroy, COR, 24:132; Denny, *Military Journal*, 146.

39. Court of Inquiry on General Harmar, ASPM, 1:21, 27; Joseph Chew, Information from Capt. Matthew Elliott, COR, 24:133-34.

40. Capt. Mathew Elliott to Col. A. McKee, Oct. 23, 1790, COR, 24:108-109.

41. General Orders, Oct. 29, 1790, ASPI, 1:105.

42. Denny, *Military Journal*, 146. Denny does not give the captains' first names, nor were their first names found in other sources.

43. Warner, "General Josiah Harmar's Campaign," 43, 52.

44. Chew, Information from Capt. Matthew Elliott, COR, 24:133-34.

45. Warner, "General Josiah Harmar's Campaign," 51.

46. Ibid., 52.

47. Enclosure: Extracts from Orders, 17 October–4 November 1790, National Archives, https://founders.archives.gov/documents/Washington/05-07-02-0040-0004.

48. Information from Blue Jacket, COR, 24:135.

49. Chew, Information from Captain Mathew Elliott, COR, 24:134.

50. Denny, *Military Journal*, 148; Governor St. Clair to the Secretary of War, Oct. 29, 1790, SCP, 188. Some sources refer to an ambush of a detachment led by Ensign Asa Hartshorn on October 20, but neither Harmar's report nor Denny's journal nor the testimony of the court of inquiry that was later held mentions such an ambush.

51. Governor St. Clair to the Secretary of War, Oct. 29, 1790, SCP, 2:188.

52. Brigadier General Harmar to the Secretary of War, Nov. 4, 1790, ASPI, 1:104.

53. Gov. St. Clair to Secretary of War, Nov. 6, 1790, SCP, 2:190.

54. The court of inquiry was held at Fort Washington in September 1791, despite the army being behind schedule to march again to the Maumee. Major General Richard Butler presided. The other members of the court were Lieutenant Colonels George Gibson and William Darke.

55. *Blue Jacket's Speech and Answer*, COR, 24:135-36.

56. Norton, *Journal*, 128-29; Leroy V. Eid, "'A Kind of Running Fight': Indian Battlefield Tactics in the Late Eighteenth Century," *Western Pennsylvania Historical Magazine* 71, no. 2 (April 1988): 149n4, https://journals.psu.edu/wph/article/view/4105/3922.

57. In some accounts, Hunt was tortured to death. But in his report to Harmar, Kingsbury never mentions torture, writing only that Hunt was "murdered." Hoffman, *Simon Girty*, 296-97, quoting Draper Manuscripts, microfilm 2-W-385-387, Draper, Draper Manuscript Collection: Harmar Papers. It is likely Kingsbury would have reported Hunt being tortured within view of the station if that had occurred.

58. Conflicting accounts place Simon Girty at the attacks on both Dunlap's Station and Baker's Station. That puts him in two places at once. The weight of opinion seems to be that Girty was at Baker's Station. Although the Indians besieging Kingsbury yelled that Girty was with them, Kingsbury never heard or saw Girty. The Indians' claim that Girty was at Dunlap's Station most likely was a psychological ploy intended to heighten the defenders' fears.

59. Report of the Secretary of War to the President, December 10, 1790, Territorial Papers of the United States, 2:314. The arts of agriculture likely included raising cattle, sheep, and hogs, in place of hunting. That was discussed with Red Jacket in Philadelphia. *Joseph Moore's Journal*, Territorial Papers of the United States, 2:634.

60. H. Knox, Secretary of War Report, Jan. 5, 1791, ASPI, 1:107; General Knox to Governor St. Clair, Sept. 14, 1798, SCP, 183.

61. The following information about Knox's assessment is from H. Knox, Secretary of War Report, Jan. 22, 1791, ASPI, 1:112, 113.

CHAPTER FIVE: ST. CLAIR'S ARMY FORMS

1. President Washington to General St. Clair, March 28, 1792, SCP, 283.

2. Instructions to Major General Arthur St. Clair, March 21, 1791, ASPI, 1:171.

3. Ibid.

4. Ibid., 1:173.

5. Ibid., 1:172.

6. Ibid.

7. Message from the Secretary of War to the Miamis, March 11, 1791, ASPI, 1:147.

8. Ward, *When Fate Summons*, 100.

9. Sargent and Denny both give the count's name as Malartie, but the correct spelling is Malartic. Winthrop Sargent, *Diary of Col. Winthrop Sargent, adjutant general of the United States' army during the campaign of MDCCXCI*, 43, Internet Archive, https://archive.org/details/diaryofcolwinthr00sarg/n11/mode/2up; Denny, *Military Journal*, 154; Arthur St. Clair, *A Narrative of the Manner in Which the Campaign against the Indians in the Year One Thousand Seven Hundred and Ninety-One, Was Conducted, under the Command of Major General St. Clair*, 221, Northern Illinois University Digital Library, https://digital.lib.niu.edu/islandora/object/niu-prairie%3A2033. The count's full name was Louis Hippolyte Joseph de Mauris, Vicomte de Malartic. Phillip J. Wolfe and Warren J. Wolfe, eds. and trans., "Prospects for the Gallipolis Settlement: French Diplomatic Dispatches," *Ohio History Journal* 103

(Spring-Summer 1994): 49n13, https://resources.ohiohistory.org/ohj/search/display.php?page =46& ipp=20&searchterm=Array&vol=103&pages=41-56.

10. *A View of the Troops Authorized by the Acts of Congress, for the Campaign of 1791*, ASPI, 1:196.

11. Letter to Maj. Gen. Richard Butler, July 14 1791, COR, 24:286.

12. Richard M. Lytle, *The Soldiers of America's First Army: 1791*, 153-55, 186-88.

13. Ibid., 159-75, 191-243.

14. Ibid., 143-46, 149.

15.Thomas Irwin, "St. Clair's Defeat: As Told by an Eye-Witness—From Original MSS.," Frazer E. Wilson ed., *Ohio History Journal* 10 (Jan. 1902): 380, https://resources.ohiohistory. org/ohj/search/display.php?page=15&ipp=20&searchterm=array&vol=10&pages=378-380.

16. George Washington to William Darke, 4 April, 1791, National Archives, https:// founders.archives.gov/documents/Washington/05-08-02-0039, and George Washington to William Darke, 7 April, 1791, National Archives, https://founders.archives.gov/documents/ Washington/05-08-02-0052.

17. Lytle, *Soldiers*, 250; Brent Tarter, "William Darke (1736-1801)," *Dictionary of Virginia Biography*, Library of Virginia, 2015, https://www.lva.virginia.gov/public/dvb/bio.asp?b= Darke_William.

18. Lytle, *Soldiers*, 271.

19. Ibid., 251-53.

20. Ibid., 272, 274; Sargent, *Diary*, 3.

21. Lytle, *Soldiers*, 272; Colonel Joseph Wood to General St. Clair, SCP, 1:377n1; Ward, *When Fate Summons*, 128.

22. Lytle, *Soldiers*, 254-58, 274-81.

23. John F. Winkler, *Wabash 1791: St. Clair's Defeat* (Oxford: Osprey, 2011), 21.

24. Compare Lytle, *Soldiers*, 71, and Calloway, *Victory with No Name*, 87, who cites Lytle, stating that Major Heart's twelve-year-old son accompanied him, with V. Allen Gray, "Capt. Jonathan Heart/Hart," The Society of the Cincinnati in the State of Connecticut, https://www.theconnecticutsociety.org/hearthart-jonathan/. The Society of the Cincinnati was formed by Henry Knox in 1783 with officers of the Continental army. It describes itself as a hereditary, patriotic organization and continues to this day. Jonathan Heart was an original member. As a hereditary society, it would have known of Heart's son. It recorded that his son, Alces Everlin Heart, was born October 10, 1782, making him only nine when the expedition started. The society recorded that Alces lived to adulthood with no mention of his accompanying St. Clair's expedition. This casts substantial doubt on the conclusion that Heart brought his son with him.

25. Lytle, *Soldiers*, 161, 280-81.

26. Referring to enlisted men, Knox gave the number of militia as 418. He based the number on musters, and 418 is the number of enlisted men in the Muster Roll of October 24. However, at least thirty-five militia had previously deserted. Several others may also have gone missing before October 24. Thus, when the militia arrived, the number of men was at least 453 and probably somewhat higher. *A Summary Statement of Facts, Relatively to the Measures Taken, in Behalf of the United States, to Induce the Hostile Indians, Northwest of the Ohio, to Peace, Previously to the Exercise of Coercion against Them; and Also a Statement of the Arrangements for the Campaign of 1791*, ASPI, 1:140; *A View of the Troops*, ASPI, 1:196; *A General Abstract of the Troops in the Service of the United States Commanded by His Excellency Arthur*

St. Clair, Major General and Commander in Chief of the Troops in the Western Territory, October 26, 1791, Manuscripts in Ohio: A Muster Roll, A Monthly Return and the Battle of Wabash, Ohio Memory, https://ohiomemory.ohiohistory.org/archives/4952.

27. Oldham County Historical Society, *History and Families Oldham County, Kentucky: First Century 1824–1924 (Nashville, TN: Turner Publishing Co., 1996)*, 19; Helen McKinney, "Oldham County," explorekyhistory.ky.gov/items/show/844.

28. St. Clair, *Narrative*, 270.

29. *Court of Inquiry on General Harmar*, ASPM, 1:31.

30. As alluded to in the Introduction, the failure to have a guide has generally not been mentioned, or has been glossed over, in accounts and critiques of the campaign.

31. St. Clair, *Narrative*, 270.

32. Ibid., 62-63; Secretary of War to the House of Representatives, November 14, 1792, *St. Clair's Defeat*, ASPM, 1:39.

33. Patrick J. Furlong, "Problems of Frontier Logistics in St. Clair's 1791 Campaign," Selected Papers from the 1983 and 1984 George Rogers Clark Trans-Appalachian Frontier History Conferences, National Park Service History Electronic Library & Archive, http://npshistory.com/series/symposia/george_rogers_clark/1983-1984/sec6.htm.

34. From Arthur St. Clair to Alexander Hamilton, 21 July 1791, National Archives, https://founders.archives.gov/?q=%20Author%3A%22St.%20Clair%2C%20Arthur%22%20Recipient%3A%22Hamilton%2C%20Alexander%22&s=1111311111&r=3.

35. J. Knox, Sec'y of War, to Maj. General A. St. Clair, 21st July 1791, COR, 24:291. The document omits Knox's first name but uses his middle initial.

36. St. Clair, *Narrative*, 96; General Knox to General Butler, August 25, 1791, SCP 2:232.

37. St. Clair, *Narrative*, 5.

38. George Washington to William Darke, 9 August, 1791, National Archives, founders.archives.gov/documents/Washington/05-08-02-0284. The text of Butler's letter to Washington is in note 1 following Washintgton's response.

39. Samuel Newman, "Captain Newman's Original Journal of St. Clair's Campaign," *Wisconsin Magazine of History* 2 (Sept. 1918): 45.

CHAPTER SIX: THE ALLIES

1. Narrative of Mr. Thomas Rhea, Who Arrived at Pittsburg, from Captivity, the 30th of June 1791, ASPI, 1:196-97; Henry Knox to Tobias Lear, 11 July 1791, National Archives, https://founders.archives.gov/?q=%20Period%3A%22Washington%20Presidency%22%20Recipient%3A%22Lear%2C%20Tobias%22&s=1111312111&r=62.

2. Sugden, *Blue Jacket*, 94, quoting Council at Huron Village, 16 August 1790, Draper Manuscripts: Frontier War Papers, 23U88. Lyman Draper, Draper Manuscript Collection: Frontier War Papers, Wisconsin Historical Society, Madison.

3. Mr. Gamelin's Journal: Memorandum of Sundry Speeches Held by Anthony Gamelin to the Chiefs of the Wabash and Miami Nations, ASPI, 1:94.

4. The Speech of the Cornplanter, Half-Town and the Great-Tree, Chiefs of the Seneca Nation, to the President of the United States of America, January 10, 1791, ASPI, 1:144, 209.

5. Message from the Cornplanter, New-Arrow, Half-Town, and Big-Tree, Chiefs of the Seneca Nation of Indians, to the President of the United States, ASPI, 1:145.

6. To George Washington from Henry Knox, 31 March, 1791, https://founders.archives.gov/documents/Washington/05-08-02-0020.

7. Leroy V. Eid, "Their Rules of War: A Summary of James Smith's Indian Woodland War," *The Register of the Kentucky Historical Society* 86, no.1 (Winter 1988): 18-19, JSTOR, https://www.jstor.org/stable/23380726.

8. Miami Tribe, Indigenous Languages Digital Archive. https://mc.miamioh.edu/ilda-myaamia/dictionary/entries/3413; https://mc.miamioh.edu/ilda-myaamia/dictionary/entries/5803.

9. Denny, *Military Journal*, 70.

10. Delaware Tribe of Indians, "About the Delaware Tribe," https://delawaretribe.org/homepage/about-the-tribe/.

11. Buser, *Tarhe*.

12. Reginald Horsman, "Egushwa," *Dictionary of Canadian Biography*, http://www.biographi.ca/en/bio/egushwa_4E.html; John Sugden, "Egushawa (1726–March 1796)," *American National Biography*, 2000, https://doi.org/10.1093/anb/9780198606697.article.2001688.

13. University of Minnesota, Duluth, *The Chippewa*, https://www.d.umn.edu/ cla/faculty/tbacig/studproj/a1041/mnansx1800/chippewa.htm; Ross, *War on the Run*, 140, 299.

14. Col. A. McKee to Sir John Johnson, Dec. 5, 1791, COR, 24:336.

15. Ironstrack, *Mihsi-maalhsa Wars, Part 2*.

16. Col. McKee to Sir John Johnson, 20th June 1791, COR, 24:262-63.

17. Weisenberg immigrated to America as a teenager, paying her way by agreeing to be sold by the ship's captain as an indentured servant. This was not an unusual arrangement for the time. She was soon out of her indentured servitude and living with William Johnson. O'-Toole, *White Savage*, 44-46.

18. Norton, *Journal*, 177.

19. Captain Joseph Brant to Sir John Johnson, Miamis Rapids 23d June 1791, COR, 24:270.

20. *Queries by Capt. Hendrick, Answered by Timothy Pickering*, COR, 24:275-76. The Mohicans are now known as the Stockbridge-Munsee. Stockbridge-Munsee Band of Mohican Indians, "Brief History: Muh-he-con-ne-ok," https://www.mohican.com/brief-history/.

21. Letter from Col. A. McKee, Foot of the Miamis Rapids July 5th 1791, COR, 24:281.

22. George Ironstrack, *The Mihsi-maalhsa Wars, Part 3, The Battle of the Wabash*, https://aacimotaatiiyankwi.org/2014/05/19/the-mihsi-maalhsa-wars-part-iii/.

23. William Heath, *William Wells and the Struggle for the Old Northwest* (Norman: University of Oklahoma Press, 2015).

24. Paul A. Hutton, "William Wells: Frontier Scout and Indian Agent," *Indiana Historical Journal* 74, no. 3 (Sept. 1978): 183, 186n6, https://scholarworks.iu.edu/journals/index.php/imh/article/view/10110/13932.

25. Speech of Lord Dorchester to the Indians, August 15, 1791, COR, 24:309-10.

26. Robert Henderson, "Why Was a British Musket Called a 'Brown Bess'?", Access Heritage, https://www.militaryheritage.com/Brown_Bess_musket_name.htm.

27. Douglas D. Scott, Joel Bohy, Nathan Boor, Charles Haecker, William Rose, and Patrick Severts, with contributions by Daniel M. Sivilich and Daniel T. Elliott, "Colonial Era Firearm Bullet Performance: A Live Fire Experimental Study for Archaeological Interpretation," Modern Heritage Foundation, https://modernheritage.net/images/Scott_etal_2017.pdf; Hugh T. Harrington, "The Inaccuracy of Muskets," *Journal of the American Revolution*, https://allthingsliberty.com/2013/07/the-inaccuracy-of-muskets/.

28. John Danielski, "The Kentucky Rifle— How America's Famous Frontier Long Gun Changed Warfare," Military History Now, May 4, 2020, https://militaryhistorynow.com/2020/05/04/the-kentucky-rifle-how-americas-famed-frontier-long-gun-changed-warfare/.

29. The Buckskinners, "Long Rifles," https://thebuckskinners.com/long-rifles/.

30. Mark Maloy, "Small Arms of the Revolution," American Battlefield Trust, https://www. battlefields.org/learn/articles/small-arms-revolution.

31. Norton, *Journal*, 130.

32. Eid, "'Kind of Running Fight,'" 154.

33. Williams, *Dunmore's War*, 48; Reuben Gold Thwaites and Louise Phelps Kellogg, eds., *Documentary History of Dunmore's War, 1774* (Madison: Wisconsin Historical Society, 1905), 264.

34. Eid, *Their Rules of War*, 19-2; Eid, "'Kind of Running Fight,'" 168.

35. Eid, .*Their Rules of War*, 8-14; Eid, "'Kind of Running Fight,'" 152-56, 166, 168. Norton, *Journal*, 129-30.

CHAPTER SEVEN: BLAND, BOUQUET, AND BAYONETS

1. Harry Schenawolf, "Loading and Firing a Brown Bess Musket in the Eighteenth Century," *Revolutionary War Journal*, March 15, 2015, https://revolutionarywarjournal.com/brown-bess/.

2. Humphrey Bland, Esq., Brigadier General of Her Majesty's Forces, *A Treatise of Military Discipline; In Which Is Laid Down and Explained the Duty of the Officer and Soldier Thro' the Several Branches of the Service*, 5th ed. (London: Printed for D. Midwinter, J. and P. Knapton, 1743), Hathi Trust, https://babel.hathitrust.org/cgi/pt?id=nyp.33433009417621&seq=265.

3. Williams, *Dunmore's War*, 126.

4. Bland, *Treatise*, 13, 135.

5. St. Clair, *Narrative*, 39.

6. Ross, *War on the Run*, 462.

7. Mary C. Darlington, ed., *History of Colonel Henry Bouquet and the Western Frontiers of Pennsylvania 1747–1767* (Pittsburgh, PA: privately published, 1920), 193, 196, https://archive.org/details/historyofcolonel00darluoft/page/n9/mode/2up.

8. Ibid., 194, 197.

9. Eid, "'Kind of Running Fight,'" 168.

10. In a letter from Bouquet to Governor John Penn, written from a camp in western Pennsylvania in 1763, "there is a humorous allusion to St. Clair." SCP, 6-7n2.

11. Williams, *Dunsmore's War*, 39, 269, 275.

12. Thwaites and Kellogg, eds., *Documentary History*, 259; Williams, *Dunmore's War*, 285.

13. Williams, *Dunmore's War*, 289.

14. Ibid., 291-92.

CHAPTER EIGHT: THE SLOW TREK THROUGH THE FOREST

1. Colonel Darke gave the distance as twenty-four miles. To George Washington from William Darke, 9-10 November 1791, National Archives, https://founders.archives.gov/documents/Washington/05-09-02-0094.

2. Newman, "Original Journal," 64.

3. Ibid., 64-66.

4. Ibid., 66, 67.

5. *A View of the Troops*, ASPI, 1:196.

6. *A Summary Statement of Facts . . . and Also a Statement of the Arrangements for the Campaign of 1791*, ASPI, 1:139-40.

7. General Knox to the President, October 1, 1791, SCP, 2:244.

8. Denny, *Military Journal*, 154.

9. Ibid., 170.

10. St. Clair, *Narrative*, 4-5.

11. Ibid., 212.

12. Winkler, *Wabash 1791*, 23.

13. Lytle, *Soldiers*, 419.

14. Instead of mortars, some secondary sources refer to carronades, while others refer to howitzers. But based on intelligence from an army deserter, John Wade, Simon Girty reported that St. Clair had two Coehorns, and Coehorns were mortars. Letter from Simon Girty to Colonel Alexander McKee, COR, 24:329.

15. Boyd L. Dastrup, "King of Battle: A Branch History of the U.S. Army's Field Artillery," US Army Center of Military History, https://history.army.mil/html/books/070/70-27/cmh-Pub_70-27.pdf; Harry Schenawolf, "Cannon Projectiles of the American Revolutionary War," *Revolutionary War Journal*, March 15, 2015, https://revolutionarywarjournal.com/cannon-projectiles/; Harry Schenawolf, "Artillery Battle Tactics during the American Revolutionary War," *Revolutionary War Journal*, January 29, 2016, https://revolutionarywarjournal.com/war-artillery-tactics/; AmericanRevolution.Org: Your Gateway to the American Revolution, "Artillery," https://www.americanrevolution.org/artillery.php.

16. Sargent, *Diary*, 8-9; Calloway, *Victory with No Name*, 86.

17. St. Clair, *Narrative*, 16.

18. Ibid., 17, 18.

19. Sargent, *Diary*, 10.

20. Quoted in Ross, *War on the Run*, 143.

21. Newman, " Original Journal," 69.

22. Ibid., 70.

23. Ibid.

24. St. Clair, *Narrative*, 18.

25. Copy of a Letter from General St. Clair to the Secretary of War, Nov. 1, 1791, ASPI, 1:136.

26. Howard E. LeWine, ed., "Biliary Colic," Harvard Health Publishing, August 16, 2023, https://www.health.harvard.edu/a_to_z/biliary-colic-a-to-z#:~:text=Biliary%20colic%20is%20a%20steady,that%20helps%20to%20digest%20fats.

27. Compare Newman, "Original Journal," 71; Denny, *Military Journal*, 157; Sargent, *Diary*, 15.

28. Sargent, *Diary*, 15.

29. Newman, "Original Journal," 71; Denny, *Military Journal*, 157.

30. Denny, *Military Journal*, 158.

31. Twenty is the number given by Denny, *Military Journal*, 158. Newman put the number at sixty. Newman, "Original Journal," 72.

32. Newman, "Original Journal," 73.

33. Sargent, *Diary*, 17.

34. Denny, *Military Journal*, 158.

35. Denny journaled the amount of flour as 1,800 pounds, about a two-day supply at a half ration of flour. Ibid. Sargent's diary gives the figure as 16,000 pounds, more than a week's supply at the full ration. Sargent, *Diary*, 17.

36. Denny, *Military Journal*, 158.

37. Some secondary sources state that the sons of Major Heart and Captain Newman continued on with the army, placing them with it when it was attacked. Definite information on Newman's son seems lacking, though Calloway states he was killed during the battle. Calloway, *Victory with No Name,* 121. Heart's son is named by Lytle, *Soldiers*, 79, and by Cal-

loway, who cites Lytle. *Victory with No Name*, 87. Neither state whether Heart's son was killed or survived. As noted, it is doubtful that Heart's son, Alces Everlin Heart, accompanied his father. See ch. 5, note 24. If Alces was with his father, perhaps both boys did continue on with the army. Given the food shortage, however, it seems they might have remained at Fort Jefferson. If so, it was a fortunate choice.

38. The quotes that follow are from George Washington, *Third Annual Address to Congress*, October 25, 1791, American Presidency Project, https://www.presidency.ucsb.edu/documents/third-annual-address-congress-0.

39. Sargent, *Diary*, 19.

40. The following muster roll information is from *A General Abstract of the Troops in the Service of the United States Commanded by His Excellency Arthur St. Clair*, October 26, 1791.

41. Copy of a Letter from General St. Clair to the Secretary of War, Nov. 1, 1791, ASPI, 1:137.

42. Denny, *Military Journal*, 159.

43. Copy of a Letter from General St. Clair, Nov. 1, 1791, ASPI, 1:137.

44. Ibid.; Denny, *Military Journal*, 159.

45. Gerry Barker, *Some Thoughts on Scouts and Spies* (Lebanon, TN: Greenleaf Press, 2017), 7.

46. St. Clair, *Narrative*, 132.

47. Ironstrack, *Mihsi-maalhsa Wars, Part 3*.

48. Declaration of John Wade, Deserter from the American Army, COR, 24:329.

49. Ibid., 328-29.

50. Schedule of Papers Submitted to the Right Honorable Henry Dundas in Letter No 13 of the 2nd December 1791, COR, 24:335.

51. Sargent, *Diary*, 20.

52. St. Clair, *Narrative*, 218-19.

CHAPTER NINE: THE SCOUT

1. Denny, *Military Journal*, 156-57.

2. When the Chickasaws undertook a scouting mission for St. Clair, they were accompanied by Captain Richard Sparks. Decades later, Sparks's brother-in-law, Colonel G. W. Sevier, was interviewed by Lyman Draper. Sevier told Draper of Sparks recounting that George Colbert and his older brother, William Colbert, another prominent Chickasaw, were with Piominko and on the scout. Russell E. Bidlack, "Richard Sparks (ca. 1757–1815): Indian Captive to U.S. Colonel," The Sparks Family Online, http://www.sparksfamilyassn.org/pages/087-A.html; Draper Manuscripts, 30-S. Lyman Draper, Draper Manuscript Collection: Draper's Notes, Wisconsin Historical Society, Madison. Winthrop Sargent journaled that George Colbert was with Piominko, while "the Elder Colbert," William, arrived at Fort Washington with twenty more Chickasaws weeks later. Sargent, *Diary*, 28. Sevier also recalled being told that Piominko and the Colberts had fourteen Chickasaws with them, whereas Sargent recorded that there were twenty, including Piominko. Bidlack, "Richard Sparks"; Draper Manuscripts, 30-S; Sargent, *Diary*, 19-20. As Sargent's account was recorded contemporaneously, it is likely to be correct.

3. Chickasaw Nation, "Chickasaw Nation Corrects Names of Famed Leaders," October 7, 2014, ICT News, https://ictnews.org/archives/native-history-chickasaw-nation-corrects-names -of-famed-leaders.

4. Only Sargent recorded that Piominko wanted to continue on to Congress but gave in to Colbert's desire to fight. Sargent is also the only one to write that Piominko gave in to Col-

bert's insisting that he lead the scouting party. Sargent, *Diary*, 21. That seems unlikely, and Sargent may have misunderstood. Denny referred to Piominko as the Chickasaw leader, as did Richard Sparks's reminisces. Denny, *Military Journal*, 160; Bidlack, "Richard Sparks."
5. Sugden, *Tecumseh*, 19.
6. Tecumseh's father, Pukeshinwau, died fighting at Point Pleasant. Tecumseh was only seven when Sparks was forced to leave the Shawnee.
7. Bidlack, *Richard Sparks*.
8. Sugden, *Tecumseh*, 20.
9. Copy of a Letter from General St. Clair, Nov. 1, 1791, ASPI, 1:137.
10. Denny recorded that they were "four riflemen," while Sargent wrote they were "five privates." Denny, *Military Journal*, 157; Sargent, *Diary*, 21.
11. Barker, *Some Thoughts*, 15-16, 17-18.
12. Ibid., 7.
13. Ibid., 22.
14. Denny journaled that Captain Sparks "had missed the enemy altogether." Denny, *Military Journal*, 171. Denny apparently misunderstood the critical difference between sending Sparks to scout the targeted towns and sending a scouting party to search out whether Indians were on the way to attack. The likely route and methods for the former were not the same as for the latter.
15. Barker, *Some Thoughts*, 13.
16. Denny, *Military Journal*, 171.

CHAPTER TEN: MORTAL STAKES
1. Sugden, *Tecumseh*, 63. That was Steven Ruddell's recollection. Lankford, *Losing the Past*, 226. Anthony Shane also grew up with Tecumseh and the Ruddells. He recalled that Tecumseh was scouting at Nettle Creek, a tributary of the Mad River, when the battle occurred. Sugden, *Tecumseh*, 63. Shane's memory seems mistaken since Confederation scouts were observing St. Clair's force and knew it was far past Nettle Creek.
2. Sugden, *Blue Jacket*, 119-21; Calloway, *Victory with No Name*, 102; Leroy V. Eid, "American Indian Military Leadership: St. Clair's Defeat 1791," *Journal of Military History* 1, no. 57 (January 1993): 71, 79-80, JSTOR, https://www.jstor.org/stable/2944223.
3. Letter from Simon Girty to Colonel Alexander McKee, COR, 24:329.
4. Norton, *Journal*, 130.
5. Similarly, at the Little Big Horn, Crazy Horse restrained premature charges. Bray, *Crazy Horse*, 224-27.
6. Corbin Douglas Clark, *Musical Culture of the Algonquin: A Study of the Musical Culture of the Algonquin Indigenous People of North America*, Liberty University, https://digital commons.liberty.edu/cgi/viewcontent.cgi?article=1390&context=honors.
7. Denny, *Military Journal*, 71, 72.
8. Letter from Simon Girty to Colonel Alexander McKee, COR, 24:329-30; St. Clair, *Narrative*, 71; Norton, *Journal*, 177. In June 1794, two captured Shawnee said that the Delaware numbered 400, which seems high; that the Shawnee could generally bring 300 into action, which also seems high for the Wabash battle; and that the Wyandot never brought more than 150 into action. *Examination of Two Shawanese Warriors, Taken Prisoners on the Miami of the Lakes, Twenty Miles above Grand Glaize, on the 22d Instant, June*, APSI 1:489.
9. Letter from Simon Girty to Colonel Alexander McKee, COR, 24:329-30.

10. William May, a captured American private, later reported hearing that Girty led the Wyandots against St. Clair. *Sworn Statement of William May*, ASPI, 1:243. It is not credible that Tarhe relinquished command of his warriors. May likely misunderstood what he heard about Girty's role or just assumed that he was in command. More than once, Girty's reputation led to his erroneously being credited with leadership. Hoffman, *Simon Girty*, 243. But May's statement is a good indication that Girty was with the Wyandots.

11. Simon Girty told a different American prisoner that James Girty shared command of the Shawnee. Sugden, *Blue Jacket*, 118. The leadership claim has no credibility. But the story suggests that James was with the Shawnee. Rather than completely lying about James's presence, Simon probably exaggerated James's role, spinning a yarn as he had about his scar to young Oliver Spencer. James's wife was Shawnee, and they lived among the Shawnee. Tanner, *Atlas*, 82; Hoffman, *Simon Girty*, 120, 248. James established a trading post in a village that became known as "Girty's Town" (now St. Mary's, Ohio). Later, James moved his trading post farther northwest to the Maumee. Tanner, *Atlas*, 84; Hoffman, *Simon Girty*, 248; Sugden, *Blue Jacket*, 131.

12. Jefferson County Local History, "George Ash: The Story of a Jefferson County Pioneer," *Madison Weekly Courier*, Jan. 28, 1874, jeffersoncountylocalhistory.org; *Cincinnati Chronicle and Literary Gazette*, "Story of George Ash," Nov. 7, 1829, 70.

13. Harrison Frech, *Anthony Shane, Metis Interpreter: A Bridge between Two Cultures: Scout, Interpreter, Town Founder, Witness to History* (Defiance, OH: Harrison Frech, 1991); Harrison Frech, researcher, "Anthony Shane, Founding Father," Oct. 5, 1996, rockfordalive.com.

14. Letter from Colonel Alexander McKee to Sir John Johnson, COR, 24:330.

15. Denny, *Military Journal*, 161.

16. Lytle, *Soldiers*, 81-82, 89-90.

17. Ibid., 162.

18. Sources spell Bartholomew Schaumburg's first and last name inconsistently. The spelling here is taken from a letter he wrote that was kept in the family's papers. The Historic New Orleans Collection, "*Manuscripts Division UPDATE*," vol. 1, no. 1., 3-4 (1982), https://www.hnoc.org/sites/default/files/file_uploads/Vol%201_Number%201.pdf.

19. Lytle, *Soldiers*, 163.

20. Benjamin Van Cleve, "Memoirs of Benjamin Van Cleve," *Quarterly Publication of the Historical and Philosophical Society of Ohio*, ed. Beverley W. Bond Jr., vol. 17, nos. 1 and 2 (January–June, 1922): 24, Internet Archive, https://ia804705.us.archive.org/20/items/memoirs ofbenjami00vancrich/memoirsofbenjami00vancrich.pdf.

21. Copy of a Letter from General St. Clair, Nov. 1, 1791, ASPI, 1:137.

22. Sargent, *Diary*, 22-23; Lytle, *Soldiers*, 83, 88.

23. William Darke to Mrs. Sarah Darke, COR, 24:331.

24. William Darke to Col. John Morrow, COR, 24:333-34.

25. William Darke to Mrs. Sarah Darke, COR, 24:332-33.

26. Denny, *Military Journal*, 163.

27. St. Clair, *Narrative*, 38.

28. St. Clair, *Narrative*, 272. This may have been Lieutenant Robert Buntin of the Kentucky militia, as he is the only Buntin in Lytle's comprehensive lists of officers in St. Clair's units. Lytle, *Soldiers*, 298.

29. St. Clair, *Narrative*, 272-73.

30. Ibid., 273.

31. Wilson, *St. Clair's Defeat*, 379.

32. St. Clair, *Narrative*, 273.

33. Sargent, *Diary*, 24; Copy of a Letter from Major General St. Clair to the Secretary for the Department of War, Nov. 9, 1791, ASPI, 1:137.

34. Denny, *Military Journal*, 164.

35. Wilson, *St. Clair's Defeat*, 379.

36. *A General Abstract of the Troops in the Service of the United States Commanded by His Excellency Arthur St. Clair*, October 26, 1791; Sargent, *Diary*, 35; Calloway, *Victory with No Name*, 127n62, citing, *inter alia*, Winthrop Sargent Papers, reel 3, 274, 282; Lytle, *Soldiers*, 135-290. The number of officers comes from reconciling the October 26 muster roll with Lytle's lists of officers.

37. Sargent, *Diary*, 35; Calloway, *Victory with No Name*, 127n62, citing, *inter alia*, Winthrop Sargent Papers, reel 3, 274, 282; Lytle, *Soldiers*, 295-300. The investigating congressional committee stated that after the detachment of "the first regiment, consisting of about three hundred effective men . . . [o]n the third of November the army consisted of about fourteen hundred effective men." St. Clair, *Narrative*, 69. This statement has been misinterpreted by some to mean that St. Clair's total force was only about fourteen hundred. But in the style of the time, the reference to "effective men" only counted enlisted men, not officers. Nor was the committee counting the militia. Thus, the committee statement of "about fourteen hundred" is consistent with, and would have been based on, the actual number of 1,380 enlisted men in the regulars, levies, and Faulkner's company. In defending himself, St. Clair wrote that he had an army of 1,600, including 300 Kentucky militia. Ibid., 131. Consistent with the practice of the time, St. Clair was referring to enlisted men and did so without counting those assigned as servants.

38. The two mortars were not deployed. Winkler, *St. Clair's Defeat*, 24. The mortars were apparently not viewed as suitable for defending the camp. Customarily they were used against fortifications, massed infantry, or infantry marching forward.

39. Sargent, *Diary*, 24, 34.

40. Copy of a Letter from Major General St. Clair to the Secretary for the Department of War, Nov. 9, 1791, ASPI, 1:137.

41. General St. Clair to the Secretary of War, Jan. 22, 1792, SCP, 2:278.

42. Denny misnamed McMickle as Martz, but Sargent correctly listed him as McMickle.

43. Cobb's father wrote to Secretary Knox that William had accepted a military appointment from the president "thou by a wrong name." "David Cobb (1748–1830) to Henry Knox," April 3, 1791, Gilder Lehrman Institute of American History, https://www.gilderlehrman. org/collection/glc0243704897; H. Clay Williams, "Cobb, General David," *Biographical Encyclopedia of Massachusetts of the Nineteenth Century*, vol. 2, 1833, 133. Cobb used the name David, his father's and his brother's first name, which explains why some sources list him as Ensign David Cobb.

44. Miami Tribe of Oklahoma, Indigenous Languages Digital Archive: Miami-Illinois, https://mc.miamioh.edu/ilda-myaamia/dictionary/entries/5538.

45. Christine Keller, Colleen Boyd, Mark Groover, and Mark Hill, *Archeology of the Battles of Fort Recovery, Mercer County, Ohio: Education and Protection*, 126, https://www.academia. edu/3321140/Archeology_of_the_Battles_of_Fort_Recovery_Mercer_County_Ohio_Education_and_Protection.

46. Ibid., 147; 131, fig. 62.

47. Christine Thompson and Kevin C. Nolan, "A Village Built over a Battlefield: Urban Archaeology and Preservation at the Battle of the Wabash," *Indiana Archaelology* 13, no. 1 (2018): 45.

48. Jefferson County Local History, "George Ash," 3; "Story of George Ash," 72. Lacrosse was the Indian sport analogous to war. Sometimes known as the "Little Brother of War," a lacrosse match could last for days with dozens of players on the field. Almost unlimited roughness was normal. Adele Conover, "Little Brother of War," *Smithsonian Magazine*, Dec. 1, 1997, https://www.smithsonianmag.com/history/little-brother-of-war-147315888/.

49. "Only where love and need are one, And the work is play for mortal stakes, is the deed ever really done, For heaven and the future's sakes." Robert Frost, "Two Tramps In Mud Time," 2, Frost Place, https://frostplace.org/wp-content/uploads/2020/09/Two-Tramps-in-Mud-Time-Poem-Text.pdf.

CHAPTER ELEVEN: NIGHT PATROL

1. Jefferson County Local History, "George Ash," 3; "Story of George Ash," 72.

2. For Crazy Horse, this was Wakan Tanka, "the Great Holy." Bray, *Crazy Horse*, 218.

3. Denny, *Military Journal*, 164, 165.

4. Brigade major was not a rank but a position on a commander's staff. In this case, it was General Butler's staff. Lytle, *Soldiers*, 31.

5. The following section about Slough's patrol is based on St. Clair, *Narrative*, 214-18. The narrative's misspelling of some last names in Slough's testimony has been corrected. See Lytle, *Soldiers*, 286, 290.

CHAPTER TWELVE: THE SOUND OF BELLS

1. Jefferson County Local History, "George Ash," 3; "Story of George Ash," 72.

2. Charles Aubrey Buser, *Wyandot Clothing*, Wyandot Nation, http://www.wyandot.org/wylife.html.

3. Thompson and Nolan, "Village," 44; Jefferson County Local History, "George Ash," 3; "Story of George Ash," 72.

4. The main events of the battle are clear. But the vagaries of human perception and recall, exacerbated by the life-and-death stress and confusion of war, have naturally left accounts that are not entirely consistent and an imprecise timeline. The lack of references to the actions of individual Native Americans during the battle reflects an unfortunate lack of information, unlike later engagements in the West, the Little Big Horn being a prime example.

5. Wilson, *St. Clair's Defeat*, 378, 379.

6. Sargent, *Diary*, 25, 34; Denny, *Military Journal*, 165.

7. Sunrise at the battle site was 7:16 AM. timeanddate.com, https://www.timeanddate.com/sun/@5154873?month=11&year=1791. First light occurs half an hour before sunrise. So the attack began at approximately 6:47 AM.

8. St. Clair, *Narrative*, 219; Sargent, *Diary*, 34; Keller et al., *Archeology of the Battles*, 140.

9. Wilson, *St. Clair's Defeat*, 379.

10. Denny, *Military Journal*, 165.

11. Van Cleve, "Memoirs," 25.

12. Ibid.

13. Keller et al., *Archeology of the Battles*, 131-32.

14. Winkler, *Wabash 1791*, 58, 61; Lytle, *Soldiers*, 239.

15. To George Washington from William Darke, 9-10 November 1791, National Archives. Denny and Sargent had conflicting impressions of what happened to the outposts. Neither was entirely correct. Denny thought the initial attack "killed and cut off nearly all of the guards." Denny, *Military Journal*, 165. But that description does not fit with Newman, Hannah, and Turner escaping the initial onslaught. Sargent thought those who made it back to camp were "never . . . effectually collected" and could no longer be counted as part of the "efficient numbers" available to fight. Sargent, *Diary*, 35. That seems overstated. Hannah and Newman certainly fought to defend the camp, and there is no suggestion that Turner did not do the same. It seems likely that a fair number of their men from the outposts followed them and also fought.

16. Denny, *Military Journal*, 165; To George Washington from William Darke, 9-10 November 1791, National Archives.

17. St. Clair, *Narrative*, 51.

18. Van Cleve, "Memoirs," 25.

19. St. Clair, *Narrative*, 221.

20. Denny, *Military Journal*, 165.

21. Sargent, *Diary*, 36.

22. Ironstrack, *Mihsi-maalhsa Wars—Part 3*.

23. Christine K. Thompson, Erin A. Steinwachs, and Kevin C. Nolan, *The Battle of the Wabash and the Battle of Fort Recovery: Mapping the Battlefield Landscape and Present Day Fort Recovery, Ohio*. 2016, 21, Ball State University, https://www.bsu.edu/-/media/www/departmentalcontent/aal/ aalpdfs/abpp-composite-map-document-final.pdf?sc_lang=en&hash=1E3 DD66 AAECE94A0BA5522F7B9D91A97C48450EE.

24. Sargent, *Diary*, 45.

25. St. Clair, *Narrative*, 222.

26. Sargent, *Diary*, 48.

27. Norton, *Journal*, 178.

28. Sargent, *Diary*, 45, 48.

29. Ibid., 46-48.

CHAPTER THIRTEEN: CHARGING TO DEFEAT

1. Copy of a Letter from Major General St. Clair to the Secretary for the Department of War, Nov. 9, 1791, ASPI, 1:137.

2. To George Washington From William Darke, 9-10 November 1791, National Archives.

3. Copy of a Letter from Major General St. Clair to the Secretary for the Department of War, Nov. 9, 1791, ASPI, 1:137. Darke claimed he ordered the bayonet charge. To George Washington from William Darke, 9-10 November 1791, National Archives. Whether that was because St. Clair's order never reached him, Darke was confused, or Darke was trying to diminish St. Clair's role, is open to question. As to his memory, Darke appears to have conflated some events before and after the charge.

4. Copy of a Letter from Major General St. Clair to the Secretary for the Department of War, Nov. 9, 1791, ASPI, 1:137.

5. To George Washington from William Darke, 9-10 November 1791, National Archives.

6. Copy of a Letter from Major General St. Clair to the Secretary for the Department of War, Nov. 9, 1791, ASPI, 1:137.

7. Norton, *Journal*, 178.

8. Sargent, *Diary*, 45.

9. Ibid., 44-45.

10. To George Washington from William Darke, 9-10 November 1791, National Archives.

11. Sargent, *Diary*, 45. Lytle and Winkler place Major Heart among those killed in the counterattack to clear the camp. Lytle, *Soldiers*, 99; Winkler, *Wabash 1791*, 75. But Heart's dying this early in the battle is inconsistent with Sargent writing that Heart's "conduct *through the day* was soldierly beyond my expectations." (Emphasis added.) Sargent, *Diary*, 45. There is significant evidence that Heart was killed later, as the retreat began. See ch. 14, note 21.

12. The illusion of smoke was, in reality, a fog-like mist formed by the reaction of cold air to still-warm, bloody scalp wounds. Charles Cist, *Sketches and Statistics of Cincinnati in 1859* (Cincinnati, OH: Moore, Wilstach, Keys & Co., 1859), 75, 84, Internet Archive. https://archive.org/details/sketchesstatisti01cist/page/10/mode/2up. Unfortunately, Fowler's descriptions of his own deeds, such as advising Colonel Darke on what to do, lack credibility.

13. To George Washington from William Darke, 9-10 November 1791, National Archives.

14. Ibid.

15. Ibid.

16. Sargent, *Diary*, 56. Sargent made these observations when he returned to the site of the battle months later.

17. Ibid., 36.

18. Denny, *Military Journal*, 166; Copy of a Letter from Major General St. Clair to the Secretary for the Department of War, Nov. 9, 1791, ASPI, 1:137.

19. Van Cleve, "Memoirs," 26.

20. Sargent, *Diary*, 45.

21. Ibid., 36-37; Copy of a Letter from Major General St. Clair to the Secretary for the Department of War, Nov. 9, 1791, ASPI, 1:137.

22. William Kincaid, "Fort Statue Honors Indian War Survivor: Carving by Local Artist Phil Wood Will Be Unveiled May 3," *Daily Standard*, April 17, 2009, https://dailystandard. com /archive/2009-04-17/stories/8528/fort-statue-honors-indian-war-survivor. Nancy Knapke was the Fort Recovery State Museum director when a statue of Nance was unveiled in 2009. The statue commemorates Nance and, in Knapke's words, the "women who lost their lives." Lytle and Calloway suggest Miller's husband was in the 2nd US Regiment. Lytle, *Soldiers*, 71; Calloway, *Victory with No Name*, 123. Winkler identifies her as an army cook whose husband was Private Horace Miller of the 1st US Regiment. Winkler, *Wabash 1791*, 74.

23. Van Cleve, "Memoirs," 26.

24. According to Lytle and Winkler, the regulars were led by Captain Patrick Phelon, as Heart had been killed clearing the camp after Darke's charge. About half a dozen soldiers crossed the river, and Phelon followed to bring them back. The blast of gunfire from the woods cut down everyone on the west side of the water. Lytle, *Soldiers*, 102. Winkler's account is similar. Winkler, *Wabash 1791*, 75. Wiley Sword describes a "forlorn" charge that was met with "tremendous fire" and says "Heart was almost immediately killed." Wiley Sword, *President Washington's Indian War*, 184. Yet Sword recounts that "the charge carried a short distance beyond the Wabash." Ibid. As to Major Heart, there is strong evidence he was killed later. See ch. 14, note 21.

25. Jefferson County Local History, "George Ash," 3; "Story of George Ash," 72. Years later, George Ash placed this incident an hour or more into the battle and said it was followed by an attack that penetrated the American camp. While the bayonet charge to the river was closer to two hours into the fight, its circumstances best explain why some Shawnee were retreating. Being driven back across the river was their only setback of the day and, at this

point, some Confederation warriors had little or no ammunition left. The final attack into the army's camp followed. The incident described by Ash is sometimes placed after one of the incursions into the army's camp, but those were less likely to cause a retreat because, from the Shawnee perspective, they were successful.

26. Jefferson County Local History, "George Ash," 3; "Story of George Ash," 72.

27. St. Clair, *Narrative*, 224; To George Washington from William Darke, 9-10 November 1791, National Archives.

CHAPTER FOURTEEN: ESCAPE AND FLIGHT

1. Lytle suggests the possibility that Little Turtle ordered the pause to consider offering surrender terms to St. Clair. Winkler infers that "the Indian commanders considered withdrawal." Winkler, *Wabash 1791*, 75. Neither idea fits the facts. It is possible, but unlikely, that the Confederation leaders would have considered offering surrender terms. It is inconceivable that leaders like Blue Jacket, Little Turtle, and Buckongahelas would have considered withdrawing from a battle they were winning, when they had only taken a few casualties. Most importantly, there was no reason to order a unilateral ceasefire while considering either idea.

2. Jefferson County Local History, "George Ash," 3; "Story of George Ash," 72.

3. Harry Shenawolf, "American Revolutionary War Artillery: Spiking Cannon So the Enemy Was Unable to Use," *Revolutionary War Journal*, July 20, 2019, https://revolutionarywarjournal.com/american-revolutionary-war-artillery-spiking-cannon-so-the-enemy-was-unable-to--use/ The vent was also known as the touchhole.

4. To George Washington from William Darke, 9-10 November 1791, National Archives.

5. Sargent, *Diary*, 44.

6. Ibid., 46.

7. Ibid., 44, 46.

8. Denny, *Military Journal*, 167.

9. Ironstrack, *Mihsi-maalhsa Wars, Part 3*.

10. Denny, *Military Journal*, 166.

11. Sargent, *Diary*, 37.

12. Cist, *Sketches*, 83.

13. Denny, *Military Journal*, 167; Sargent, *Diary*, 37.

14. St. Clair, *Narrative*, 51.

15. Sargent, *Diary*, 38.

16. William David Butler, John Cromwell Butler, and Joseph Marion Butler, *The Butler Family in America*, 161, Seeking My Roots, https://www.seekingmyroots.com/members/ files/ G000189.pdf. The family history quotes a letter written by Edward Butler to his brother Percival seven days later. Edward's letter does not contain a quote sometimes attributed to Richard Butler in which he purportedly told Edward, "I am mortally wounded. Leave me to my fate and save our brother." Sword, *President Washington's Indian War*, 185, 361n54. That language does not ring true, and if it had been said it surely would have been in Edward's contemporaneous letter. Instead, the purported quote comes from a letter written decades later by Edward's son, after he was grown and had attained the rank of colonel. Butler et al., *Butler Family*, 285.

17. A letter dated December 20, 1791, and published in the *Providence Gazette and County Journal*, January 14, 1792, describes the scene. Lytle, *Soldiers*, 103. The letter refers to the recipient of Butler's ring, sword, and watch only as "one of the gentlemen" and does not men-

tion Edward or Thomas Butler. Sixty years later, the Gaither family returned General Butler's sword to his family. Butler et al., *Butler Family*, 162.

18. Van Cleve, "Memoirs," 26.

19. Sargent, *Diary*, 46.

20. Sargent placed the time of the breakout at 9:30 AM. Sargent, *Diary*, 39. Whether he estimated from the sun or had a pocket watch is unknown.

21. Major Heart was a member of The Society of the Cincinnati in the State of Connecticut. According to the society, he was fatally shot "while covering the retreat." Gray, "Capt. Jonathan Heart/Hart." See ch. 5, note 24 regarding the society. Heart was also a Mason and a member of the first Masonic lodge in the Northwest Territory. According to the history of his lodge, Heart was ordered "to charge the . . . Indians in order to check them and gain time for the retreating army . . . but in the charge he . . . was killed." Oliver A. Roberts, "American Battle Abbey Roll, No. 1," *New England Craftsman* 6, no. 3 (December 1910): 72, Masonic Genealogy, http://masonicgenealogy.com/MediaWiki/index.php?title=AmericanUnion.

22. Wilson, *St. Clair's Defeat*, 380.

23. Van Cleve, "Memoirs," 26, 27.

24. Copy of a Letter from Major General St. Clair to the Secretary for the Department of War, Nov. 9, 1791, ASPI, 1:137.

25. Denny, *Military Journal*, 167, 168.

26. Sargent, *Diary*, 43.

27. Sargent claimed that "the determined resolution" of those too "(incapacitated from wounds to quit the field, yet who as soon as the fate of the day became certain, charged their pieces with a coolness and deliberation that reflects the highest honor upon their memory) and the firing of Musketry in Camp after we quitted it, leaves . . . very little room for doubt that their latest efforts were professionally brave and that where they could pull a trigger they avenged themselves." Sargent, *Diary*, 38. The usually cool-headed Sargent seems to have painted an idealized, imagined picture. It is not plausible that all those left behind still had a gun and were physically and mentally capable of "charging their pieces," or even of cocking and firing a musket or pistol. This is not to suggest that none of the abandoned wounded died fighting, only that many did not. In substantial part, the shots that were heard were more likely fired in celebration or to finish off wounded soldiers who looked like they could still fight.

28. Norton, *Journal*, 178.

29. William Walker to Charles Cist, June 17, 1852, William Walker collection (manuscript), 1852–1863, Chicago Historical Society Research Center, MSS Alpha 1 W, Chicago. Walker had close ties to the Wyandot. Ibid.

30. Other versions differ in detail, sometimes describing Butler in more heroic terms. All agree that Richard Butler was tomahawked.

31. Norton, *Journal*, 178.

32. Van Cleve, "Memoirs," 27.

33. Sword, *President Washington's Indian War*, 190n78, citing *Columbian Centinel*, January 11, 1792, Burton Collection; 4 U 100-130, Draper Manuscripts. Burton Historical Collection, Detroit Public Library; Lyman Draper, Draper Manuscript Collection: Frontier War Papers, Wisconsin Historical Society, Madison.

34. In early April 1792, Turner was offered a new appointment as an ensign but declined it. That spring, Ebenezer Denny met Turner in Philadelphia. Denny thought that Turner either was, or was feigning to be, mentally disturbed. To George Washington From William Darke,

25 April 1792, National Archives, https://founders.archives.gov/documents/Washington/05-10-02-0193; Denny, *Military Journal*, 173. On that somewhat mysterious note, our knowledge of Samuel Turner ends. It is certainly possible Turner was suffering from what we now know as post-traumatic stress disorder.

35. *St. Clair's Defeat*, 14. McDowell's first name is not given, but the only McDowells in St. Clair's army were privates named James and John. Lytle, *Soldiers*, 370.

36. Kincaid, *Fort Statue.*

37. Wilson, *St. Clair's Defeat*, 14.

38. Ibid.

39. Copy of a Letter from Major General St. Clair to the Secretary for the Department of War, Nov. 9, 1791, ASPI, 1:138.

40. Denny, *Military Journal*, 168.

41. Sargent, *Diary*, 39.

42. Van Cleve, "Memoirs," 27.

43. Denny, *Military Journal*, 167.

44. To George Washington from William Darke, 9-10 November 1791, National Archives.

45. Denny, *Military Journal*, 171-74; Sargent, *Diary*, 42-43. The casualty numbers recorded by Denny and Sargent have been adjusted to account for Captain Darke and Colonel Gibson dying of their wounds.

46. Sargent, *Diary*, 36. The numbers Sargent gives here total only 881, including 64 officers. Sargent obviously received additional information, as he later names 68 officers killed, wounded, or missing. Ibid., 42-43. That list matches Denny's. *Military Journal*, 171-74.

47. Sargent, *Diary*, 42-43.

48. Ibid., 42; *Monthly Return of the Second United States Regiment*, December 1, 1791, Manuscripts in Ohio: A Muster Roll, A Monthly Return and the Battle of Wabash, Ohio Memory, https://ohiomemory.ohiohistory.org/archives/4952.

49. *Monthly Return of the Second United States Regiment*, December 1, 1791, Ohio Memory. Additionally, the monthly return notes that fifty privates from Phelon's, Newman's, and Hughes's companies "cannot at present be accounted for." Lytle states that Hughes was on a recruiting assignment in Rhode Island. Lytle, *Soldiers*, 193-94. But the monthly return shows that Hughes was "sick present." The monthly return also shows that eighteen men had deserted. Most, if not all, would have deserted after the battle.

50. Lytle, *Soldiers*, 296, 303.

51. Sargent, *Diary*, 36; Wilson, *St. Clair's Defeat*, 380.

52. Sargent, *Diary*, 48.

53. Calloway, *Victory with No Name*, 127.

54. Col. A. McKee to Sir John Johnson, 5th Dec. 1791, COR, 24:336. Consistent with McKee's description of "many prisoners," over the next nine years, both official and unofficial reports claimed to identify more than a dozen other soldiers who were taken prisoner and held captive. Gaff, *Field of Corpses*, 402-403, n8.

55. Information Given by Sergeant Reuben Reynolds, of Connecticut, Belonging to Captain Buel's Company of the Second Regiment, ASPI, 1:244.

56. Spencer, *Indian Captivity*, 96.

57. Calloway, *Victory with No Name*, 127.

58. Claims of torture came from Winthrop Sargent and Captain Robert Buntin, who were part of a mission that returned to the battlefield three months later to try to recover the lost cannons. With twenty inches of snow covering the field, Sargent described how "at every

tread of the horse's feet, dead bodies were exposed to view, mutilated, mangled and butchered with the most savage barbarity; and indeed there seems to have been no act of indecent cruelty or torture which was not practiced on this occasion, to the women as well as the men." Sargent, *Diary*, 55. Severed limbs were seen. Stakes "as thick as arms" had been driven through some of the women's bodies. Dillon, *History of Indiana*, 284, quoting a letter from Captain Robert Buntin to General St. Clair, February 13, 1792. Sargent and Buntin thought these were signs of torture, though neither reported any evidence of burning. But given the absence of reports of torture from the prisoners who were taken away unharmed, torture can be ruled out. Contrary to what Sargent and Buntin imagined, it is likely that the wounded were quickly dispatched with tomahawks, clubs, or knives. Some of the mutilation, mangling, and butchery would have come from slashing tomahawks that first wounded then killed, from scalp knives, and from deliberate defacement, a common practice of the time and culture. Some would also have come from scavengers like vultures, crows, opossums, coyotes, and foxes.

59. Sargent, *Diary*, 39; Col. A. McKee to Sir John Johnson, Dec. 5, 1791, COR, 24:336.

60. Norton, *Journal*, 178.

61. Col. A . McKee to Sir John Johnson, Detroit, 5th December 1791, COR, 24:336-37.

CHAPTER FIFTEEN: THE CONSEQUENCES OF VICTORY

1. Simon Pokagon, "The Massacre of Fort Dearborn at Chicago: Gathered from the Traditions of the Indian Tribes Engaged in the Massacre, and from the Published Accounts," *Harper's New Monthly Magazine*, vol. 98, no. 586, March 1899, 650, Amherst College Digital Collections, https://acdc.amherst.edu/view/NativeLiterature/E356-C53_P65_1899?from_search=1.

2. Statement Relative to the Frontiers Northwest of the Ohio, ASPI, 1:199.

3. The excerpts from the House's meeting as a committee of the whole are from Annals of Congress, House of Representatives, 2nd Cong., 1st sess., Library of Congress, https://memory.loc.gov/cgi-bin/ampage?collId=llac&fileName=003/llac003.db& recNum=2.

4. Report of the Secretary of War to the President, Territorial Papers of the United States, 2:314; H. Knox, Secretary of War Report, Jan. 22, 1791, ASPI, 1:113.

5. *The CAUSES of the existing HOSTILITIES between the UNITED STATES and certain Tribes of Indians north-west of the OHIO stated and explained from official and authentic Documents, and published in obedience to the orders of the PRESIDENT of the UNITED STATES*, January 26, 1792, Territorial Papers of the United States, 2:361.

6. Ibid.

7. Senator Benjamin Hawkins to the President of the United States, Senate Chamber, 10 Feb. 1792, Territorial Papers of the United States, 2:367, 368.

8. William Patrick Walsh, "The Defeat of Major General Arthur St. Clair, November 4, 1791: A Study of the Nation's Response 1791–1793" (PhD diss., Loyola eCommons, 1977), 45, Loyola eCommons, https://ecommons.luc.edu/cgi/viewcontent.cgi?referer=&httpsredir =1&article=2772&context=luc_diss.

9. *Causes of the Failure of the Expedition against the Indians, in 1791, under the Command of Major General St. Clair, Communicated to the House of Representatives, on the 8th of May, 1792*, ASPM, 1:40, 41.

10. Absalom Baird to Washington, June 28-29, 1792, 4U20, Lyman C. Draper, Draper Collection of Manuscripts: Frontier Papers, Wisconsin Historical Society, Madison; To George

Washington from Alexander Hamilton, 2 September, 1794, n9, National Archives, https://founders.archives.gov/documents/Hamilton/01-17-02-0146.

11. Some believe that Wells entered into a "family compact" with Little Turtle and with the Porcupine to work for peace, though fighting on opposite sides. George Ironstrack, *The Mihsi-maalhsa Wars, Part 4, The Battle of Taawaawa Siipiiwi*, https://aacimotaatiiyankwi.org/2016/01/01/mihsi-maalhsa-wars-part-iv-the-battle-of-the-taawaawa-siipiiwi/, citing Harvey Lewis Carter, *The Life and Times of Little Turtle: First Sagamore of the Wabash* (Champaign: University of Illinois Press, 1986), 112-121. More believable is that Wells agreed with his adoptive father and with his Miami father-in-law not to harm each other.

12. Sugden, *Blue Jacket*, 138-39.

13. The following information about the intertribal conference is from *Proceedings of a General Council of Indians*, COR, 24:485-95.

14. *The Speech of the Cornplanter and New Arrow Major General Wayne*, Chinuchshungutho, 8th December, 1792, ASPI, 1:337.

15. Memorandum of Instructions Given to Captain Hendricks by Colonel Pickering, Niagara, 4th June, 1798, ASPI, 1:346.

16. Suggestions Given to Gov. J. G. Simcoe by the Commissioners of the United States, COR, 24:545.

17. Reply of Col. J. G. Simcoe to Commissioners of the United States, COR, 24:546.

18. Letter from James Seagrave to the Chiefs and Head-men of the Cussetah and Coweta towns, dated, St. Mary's, 20th February, 1793, ASPI, 1:375; James Seagrave to Alexander Cornell, dated, St. Mary's, 20th February, 1793, ASPI, 1:375; James Seagrave to Fine Bones, Chief of the Broken Arrow, dated, St. Mary's, 20th February, 1793, ASPI, 1:376; James Seagrave to the leader of the Coweta, dated, St. Mary's, 20th February, 1793, ASPI, 1:376; James Seagrave to the White Lieutenant of the Oakfuskees, dated, St. Mary's, 20th February, 1793, ASPI, 1:376-77.

19. Sugden, *Blue Jacket*, 138-39.

20. Letter to General Knox, on Lake Erie, 21st of August, 1793, ASPI, 1:359.

21. To Messrs. B.L. B.R. T.P. Commissioners of the United States, July 30-In Council at Major Elliot's, Near the Mouth of the Detroit River, ASPI, 1:352.

22. The following information about the American negotiators' response is from *Speech of the Commissioners of the United States to the Deputies of the Confederated Indian Nations Assembled at the Rapids of the Miami River*, July 31, ASPI, 1:352-53.

23. In Council: Present as Yesterday, August 1, 1793, ASPI, 1:354.

24. Ibid.

25. The Seven Nations of Canada was an alliance of seven village communities in the St. Lawrence River system that dated back to the days of New France. It included Iroquois, predominantly Mohawk, Onondaga and Oneida, Algonquin, Huron, Abenaki, and Nippissing. Thus, the alliance included former enemies. Darren Bonaparte, *The Seven Nations of Canada: The Other Iroquois Confederacy, The Wampum Chronicles*, http://www.wampumchronicles.com/sevennations.html.

26. Estimate of Settlers North of the Ohio, Territorial Papers of the United States, 2:470.

27. *Mr. Gamelin's Journal*, ASPI, 1:94.

28. The excerpts from the council's response are from To the Commissioners of the United States, August 16th, 1793, at the Mouth of the Detroit river, ASPI, 1:356, 357.

29. *Proceeding of a Council Held at Buffalo Creek, 10th October, 1793*, ASPI, 1:478.

30. Message from the Secretary of War to the Sachems, Chiefs, and Warriors of the Six Nations, ASPI, 1:478.

CHAPTER SIXTEEN: THE IRONY OF FALLEN TIMBERS

1. In the future, Harrison and Tecumseh would oppose each other, both politically and militarily.

2. Archaeological Conservancy, "Fort Greenville (Ohio)," https://www.archaeologicalconservancy.org/fort-greenville-ohio/.

3. Touring Ohio, "Fort Miamis," http://touringohio.com/history/fort-miamis.html.

4. Copy of a Letter from Major General Wayne to the Secretary of War, dated Head Quarters, Greenville, 7th July, 1794, ASPI, 1:488; James Neill's Information to the Secretary of War, Taken 21st October, 1794, ASPI, 1:495.

5. John F. Winkler, *Fallen Timbers: The U.S. Army's First Victory* (Oxford: Osprey, 2013), 28; Sugden, *Blue Jacket*, 170.

6. Sugden, *Blue Jacket*, 173; Sugden, *Tecumseh*, 88; Winkler, *Fallen Timbers*, 27.

7. *Examination of a Shawnee Prisoner, Taken by Captain Wells, on the Evening of the 11th of August, 1794, Near the Foot of the Rapids*, ASPI, 1:494.

8. Sugden, *Blue Jacket*, 176; Sugden, *Tecumseh*, 89; Winkler, *Fallen Timbers*, 62.

9. Copy of a Letter from Major General Wayne to the Secretary of War, Dated Head Quarters, Grand Glaize, 28th August, 1794, ASPI, 1:491.

10. Ibid.

11. Sugden, *Blue Jacket*, 179.

12. *A Return of the Killed, Wounded, and Missing, of the Federal Army, Commanded by Major General Wayne, in the Action of the 20th August, 1794, Fought on the Banks of the Miami, at the Post of the Rapids, in the Vicinity of the British Post*, ASPI, 1:492. Wayne substantially overestimated the number of Indian combatants at two thousand and the number of Indian casualties as being at least double his own.

13. *A Proclamation*, Feb. 22, 1795, SCP 2:343, n1.

14. In Council: Present as before, July 22, 1795, ASPI, 1:571. One noted author has described Tarhe as simply warning the Americans, apparently focusing only on the beginning of his speech.

15. In Council: Present as before, July 27, 1795, ASPI, 1:574.

16. In Council: Present as before, July 22, 1795, ASPI, 1:575.

17. The Treaty of Greenville 1795: Wyandots, Delawares, etc. (concluded August 3, 1795), Avalon Project, https://avalon.law.yale.edu/18th_century/greenvil.asp; ASPI, 1:562-63.

18. The Secretary of War to the President, War Office, September 28, 1795, Territorial Papers of the United States, 2:557.

19. Tanner, *Atlas*, 101.

20. Bureau of the Census, *Contents-Ohio*, 7, 2, https://www2.census.gov/prod2/decennial/documents/06229686v32-37ch3.pdf.

21. Bob Blaisdell, *Great Speeches by Native Americans* (Mineola, NY: Dover Publications, 2000), 86, citing H. B. Cushman, *History of the Choctaw, Chickasaw and Natchez Indians* (Greenville, TX: Headlight Printing, 1899), 311.

22. Pokagon, "Massacre of Fort Dearborn," 650.

CHAPTER SEVENTEEN: THE INVESTIGATION OF DEFEAT

1. George MacDonald Fraser, *Flashman* (New York: New American Library, 1970), 242. In the full quote, Flashman adds "in my case, [it's] all panic."

2. All quotes are from Copy of a Letter from Major General St. Clair to the Secretary for the Department of War, Nov. 9, 1791, ASPI, 1:137-138.

3. Ibid., 1:138; St. Clair, *Narrative*, 148.

4. Copy of a Letter from Major General St. Clair to the Secretary for the Department of War, Nov. 9, 1791, ASPI, 1:138.

5. St. Clair, *Narrative*, 147-48.

6. Ibid., 101-102.

7. Ibid.

8. Ibid., 148.

9. Ibid., 54.

10. From George Washington to the United States Senate and House of Representatives, 12 December 1791, see commentary between the correspondence and note 1, National Archives, https://founders.archives.gov/documents/Washington/05-09-02-0166.

11. To George Washington from William Darke, 9-10 November 1791, National Archives.

12. Wilson, *St. Clair's Defeat*, 380.

13. Sargent, *Diary*, 35.

14. Ibid., 35.

15. Ibid., 56.

16. Ibid., 35.

17. All quotes are from *General Armstrong to the President*, December 23, 1791, SCP, 2:277. The St. Clair papers do not have any answering correspondence from Washington.

18. All quotes are from Statement Relative to the Frontiers Northwest of the Ohio, Dec. 26, 1791, ASPI, 1:198.

19. Ibid.

20. General St. Clair to the President, March 26, 1792, SCP 2:283.

21. President Washington to General St. Clair, March 28, 1792, SPC 2:283-84.

22. General St. Clair to President Washington, March 31, 1792, SCP 2:285.

23. President Washington to General St. Clair, April 4, 1792, SCP 2:285.

24. All quotes are from Abraham D. Sofaer, "Executive Power and the Control of Information: Practice under the Framers," *Duke Law Review* 1977, no. 1 (March 1977): 1, 6n29, 31, https://scholarship.law.duke.edu/cgi/viewcontent.cgi?article=2608&context=dlj.

25. St. Clair, *Narrative*, 198-99. The *Narrative* misspells Mentges as Mentgetz.

26. *Causes of the Failure of the Expedition*, ASPM, 1:37-39.

27. Ibid., 1:41-44.

28. Ibid., 1:37.

EPILOGUE: ENDURING LESSONS

1. Schoenfield and Schoenfield, *Legal Negotiations*, 254-56.

2. "Bridge is a game of incomplete information." Eric Rodwell, *The Rodwell Files* (Toronto: Master Point Press, 2011), 375.

3. Schoenfield and Schoenfield, *Legal Negotiations*, 263.

4. Ibid., 296.

5. Simon Parkin, *A Game of Birds and Wolves: The Ingenious Young Women Whose Secret Board Game Helped Win World War II* (Boston: Little, Brown, 2020), 95-96. In World War II, war gaming was critical in winning the Battle of the Atlantic.

6. Smith, *Historical Account*, 41, 44-45, 46.

7. Ibid., 45.

8. Martin West, *Bouquet's Expedition against the Ohio Indians in 1764 by William Smith* (Kent, OH: Kent State University Press, 2017), https://www.kentstateuniversitypress.com/2015/bouquets-expedition-against-the-ohio-indians-in-1764-by-william-smith/.

9. St. Clair, *Narrative*, 39.

10. Smith, *Historical* Account, 46.

11. Ibid., 58.

12. Ross, *War on the Run*, 462.

13. Ohio Department of Natural Resources, *History of Ohio State Forests*; Carman, *Indiana Forest Management*.

14. Thomas A. Albright, "Forests of Ohio 2017," 1, US Department of Agriculture, Forest Service, https://www.fs.usda.gov/nrs/pubs/ru/ru_fs171.pdf; US Department of Agriculture, Forest Service, *Forests of Indiana, 2021*, 2022, 1, https://www.fs.usda.gov/nrs/pubs/ru/ru_fs368.pdf.

15. Forest Resources Association, *Forest Carbon Report: Ohio*, https://cdn.ymaws.com/www.ohioforest.org/resource/resmgr/timber_talk/2020/september/Ohio_Forest_Carbon_Report_20.pdf.

16. Helen N. Alves-Pinto, Carlos L. Cordeiro, Jonas Geldmann, Harry D. Jonas, Marilla Palimbo Gaiarsa, Andrew Balmford, James E. M. Watson, Agnieszka Ewa Latawiec, and Bernard Strassburg, "The Role of Different Governance Regimes in Reducing Native Vegetation Conversion and Promoting Regrowth in the Brazilian Amazon," *Biological Conservation* 267, 109473 (March 2022), 4, https://www.sciencedirect.com/science/article/abs/pii/S00063207 2200026X.

17. Donald M. Waller and Nicholas J. Reo, "First Stewards: Ecological Outcomes of Forest and Wildlife Stewardship by Indigenous Peoples of Wisconsin, USA," *Ecology and Society* 23, no.1 (March 2018): 45-59, JSTOR, https://www.jstor.org/stable/26799060.

18. Rainforest Trust, *The Peruvian Amazon*, https://www.rainforesttrust.org/our-impact/success-stories/the-peruvian-amazon/.

19. Rainforest Trust, *New Project Launch in Peruvian Amazon Will Save 3.8 Million Acres*, April 21, 2023, Newsletter email to the author.

20. Rainforest Trust, *New Project Launch in the Brazilian Amazon*, January 26, 2023, Newsletter email to the author.

21. "The effects of a changing climate are a national security issue with potential impacts to Department of Defense . . . missions, operational plans, and installations." Department of Defense, *Report on Effects of a Changing Climate to the Department of Defense*, January 2019, 2, https://media.defense.gov/2019/Jan/29/2002084200/-1/-1/1/CLIMATE-CHANGE-REPORT-2019.PDF. The report found that of seventy-nine military bases surveyed, approximately two-thirds were threatened with climate-change-related risks, some of them with multiple risks.

22. Frost, "Two Tramps in Mud Time," 2.

BIBLIOGRAPHY

PRIMARY SOURCES

American State Papers, Indian Affairs. Vol. 1. Library of Congress. https://memory. loc.gov/cgi-bin/ampage?collId=llsp&fileName =007/llsp007.db&recNum=.

American State Papers, Military Affairs. Vol. 1. Library of Congress. https://memory. loc.gov/cgi-bin/ampage?collId=llsp&fileName =016/llsp016.db&recNum=4.

Annals of Congress. House of Representatives, 2nd Cong., 1st sess. Library of Congress. https://memory.loc.gov/cgi-bin/ampage?collId=llac&fileName=003/llac 003.db&recNum=2.

Bland, Humphrey. *A Treatise of Military Discipline; In Which Is Laid Down and Explained the Duty of the Officer and Soldier Thro' the Several Branches of the Service.* 5th ed. London: Printed for D. Midwinter, J. and P. Knapton, 1743. Hathi Trust. https://babel.hathitrust.org/cgi/pt?id=nyp.33433009 417621&seq=265.

Blue Jacket, George. *A Story of the Shawanoes.* Eastern Shawnee Tribe of Oklahoma Digital Collection. https://ohiomemory. org/digital/collection/p16007coll27/id/ 364#:~:text=George%20Bluejacket%20was%20the%20son,signed%20the%20Tr eaty%20of%20Greeneville.

Bureau of the Census. *Contents—Ohio.* https://www2.census.gov/prod2/decennial/ documents/06229686v32-37ch3.pdf.

"Cobb, David (1748—1830) to Henry Knox," April 3, 1791, Gilder Lehrman Institute of American History. https://www.gilderlehrman.org/collection/glc02437 04897.

Colonial Office Records. Vol. 24. Michigan Historical Collections. https://quod.lib. umich.edu/cgi/t/text/text-idx?c=moa;idno=0534625.0024.001.

Denny, Ebenezer. *Military Journal of Major Ebenezer Denny: An Officer in the Revolutionary and Indian Wars.* https://exploreuk.uky.edu/catalog/ xt76dj58d796# page/1/mode/1up.

Draper, Lyman. Draper Manuscript Collection: Draper's Notes (S series). Wisconsin Historical Society. Madison, Wisconsin.

———. Draper Manuscript Collection: Frontier War Papers, 1754–1885 (U series). Wisconsin Historical Society. Madison, Wisconsin.

———. Draper Manuscript Collection: Harmar Papers (W series). Wisconsin Historical Society. Madison, Wisconsin.

———. Draper Manuscript Collection: Tecumseh MSS (YY series). Wisconsin Historical Society. Madison, Wisconsin.

Franklin, Benjamin. Correspondence. National Archives, Founders Online. https://founders.archives.gov/?q=%20Author%3A%22Franklin%2C%20Benjamin%22&s=1111211111&r=1.

A General Abstract of the Troops in the Service of the United States Commanded by His Excellency Arthur St. Clair, Major General and Commander in Chief of the Troops in the Western Territory. October 26, 1791. Manuscripts in Ohio: A Muster Roll, A Monthly Return and the Battle of Wabash. Ohio Memory. https://ohio memory.ohiohistory.org/archives/4952.

Hamilton, Alexander. Correspondence. National Archives, Founders Online. https://founders.archives.gov/about/Hamilton.

Hay, Henry. *Narrative of Life on the Old Frontier: Henry Hay's Journal from Detroit to the Mississippi (i.e. Miami) River.* Edited by Milo M. Quaife. Madison, WI: Historical Society of Wisconsin, 1915. Hathi Trust. https://babel.hathitrust.org/cgi/pt?id=osu.32435015062847&seq=3.

The Historic New Orleans Collection. *Manuscripts Division UPDATE.* Vol. 1, no. 1 (1982): 3-4. https://www.hnoc.org/sites/default/files/file_uploads/Vol%201_Number%201.pdf.

Irwin, Thomas. "St. Clair's Defeat: As Told by an Eye-Witness—From Original MSS." Edited by Frazer E. Wilson. *Ohio History Journal* 10 (Jan. 1902): 378-380. Ohio History Connection. https://resources.ohiohistory.org/ ohj/search/display.php?page=15&ipp=20&searchterm=array&vol=10&pages=378-380.

Knox, Henry. Correspondence. National Archives, Founders Online. https://founders.archives.gov/?q=%20Period%3A%22Washington%20Presidency%22%20Author%3A%22Knox%2C%20Henry%22&s=1111211121&r=1.

Miami Tribe of Oklahoma. Indigenous Languages Digital Archive: Miami-Illinois. https://mc.miamioh.edu/ilda-myaamia/dictionary.

Monthly Return of the Second United States Regiment. December 1, 1791. Manuscripts in Ohio: A Muster Roll, A Monthly Return and the Battle of Wabash. Ohio Memory. https://ohiomemory.ohiohistory.org/archives/4952.

Native Languages of the Americas. "Shawnee Pronunciation and Spelling Guide." http://www.native-languages.org/shawnee_guide.htm.

Newman, Samuel. "Captain Newman's Original Journal of St. Clair's Campaign." *Wisconsin Magazine of History* 2, no. 1 (Sept. 1918): 44-73. https://content.wisconsinhistory.org/digital/collection/wmh/id/855.

North, William. Brigadier General William North, Muskingum to ___. Northwest Territory Collection, 1721–1825, M0367 box 1, folder 26 1786 08 07 005, Indiana Historical Society. https://images.indianahistory.org/ digital/collection/ONWT/ id/242/.

Northwest Ordinance (1787). National Archives. https://www.archives.gov/ milestones-documents/northwest-ordinance.

Norton, John. *The Journal of Major John Norton, 1816*. Edited by Carl F. Klink and James J. Talman. Toronto: Champlain Society, 1970.

Rogers, Robert. *A Concise Account of North America*. London: Robert Rogers, 1765.

The Royal Proclamation—October 7, 1763: By The King. A Proclamation. George R. Avalon Project. https://avalon.law.yale.edu/18th_century/proc 1763.asp.

Sargent, Winthrop. *Diary of Col. Winthrop Sargent, adjutant general of the United States' army during campaign of MDCCXCI*. Internet Archive. https://archive. org/details/diaryofcolwinthr00sarg/page/11/mode/2up.

Smith, William. *An Historical Account of the Expedition against the Ohio Indians, in the year MDCCLXIV. Under the Command of Henry Bouquet Esq., Colonel of Foot, and Now Brigadier General in America*. 1765. Internet Archive. https:// archive.org/details/cihm_41689/page/n5/mode/2up.

Spencer, O. M. *Indian Captivity: A True Narrative of the Capture of Rev. O. M. Spencer by the Indians in the Neighborhood of Cincinnati*. Edited by Milo M. Quaife. Chicago: R. R. Donnelly & Sons, 1917. Internet Archive. https://archive. org/details/omspencercapti00spenrich/page/n9/mode/2u.

St. Clair, Arthur. Correspondence. National Archives, Founders Online. https:// founders.archives.gov/?q=%20Author%3A%22St.%20Clair%2C%20Arthur%22 &s=1111211111&r=1.

———. *A Narrative of the Manner in Which the Campaign against the Indians in the Year One Thousand Seven Hundred and Ninety-One, Was Conducted, under the Command of Major General St. Clair*. Northern Illinois University Digital Library. https://digital.lib.niu.edu/islandora/object/niu-prairie%3A2033.

———. Papers. vol. 2. Hathi Trust. https://babel.hathitrust.org/cgi/pt?id=nyp.3343 3081765376&seq=14.

Stockbridge-Munsee Band of Mohican Indians. "Brief History: Muh-he-con-ne-ok." https://www.mohican.com/brief-history/.

"Story of George Ash." *Cincinnati Chronicle and Literary Gazette*, Nov. 7, 1829, 70. Reprinted in *George Ash: The Story of a Jefferson County Pioneer*. Jefferson County Local History. As published in the *Madison Weekly Courier*, Jan. 28, 1874. http://www.jeffersoncountylocalhistory.org/oralgeorgeash.

Territorial Papers of the United States, vol. 2. Hathi Trust. https://babel.hathitrust. org/cgi/pt?id=mdp.39015071159142&seq=9.

Treaty of Fort Harmar (1789). Treaty with the Wyandot, etc.: 1789. Avalon Project. https://avalon.law.yale.edu/18th_century/wya1789.asp.

Treaty of Fort McIntosh (1785). Treaty with the Wyandot, etc.: 1785. Avalon Project. https://avalon.law.yale.edu/18th_century/wya1785.asp.

Treaty of Greenville 1795: Wyandots, Delawares, etc. (concluded August 3, 1795). Avalon Project. https://avalon.law.yale.edu/18th_century/greenvil. asp.

Van Cleve, Benjamin. "Memoirs of Benjamin Van Cleve." *Quarterly Publication of the Historical and Philosophical Society of Ohio.* Edited by Beverley W. Bond Jr. Vol. 17, nos. 1 and 2 (January–June, 1922): 7-71. Internet Archive. https://ia804 705.us.archive.org/20/items/memoirsofbenjami00vancrich/memoirsofben-jami00vancrich.pdf.

Walker, William. William Walker collection (manuscript), 1852–1863. Chicago Historical Society Research Center, Chicago.

Washington, George. Correspondence. National Archives, Founders Online. https://founders.archives.gov/?q=%20Author%3A%22Washington%2C%20George%2 2&s=1111211111&.

———. *Third Annual Address to Congress.* American Presidency Project. https://www.presidency.ucsb.edu/documents/third-annual-address-congress-0.

Wolfe, Phillip J., and Warren J. Wolfe, eds. and trans. "Prospects for the Gallipolis Settlement: French Diplomatic Dispatches." *Ohio History Journal* 103 (Spring-Summer 1994): 41-56. https://resources.ohiohistory.org/ohj/search/display.php?page=46&ipp=20&searchterm=Array&vol=103&pages=41-56.

SECONDARY SOURCES

Albright, Thomas A. "Forests of Ohio 2017," 1-4. US Department of Agriculture. Forest Service. https://www.fs.usda.gov/nrs/pubs/ru/ru_fs171.pdf.

Allen, Robert S. *The British Indian Department and the Frontier in North America, 1755–1830.* Appendix D, "Indian Leaders and Notables of the British Indian Department, 1755–1830." (Oct. 24, 2006). Parks Canada. http://parkscanadahistory.com/series/chs/14/chs14-1n.htm.

Alves-Pinto, Helen N., Carlos L. Cordeiro, Jonas Geldmann, Harry D. Jonas, Marilla Palimbo Gaiarsa, Andrew Balmford, James E. M. Watson, Agnieszka Ewa Latawiec, and Bernard Strassburg. "The Role of Different Governance Regimes in Reducing Native Vegetation Conversion and Promoting Regrowth in the Brazilian Amazon." *Biological Conservation* 267, 109473 (March 2022). Science Direct. https://www.sciencedirect.com/science/article/abs/pii/S000632072200026X.

AmericanRevolution.Org: Your Gateway to the American Revolution. "Artillery." https://www.americanrevolution.org/artillery.php.

Anson, Bert. *The Miami Indians.* Norman: University of Oklahoma Press, 2000.

Archaeological Conservancy. "Fort Greenville (Ohio)." https://www.archaeologicalconservancy.org/fort-greenville-ohio/.

Axtell, James. "The White Indians of Colonial America." *William and Mary Quarterly* 32, no. 1 (Jan. 1975): 55-88. JSTOR. https://www.jstor.org/stable/1922594.

Barker, Gerry. *Some Thoughts on Scouts and Spies.* Lebanon, TN: Greenleaf Press, 2017.

Bidlack, Russell E. "Richard Sparks (ca. 1757–1815): Indian Captive to U.S. Colonel." 1671-88. The Sparks Family Online. http://www.sparksfamilyassn.org/pages/087-A.html.

Blaisdell, Bob. *Great Speeches by Native Americans*. Mineola, NY: Dover, 2000.

Bonaparte, Darren. "The Seven Nations of Canada: The Other Iroquois Confederacy." The Wampum Chronicles. http://www.wampumchronicles.com/sevennations.html.

Bray, Kingsley M. *Crazy Horse: A Lakota Life*. Norman: University of Oklahoma Press, 2006.

Broberg, Lisa Louise. "Sexual Mores among the Eastern Woodland Indians." Master's thesis, William and Mary, 1984. ScholarWorks. Dissertations, Theses, and Masters Projects. Paper 1539625275. https://dx.doi.org/ doi:10.21220/s2-hd8b-0y78.

The Buckskinners. "Long Rifles." https://thebuckskinners.com/long-rifles/.

Buser, Charles Aubrey. "Tarhe." Wyandot Nation of Kansas. http://www. wyandot. org/sachem.htm.

———. "Wyandot Clothing." Wyandot Nation of Kansas. http://www. wyandot. org/wylife.html.

Butler, William David, John Cromwell Butler, and Joseph Marion Butler. *The Butler Family in America*. St. Louis: Shallcross Printing, 1909. Seeking My Roots. https://www.seekingmyroots.com/members/files/G000189. pdf.

Calloway, Colin G. *The Victory with No Name: The Native American Defeat of the First American Army*. New York: Oxford University Press, 2015.

Carman, Sam F. "Indiana Forest Management History and Practices." 2013. US Department of Agriculture. Forest Service. https://www.fs.usda.gov/research/tree search/42897.

Carter, Harvey Lewis. *The Life and Times of Little Turtle: First Sagamore of the Wabash*. Champaign: University of Illinois Press, 1986.

Chickasaw Nation. "Chickasaw Nation Corrects Names of Famed Leaders." October 12, 2014. ICT News. https://ictnews.org/archive/native-history-chickasaw-nation-corrects-names-of-famed-leaders.

Cist, Charles. *Sketches and Statistics of Cincinnati in 1859*. Cincinnati, Ohio: Moore, Wilstach, Keys, 1859. Internet Archive. https://archive.org/details/ sketchessta-tisti01cist/page/10/mode/2up.

Clark, Corbin Douglas. *Musical Culture of the Algonquin: A Study of the Musical Culture of the Algonquin Indigenous People of North America*. Liberty University. https://digitalcommons.liberty.edu/cgi/viewcontent.cgi?article=1390&context= honors.

Coleman, Christopher B. "Letters from Eighteenth Century Indiana Merchants." *Indiana Quarterly Magazine of History* 5, no. 4 (December 1909): 137-159. IUScholarWorks Journals. https://scholarworks.iu.edu/journals/index.php/imh/article/view/5703/5127.

Conover, Adele. "Little Brother of War." *Smithsonian Magazine*, Dec. 1, 1997. https://www.smithsonianmag.com/history/little-brother-of-war-147315888/.

Cushman, H. B. *History of the Choctaw, Chickasaw and Natchez Indian*. Greenville, TX: Headlight Printing, 1899.

Danielski, John. "The Kentucky Rifle— How America's Famous Frontier Long Gun Changed Warfare." Military History Now, May 4, 2020. https://militaryhistorynow.com/2020/05/04/the-kentucky-rifle-how-americas-famed-frontier-long-gun-changed-warfare/.

Darlington, Mary C., ed. *History of Colonel Henry Bouquet and the Western Frontiers of Pennsylvania 1747–1767*. Pittsburgh, PA: privately published, 1920. Internet Archive. https://archive.org/details/historyofcolonel00darluoft/page/n9/mode/2up.

Dastrup, Boyd L. *King of Battle: A Branch History of the U.S. Army's Field Artillery*. US Army Center of Military History. https://history.army.mil/ html/books/070/70-27/cmhPub_70-27.pdf.

Davis, Wade. *Photographs*. Madeira Park, BC: McIntyre & Douglas, 2016.

Delaware Tribe of Indians. "About the Delaware Tribe." https://delawaretribe.org/home-page/about-the-tribe/.

Digital History. Explorations: The Revolution, "Slavery, The American Revolution, and the Constitution." https://www.digitalhistory.uh.edu/ active_learning/explorations/revolution/revolution_slavery.cfm#:~:text=Several%20thousand%20slaves%20won%20their,the%20colony%27s%20prewar%20total%2C%20escaped.

Dillon, John. *History of Indiana, from the Earliest Exploration by Europeans*. Indianapolis, IN: Bingham & Doughty, 1859. https://digital.library.pitt.edu/ islandora/object/pitt:31735054853399.

Edward Clown Family, as told to William B. Matson. *Crazy Horse: The Lakota Warrior's Life & Legacy*. Layton, UT: Gibbs Smith, 2016.

Eid, Leroy V. "American Indian Military Leadership: St. Clair's Defeat 1791." *Journal of Military History* 1, no. 57 (January 1993): 71-88. JSTOR. https://www.jstor.org/stable/2944223.

———. "'A Kind of Running Fight': Indian Battlefield Tactics in the Late Eighteenth Century." *Western Pennsylvania Historical Magazine*, no. 2 (April 1988): 147-171. https://journals.psu.edu/wph/article/view/4105/ 3922.

———. "Their Rules of War: A Summary of James Smith's Indian Woodland War." *Register of the Kentucky Historical Society* 86, no. 1 (Winter 1988): 4-23. JSTOR. https://www.jstor.org/stable/23380726.

Farrell, David R. "Adhemar, Saint-Martin, Toussaint-Antoine." *Dictionary of Canadian Biography*, 1983. http://www.biographi.ca/en/bio/adhemar_ toussaint_antoine_5E.html.

Fleming, Deborah. "Resurrection of the Wild: Ohio Ecology as Regeneration," *Organization & Environment* 13, no. 4 (December 2000): 486-492. JSTOR. https://www.jstor.org/stable/26161500.

Forest Resources Association. *Forest Carbon Report: Ohio*. https://cdn. ymaws.com/www.ohioforest.org/resource/resmgr/timber_talk/2020/september/Ohio_Forest_Carbon_Report_20.pdf.

"Fort Recovery, Ohio, USA—Sunrise, Sunset, and Day Length, November 1791." Time and Date AS. https://www.timeanddate.com/sun/@5154873? month=11& year=1791.Fort Wayne and Allen County Public Library Staff, eds. *St. Clair's Defeat*. Fort Wayne, IN: Boards of the Public Library of Fort Wayne and Allen County, Indiana, 1954.

Fraser, George MacDonald. *Flashman*. New York: New American Library, 1970.

Frech, Harrison. *Anthony Shane, Metis Interpreter: A Bridge between Two Cultures: Scout, Interpreter, Town Founder, Witness to History*. Defiance, OH: Harrison Frech, 1991.

———, researcher. "Anthony Shane, Founding Father." Oct. 5, 1996. rockfordalive. com. https://rockfordalive.com/schs/log-house-history.

Furlong, Patrick J. "Problems of Frontier Logistics in St. Clair's 1791 Campaign." Selected Papers from the 1983 and 1984 George Rogers Clark Trans-Appalachian Frontier History Conferences. National Park Service History Electronic Library & Archive. http://npshistory.com/series/symposia/george_rogers_clark/1983-1984/sec6.htm.

Gaff, Alan C. *Field of Corpses: Arthur St. Clair and the Death of an American Army* (Nashville, TN: Knox Press, 2023).

Gray, V. Allen. "Capt. Jonathan Heart/Hart." The Society of the Cincinnati in the State of Connecticut. https://www.theconnecticutsociety.org/heart hart-jonathan/.

Harrington, Hugh T. "The Inaccuracy of Muskets." July 15, 2013. *Journal of the American Revolution*. https://allthingsliberty.com/2013/07/the-inaccuracy-of-muskets/.

Harvey, Eleanor Jones. "Who Was Alexander Von Humboldt?" *Smithsonian Magazine*, March 24, 2020. https://www.smithsonianmag.com/smithsonian-institution/who-was-alexander-von-humboldt-180974473/.

Heath, William. *William Wells and the Struggle for the Old Northwest*. Norman: University of Oklahoma Press, 2015.

Henderson, Robert. "Why Was a British Musket Called a 'Brown Bess'"? Access Heritage. https://www.militaryheritage.com/Brown_Bess_musket_ name.htm.

Hickey, Donald R. *Tecumseh's War: The Epic Conflict for the Heart of America*. Yardley, PA: Westholme Publishing, 2023.

Hoffman, Phillip W. *Simon Girty, Turncoat Hero: The Most Hated Man on the Early American Frontier*. Illustrated ed. Staunton, VA: American History Press, 2009.

Horsman, Reginald. "Egushwa." *Dictionary of Canadian Biography*, 1979. http://www.biographi.ca/en/bio/egushwa_4E.html.

———. "Elliott, Matthew." *Dictionary of Canadian Biography*, 1983. http://www.biographi.ca/en/bio/elliott_matthew_5E.html.

———. "McKee, Alexander." *Dictionary of Canadian Biography*, 1979. http://www.biographi.ca/en/bio/mckee_alexander_4E.html.

Hughes, J. Donald. "Forest Indians: The Holy Occupation." *Environmental Review* 1, no. 2 (1976): 2-13. JSTOR. https://www.jstor.org/stable/3984362 ?seq=7.

Hurt, R. Douglas. *The Ohio Frontier: Crucible of the Old Northwest 1720-1830.* Bloomington: Indiana University Press, 1996.

Hutton, Paul A. "William Wells: Frontier Scout and Indian Agent." *Indiana Historical Journal* 74, no. 3 (Sept. 1978): 183-222. JSTOR. https://www.jstor.org/ stable/27790311.

Ironstrack, George. "The Mihsi-maalhsa Wars, Part 2, The Battle of Kiihkayonki." Aacimotaatiiyankwi. https://aacimotaatiiyankwi.org/2014/03/31/the-mihsi-maalhsa-wars-part-ii/.

———. "The Mihsi-maalhsa Wars, Part 3, The Battle of the Wabash." Aacimotaatiiyankwi. https://aacimotaatiiyankwi.org/2014/05/19/the-mihsi-maalhsa-wars-part-iii/.

———. "The Mihsi-maalhsa Wars, Part 4, The Battle of Taawaawa Siipiiwi." Aacimotaatiiyankwi. https://aacimotaatiiyankwi.org/2016/01/01/mihsi-maalhsa-wars-part-iv-the-battle-of-the-taawaawa-siipiiwi/.

Keller, Christine, Colleen Boyd, Mark Groover, and Mark Hill. *Archeology of the Battles of Fort Recovery, Mercer County, Ohio: Education and Protection.* 2011. https://www.academia.edu/3321140/Archeology_of_the_ Battles_of_Fort_Recovery_Mercer_County_Ohio_Education_and_Protection.

Kincaid, William. "Fort Statue Honors Indian War Survivor: Carving by Local Artist Phil Wood Will Be Unveiled May 3." *Daily Standard*, April 17, 2009. https://dailystandard.com/archive/2009-04-17/stories/8528/fort-statue-honors-indian-war-survivor.

Lankford, George E. "Losing the Past: Draper and the Ruddell Indian Captivity." *Arkansas Historical Quarterly* 49 no. 3 (Autumn 1990): 214-239. JSTOR. https://www.jstor.org/stable/40030798.

Lazarus, Edward. *Black Hills White Justice: The Sioux Nation Versus the United States, 1775 to the Present.* New York: HarperCollins, 1991.

LeWine, Howard E., ed. "Biliary Colic." Harvard Health Publishing. August 16, 2023. https://www.health.harvard.edu/a_to_z/biliary-colic-a-to-z#:~:text=Biliary%20colic%20is%20a%20steady,that%20helps%20to%20digest%20fats.

Library of Congress. "Thomas Jefferson: The West." https://www.loc.gov/exhibits/jefferson/jeffwest.html.

Lytle, Richard M. *The Soldiers of America's First Army: 1791.* Lanham, MD: Scarecrow Press, 2004.

Maloy, Mark. "Small Arms of the Revolution." American Battlefield Trust. https://www.battlefields.org/learn/articles/small-arms-revolution.

McKinney, Helen. "Oldham County." https://explorekyhistory.ky.gov/items/show/844.

Nierenberg, Cari. "What Is Stockholm Syndrome?" June 27, 2019. Live Science. https://www.livescience.com/65817-stockholm-syndrome.html.

Ohio Department of Natural Resources. "History of Ohio State Forests." https://ohiodnr.gov/discover-and-learn/safety-conservation/about-ODNR/forestry/state-forest-management/state-forest-history.

Oldham County Historical Society. *History and Families Oldham County, Kentucky: First Century 1824–1924*. Nashville, TN: Turner Publishing, 1996.

O'Toole, Fintan. *White Savage: William Johnson and the Invention of America*. New York, Farrar, Straus and Giroux, 2005.

Parkin, Simon. *A Game of Birds and Wolves: The Ingenious Young Women Whose Secret Board Game Helped Win World War II*. Boston, MA: Little, Brown, 2020.

Piqua Shawnee Tribe. "Nonhelema Hokolesqua (Cornstalk's Sister) c.1718–1786." *Piqua Shawnee Tribe: History, Culture* (blog). August 31, 2018. https://piquashawnee.blogspot.com/2018/08/.

Pokagon, Simon. "The Massacre of Fort Dearborn at Chicago: Gathered from the Traditions of the Indian Tribes Engaged in the Massacre, and from the Published Accounts." *Harper's New Monthly Magazine*, vol. 98, no. 586, March 1899, 649-56. Amherst College Digital Collections. https:// acdc.amherst.edu/view/NativeLiterature/E356-C53_P65_1899?from_ search=1.

Rainforest Trust. "Climate." https://www.rainforesttrust.org/fighting-climate-change/.

———. *New Project Launch in the Brazilian Amazon*, January 26, 2023. Newsletter email to the author.

———. *New Project Launch in Peruvian Amazon Will Save 3.8 Millon Acres*, April 21, 2023. Newsletter email to the author.

———. "The Peruvian Amazon." https://www.rainforesttrust.org/our-impact/success-stories/the-peruvian-amazon/.

Redmond, Edward. "Washington as Land Speculator." Library of Congress. https://www.loc.gov/collections/george-washington-papers/articles-and-essays/george-washington-survey-and-mapmaker/washington-as-land-speculator/.

Roberts, Andrew. *Churchill: Walking with Destiny*. New York: Viking, 2018.

———. *The Last King of America: The Misunderstood Reign of George III*. New York: Viking, 2021.

Roberts, Oliver A. "American Battle Abbey Roll," No. 1. *New England Craftsman* 6, no. 3 (December 1910). Masonic Genealogy. http://masonicgenealogy.com/MediaWiki/index.php?title=AmericanUnion.

Ross, John F. *War on the Run: The Epic Story of Robert Rogers and the Conquest of America's First Frontier*. New York: Bantam, 2011.

Schenawolf, Harry. "American Revolutionary War Artillery: Spiking Cannon So the Enemy Was Unable to Use." *Revolutionary War Journal*, July 20, 2019. https://revolutionarywarjournal.com/american-revolutionary-war-artillery-spiking-cannon-so-the-enemy-was-unable-to-use/.

———. "Artillery Battle Tactics during the American Revolutionary War." *Revolutionary War Journal*, January 29, 2016. https://revolutionarywarjournal.com/war-artillery-tactics/.

———. "Cannon Projectiles of the American Revolutionary War." *Revolutionary War Journal*, March 15, 2015. https://revolutionarywarjournal. com/cannon-projectiles/.

———. "Loading and Firing a Brown Bess Musket in the Eighteenth Century." *Revolutionary War Journal*, October 1, 2014. https://revolutionarywarjournal.com/brown-bess/.

Schoenfield, Mark K., and Rick M. Schoenfield. *Legal Negotiations: Getting Maximum Results*. New York: Shepards/McGraw-Hill, 1988.

Scott, Douglas D., Joel Bohy, Nathan Boor, Charles Haecker, William Rose, and Patrick Severts, with contributions by Daniel M. Sivilich and Daniel T. Elliott. "Colonial Era Firearm Bullet Performance: A Live Fire Experimental Study for Archaelogical Interpretation." Modern Heritage Foundation. https://modern-heritage.net/images/Scott_etal_2017.pdf.

Sofaer, Abraham D. "Executive Power and the Control of Information: Practice under the Framers." *Duke Law Review* 1977, no. 1 (March 1977): 1-57. https://scholarship.law.duke.edu/cgi/viewcontent.cgi?article=2608& context=dlj.

Stevens, Wayne E. *The Organization of the Fur Trade 1760–1800. Mississippi Valley Historical Review* 3, no. 2 (Sept. 1916): 172-202 . JSTOR. https://archive.org/details/jstor-1886434/page/n1/mode/2up.

Sugden, John. *Blue Jacket: Warrior of the Shawnees*. Lincoln: University of Nebraska Press, 2000.

———. "Egushawa (1726–March 1796)." *American National Biography*, 2000. https://doi.org/10.1093/anb/9780198606697.article.2001688.

———. *Tecumseh: A Life*. New York: Henry Holt, 1997.

Swanton, John Reed. "The Indian Tribes of North America." Smithsonian Institute, *Bureau of American Ethnology Bulletin* 145. Baltimore: Genealogical Publishing, 2003.

Sword, Wiley. *President Washington's Indian War: The Struggle for the Old Northwest 1790–1795*. Norman: University of Oklahoma Press, 1993.

Tanner, Helen Hornbeck, ed. *Atlas of Great Lakes Indian History*. Norman: University of Oklahoma Press, 1987.

Tarter, Brent. "William Darke (1736-1801)." *Dictionary of Virginia Biography*. Library of Virginia, 2015. https://www.lva.virginia.gov/public/dvb/ bio.asp?b= Darke_William.

Thompson, Christine K., Erin A. Steinwachs, and Kevin C. Nolan. *The Battle of the Wabash and the Battle of Fort Recovery: Mapping the Battlefield Landscape and Present Day Fort Recovery, Ohio*. March 2016. Ball State University. https://www.bsu.edu/-/media/www/departmentalcontent/ aal/aalpdfs/abpp-composite-map-document-final.pdf?sc_lang =en&hash=1E3DD66AAECE94A0 BA5522F7 B9D91A97C48450EE.

Thompson, Christine, and Kevin C. Nolan. "A Village Built over a Battlefield: Urban Archaeology and Preservation at the Battle of the Wabash." *Indiana Archaeolology* 13, no. 1 (2018): 43-47.

Thwaites, Reuben Gold, and Louise Phelps Kellogg, eds. *Documentary History of Dunmore's War, 1774*. Madison: Wisconsin Historical Society, 1905.

Touring Ohio. "Fort Miamis." http://touringohio.com/history/fort-miamis.html.

Treeplantation.com. "Tree Spacing Calculator." https://treeplantation.com/ tree-spacing-calculator.html.

University of Minnesota, Duluth. *The Chippewa.* https://www.d.umn.edu/ cla/faculty/tbacig/studproj/a1041/mnansx1800/chippewa.htm.

US Department of Agriculture. Forest Service. *Forests of Indiana, 2021.* 2022. https://www.fs.usda.gov/nrs/pubs/ru/ru_fs368.pdf.

———. Forest Service. *A History of the Daniel Boone National Forest 1770–1990,* ch. 24, "Early Forests and Forest Industry in Eastern Kentucky." http://npshistory.com/publications/usfs/region/8/daniel-boone/ history/chap24.htm.

———. Forest Service. *Timeline of Activity on the Lands of the Hoosier National Forest.* https://www.fs.usda.gov/detail/hoosier/learning/history-culture/? cid=fseprd576 369.

_____. Forest Service. Wayne National Forest. "Early Settlement."https://www.fs.usda.gov/detail/wayne/about-forest/?cid=fsm9_006138.

US Department of Defense. *Report on Effects of a Changing Climate to the Department of Defense,* January 2019, 2. https://media.defense.gov/2019/Jan/29/2002 084200/-1/-1/1/CLIMATE-CHANGE-REPORT-2019.PDF.

US Geological Survey. St. Marys River at Rockford, OH-04180988. https://waterdata.usgs.gov/monitoring-location/04180988/#parameterCode=00065&period=P7D&showMedian=false.

Waller, Donald M., and Nicholas J. Reo. "First Stewards: Ecological Outcomes of Forest and Wildlife Stewardship by Indigenous Peoples of Wisconsin, USA." *Ecology and Society* 23, no.1 (March 2018): 45-59. JSTOR. https://www.jstor.org/stable/26799060.

Walsh, William Patrick. "The Defeat of Major General Arthur St. Clair, November 4, 1791: A Study of the Nation's Response 1791–1793." PhD diss., Loyola eCommons, 1977. Loyola eCommons. https://ecommons.luc.edu/ cgi/viewcontent.cgi? referer=&httpsredir=1&article=2772&context=luc_diss.

Ward, Harry M. *When Fate Summons: A Biography of General Richard Butler, 1743–1791.* Washington, DC: Academica Press, 2014.

Warner, Michael S. "General Josiah Harmar's Campaign Reconsidered: How the Americans Lost the Battle of Kekionga." *Indiana Magazine of History* 83, no. 1 (March 1987): 43-64. JSTOR. https://www.jstor.org/stable/ 27791042.

West, Martin. *Bouquet's Expedition against the Ohio Indians in 1764 by William Smith.* Kent, OH: Kent State University Press, 2017. https://www. kentstateuniversitypress.com/2015/bouquets-expedition-against-the-ohio-indians-in-1764-by-william-smith/.

Williams, Glenn F. *Dunmore's War: The Last Conflict of America's Colonial Era.* Yardley, PA: Westholme, 2017.

Williams, H. Clay. "Cobb, General David." *Biographical Encyclopedia of Massachusetts of the Nineteenth Century.* Vol. 2, 1833.

Winger, Otho. "The Indians Who Opposed Harmar." *Journal of Ohio History* (Jan.-March 1941): 55-59, Ohio History Connection, https://resources. ohiohistory.org/ohj/browse/displaypages.php?display[ ]=0050&display[ ]=55&display[ ]=59.

Winkler, John F. *Fallen Timbers: The U.S. Army's First Victory*. Oxford: Osprey, 2013.

———. *Wabash 1791: St. Clair's Defeat*. Oxford: Osprey, 2011.

Wright, Muriel H. "A Guide to the Indian Tribes of OK: Cayuga." July 2, 2015. Seneca Cayuga Nation. https://sctribe.com/history/07-02-2015/ guide-indian-tribes-ok-cayuga.

———. "A Guide to the Indian Tribes of OK: Seneca." May 23, 2016. Seneca Cayuga Nation. https://sctribe.com/history/05-03-2016/guide-indian-tribes-ok-seneca.

Wulf, Andrea. "Founding Gardeners: The Revolutionary Generation, Nature, and the Shaping of the American Nation." 2013. https://agrarianstudies.macmillan. yale.edu/sites/default/files/files/colloqpapers/04wulf.pdf.

Wulff, Frederick. *Alexander McKee—The Great White Elk: British Indian Agent on the Colonial Frontier*. Parker, CO: Outskirts Press, 2013.

ACKNOWLEDGMENTS

Thanks to my publisher, Bruce H. Franklin, who recognized the importance of this book's environmental theme and encouraged me to search for more detail on this aspect of the conflict, particularly for the words of Native American leaders. As a result, the book is better. Thanks also to Bruce and to his team at Westholme Publishing, especially cartographer and illustrator Tracy Dungan, cover art designer Trudi Gershenov, and copy editor Ron Silverman, for bringing this project to fruition.

The book's environmental theme connects to a 2018 Rainforest Trust trip I took to the Malay Peninsula and Borneo. Led by Paul Salaman, we hiked in the rainforest, met the amazing men and women of the Rimba nongovernmental organization, boated along the Kinabatangan River and its tributaries, and traveled to the Danum Valley. The beauty of old growth forests and the fauna we saw shockingly contrasted with the destruction of deforestation. The trip exponentially deepened my understanding of the essential role of forests in preserving both a reasonable climate and the earth's priceless biodiversity, and, conversely, my awareness of the existential danger of widespread deforestation.

Thanks to my brother, Mark, and to Charles Sheaff for reviewing an early draft of the Manuscript and for their feedback and encouragement.

Much appreciation to the anonymous folks who have scanned countless historical documents and to the websites that have made them available online. This saved innumerable hours and substantial travel, making it far easier to find relevant reports, correspondence, and transcripts. The websites can be found in numerous footnotes and in the primary sources listed in the bibliography.

My deep gratitude to friends and family who helped me through the most difficult time of my life and who continue to enrich my life. To Ed Rotberg and Margie Determan, and Floyd Kaufman, who flew halfway across the country and moved in for a few weeks. To Blythe Olshan-Findley and Dave Findley and their countless dinner invitations. To Rabbi Andrea Cosnowsky for her skilled listening and counsel. Here again to my brother Mark, and to my sister-in-law, Barbara; to Laura Schoenfield and Kevin Lane; to Jeff and Rachel Schoenfield; and to my great-nephews and great-nieces. Thanks also to Tony DiVincenzo and his family, to Faith and Del Myers, and to David Bogolub.

Finally, to Kelly Moses, I'm so glad for your love and sense of adventure.

INDEX